CISTERCIAN STUDIES SERIES: NUMBER EIGHTY-FIVE

THE FINANCES OF THE CISTERCIAN ORDER IN THE FOURTEENTH CENTURY

by Peter King

THE FINANCES
THE
IN THE FOURTEENTH

CISTERCIAN STUDIES SERIES: NUMBER EIGHTY-FIVE

OF
CISTERCIAN ORDER
CENTURY

❧ BY PETER KING

CISTERCIAN PUBLICATIONS
Kalamazoo, Michigan
1985

© Copyright, Cistercian Publications Inc., 1985.

Available in Britain and Europe from
A.R. Mowbray & Co Ltd
St Thomas House   Becket Street
Oxford OX1 1TB

in all other areas from

Cistercian Publications
WMU Station
Kalamazoo, Michigan 49008

The work of Cistercian Publications is made possible in part by support from Western Michigan University.

Typeset by Gale Akins, Kalamazoo
Printed in the United States of America

Library of Congress Cataloguing in Publication Data

King, Peter, M.A.
    The finances of the Cistercian Order in the fourteenth century.

    (Cistercian studies series ; no. 85)
    Bibliography: p. 227
    1. Cistercians—Finance—History.   I. Title.
II. Series.
BX3406.2.K56 1985   225'.12   85-4119
ISBN 0-87907-885-5

CONTENTS

To Bridget and Stephen

THE FINANCES OF THE CISTERCIAN ORDER
IN THE FOURTEENTH CENTURY

by Peter King

PREFACE

I should never have undertaken research on the finances of the Cistercian Order but for a meeting with Professor A.O. Johnsen at Utstein Kloster in Norway in September 1965. During a conversation he told me of the neglected financial records of the Order at Dijon. Later that year he invited me to join him in making an edition of the Order's Tax Book at Dijon. In this way I was introduced to a new line of research, and for some years enjoyed the enriching experience of working side by side with one of the outstanding medievalists of his time.

Dr Adriano Franceschini of Ferrara in Italy called my attention to the Tax Book of the Cistercian Order at Modena, on which he was then working. He allowed me a preview of his article on the subject, and later sent me a complete microfilm of the manuscript, which I could use for my research. My debt to his generosity is apparent in every part of this book.

Dr Richard de Lavigne, my colleague in St Andrews and my friend for over twenty-five years, has always made his detailed knowledge of French history available to me. He read the typescript of this book and took infinite pains with his criticisms and suggestions. I am grateful to him for many improvements in the text, and for saving me from several blunders.

I have received help from Dr Katherine Walsh of the University of Innsbruck in Austria, and valuable technical advice from Dr Michael Prestwich of the University of Durham in England. I owe a considerable debt to M. Jean Rigault, conservateur-en-chef of the superbly ordered *Archives Dé-*

partementales de la Côte d'Or at Dijon, where it is always a pleasure to work. Over the years I have come to rely on the courtesy and efficiency of the devoted staff of St Andrews University Library, especially Miss J. Gray, the assistant librarian, Miss M.M. Fowler, and Miss J.M. Young.

My wife Christine checked the bibliography, corrected my eccentric spelling, and helped to add the sums.

Finally I wish to express my gratitude to Professor D.E.R. Watt, the Chairman of the Department of Mediaeval History in St Andrews. Without his kindness and support I should not have been able to write a book in the academic year 1981–2, which was so fateful for this university and for many others in the United Kingdom.

P.K.

St Andrews,
Feast of St Bernard, 1982

ABBREVIATIONS
(for details see bibliographies)

Sources Consulted

Accts	Dijon, *Archives de la Côte d'Or*, 11 H 1160.
CB	*The Coucher Book of Furness Abbey.*
CCR	*Calendar of Close Rolls.*
Chron. Fordun.	*Johannis de Fordun Chronica Gentis Scotorum.*
MTB	Modena, MS Latino 142.
Orig.	Janauschek, *Originum Cisterciensium.*
Statuta	*Statuta capitulorum generalium.*
TB	*The Tax Book of the Cistercian Order.*

Financial Units

fl.	florin
gr.	gros
l.	livre
t.	tournois (of Tours)

CHAPTER ONE

The Financial Records of the Cistercian Order in the Fourteenth Century, And Their Survival.

THE SOLDIERS OF THE IMPERIAL and Catholic army who sacked the abbey of Cîteaux in 1636 made a point of destroying its muniments, and took special pleasure in tearing up papal bulls.[1] More archives were lost in the eighteenth century, particularly after the dissolution of the abbey in the French Revolution. Although the property records of the mother house of the Cistercians survived in some bulk, documentation relating to the history of the Order was almost entirely lost.[2] Only the Order's financial records are still moderately complete. Most of them are in the *Archives de la Côte-d'Or* at Dijon, where the surviving archives of Cîteaux are now preserved. When supplemented by material in Sens, Troyes, and elsewhere, they form a continuous series, illustrating the financial history of a great medieval religious Order from the last years of the thirteenth century to the eve of the Reformation.[3] All this material has been listed in archival catalogues for many years, but it has never been used. Those who sought to write the history of the Cistercians during the late Middle Ages, no doubt, were disappointed to find so many Accounts. Such material hardly seemed central to the life and mission of a great religious Order. It may be admitted that making ends meet and paying off debts were always subordinate to the chief purpose of the monastic life. Yet Cisterican history in the fourteenth and fifteenth centuries is so badly documented that no kind of material should be ignored. The study which follows, one hopes, provides the context within which the Order's financial records can be placed, so that in future historians may exploit them with confidence.

From 1235 the Cistercian Chapter General found it necessary to organise Collections from all the abbeys of the Order. In the thirteenth century it was usual to ask contributors to send the money to the Fairs of Champagne.[4] Here a senior member of the Order, sometimes the bursar of Cîteaux, waited, and made a record, perhaps on rolls or on wax tablets, of what had been paid. This material was later collated at Cîteaux, and formed the basis for the Order's official Accounts.

Some of the Accounts still show traces of the materials upon which they were based. The Accounts of 1290, for instance, which are the oldest to survive, record the money which was paid in at Troyes and Provins in that year.[5] Separate records of some kind must have been kept in both places and later collated. Records kept in three separate collecting centres in 1340 have been copied, practically unchanged, into the Order's Accounts for that year.[6] The work of collation was supervised by a senior member of the Order. It was his task to dictate to a scribe, who wrote down what he heard legibly and arranged the material neatly on a page. In the late thirteenth century this operation was under the direction of the bursar of Cîteaux. According to Benedict XII's bull *Fulgens sicut stella* of 1335, the task of collecting money for the Chapter General was to be entrusted to three abbots who were known as *receptores*.[7] In the decades which followed the promulgation of the bull, they took over the task of compiling the Order's Accounts. The work of dictating to the scribe was done for some years by Jean, abbot of Jouy, who left the mark of a strong personality on their pages. He referred frequently to himself in the first person singular—'I, Jean, abbot of Jouy'—and called the Accounts 'my register'.[8]

The Accounts were the most important of the Order's

financial records. They set down what had been paid and what was owed by every individual house, as well as the Order's total income and expenditure. Their arrangement reflected, to some extent, the traditional organisation of the White Monks. In the early days, a Cistercian abbey which exceeded a certain size had sent a colony of its monks to found a new house elsewhere. The founding abbey always maintained its links with the new monastery. In Cistercian parlance it was the 'mother house' and the colony its 'daughter'. The abbot of the mother house was often called, by a curious mixture of genders, the 'father abbot', and he retained the right to carry out visitations at the daughter house. Cîteaux was the mother house of the whole Order, and the abbots of its four 'eldest daughters'—La Ferté, Pontigny, Clairvaux, and Morimond—had a special place in the Order's government. With the abbot of Cîteaux they formed a kind of inner Council of five seniors. All Cistercian abbeys could trace the lines of their foundations back to one of these five. The houses of the Order were therefore often grouped according to their five 'generations'. These groupings could be used for administrative purposes, as was especially the case in financial matters. Father abbots were often responsible for making sure that contributions were paid, and in the Order's Accounts the abbeys were listed according to generations.

On St Lambert's day, 17 September, after the Chapter General was officially over, the diffinitors, who formed a kind of inner steering committee in the Chapter General, met the five seniors of the Order in the town house of the abbot of Cîteaux at Dijon. Here the final state of the Order's finances was considered. This annual audit had been ordered by pope Benedict XII.[9] Those present at the meeting accepted the implications of the audit in the name of the Order, taking responsibility for debts and disposing of surplus. Formal documents recording this part of the proceedings have survived.[10] The totals presented on 17 September were based upon an actual physical counting out of the money,[11] checked, no doubt, against the Accounts, in whatever state of readiness they were on 17 September. It has to be remembered that money was being paid in all the time that the Chapter General was in session. It would not have been possible, therefore, to have the Accounts in their final form by St Lambert's day. The fair copies now in the archives must have been compiled from various materials during more tranquil days, after everybody had gone home. This would explain their generally neat appearance. Thus the *Summae,* which appear at the end of the Accounts for each year, always refer to the St Lambert's day Audit in the past tense: 'In the year 1339, when the Audit took place on St Lambert's day, the Order's debt was . . . ';[12] 'In the year 1340 at the end of the Chapter, these were the debts of the Order for the year. . .';[13] 'In the above year (1347) after the Audit on St Lambert's day at Dijon, the following was the situation of the Order . . . ' .[14]

Whilst the Chapter General, in order to overcome its financial crises, was increasingly obliged to rely on compulsory Collections, the mother house had, from the twelfth century, endowments to help it meet the cost of hospitality when Chapter was meeting. These endowments consisted of churches and rents from royal or baronial estates throughout Christendom. Some rich Cistercian abbeys also undertook to support the Chapter General by paying annual rents. Sometimes they set aside pieces of land for this purpose. There was, therefore, a small archive of deeds relating to these properties and rents. At some time during the early fourteenth century, these endowments were divided up between the mother house and the Chapter General.[15] It must be presumed that the documents were redistributed also. Certain lists of the endowments of the Chapter General[16] seem to be based on archive material. During the last two decades of the fourteenth century Cîteaux successfully claimed back all these endowments, and the documents with them.[17]

During the thirteenth century father abbots decided how much individual daughter houses must contribute to Collections. This led to arguments and the desire to record once and for all how much each house had to pay. In the fourteenth century there were demands within the Order for the compilation of a central register of assessments. In 1318 and 1320 the Chapter General ordered all father abbots to send in reports about the economic state of their daughter houses, and how much they had paid at the last Collection.[18] It is more than possible that not all father abbots replied, and that some of the information sent in was unreliable. A more systematic enquiry was set on foot in 1326 by commissaries of the Chapter General, appointed for every province.[19] The endless disputes and negotiations about assessments,[20] however, made the compilation of a reliable and up-to-date master list almost impossible. Several lists may, in the end, have come into being, and may have been used at Cîteaux at various times. None of them can have been definitive. Two have been used for this study, but it is possible that others will be found. In the summer of 1980 a bookseller in Belgium advertised in his catalogue a Cistercian manuscript of the fourteenth and fifteenth centuries which contained a list of all the abbeys of the Order and a quota against each one for the Order's taxes. Before a scholar could look at it the manuscript was sold and has since disappeared from view.[21]

The financial archives of the Order, therefore, consisted of the records of the Audit on 17 September, the annual Accounts, one or more registers of assessments, and documents relating to endowments. It is unlikely that there was ever a central archive where all these things could be kept together. The Order had no specialised financial staff. The *receptores* were abbots who combined their ordinary duties with attention to the Order's financial affairs at certain times of the year. Their task was to supervise the collection of money at various centres, have it counted, and give instructions for the drawing up of Accounts. There is evidence that on occasion they were unable to cope with the rush of work at the Chapter General.[22] When they had done their work they returned home to their respective abbeys. Jean, abbot of Jouy, who took so possessive a view of the Accounts,[23] may have taken them home, and returned with them the following year. He may also have had a book of assessments in his luggage. The present Tax Book at Dijon is small and easily transportable. Even though it is a fifteenth-century copy, it may well derive its size and format from the original.

What happened to the records of endowments in the fourteenth century is a mystery. They may have been kept at Cîteaux under the charge of the abbey's bursar. This official was an obedientiary of the Mother House, but his presence at the centre of the Order's government must have given him wide influence and experience in a variety of financial matters. In 1290 and 1294 he was in charge of Collections throughout the Order.[24] Even after the three *receptores* took charge of this operation, the bursar remained important. There were always abbots who preferred to pay their quotas to him. He naturally took charge of anything sent whilst the Chapter General was not meeting. His failure to account to the *receptores* for such money was a frequent cause of argument.[25] In the meantime, money paid, rightly or wrongly, to the bursar was recorded in the bursar's Accounts, which therefore always contained material relevant to the finances of the Order as a whole.[26] In the latter part of the fourteenth century, when income from Collections was much reduced,[27] the bursar gained control of almost all the financial organisation which survived. It was probably at this period that he obtained the Order's Accounts for 1337-47, and bound them into the book of his own Accounts, which begin in 1366-67.[28] It was a symbol of his victory over the *receptores*. The other financial records of the Order must have passed into his possession at the same time.

Thus the fourteenth century records of the Order's financial organisation came to be stored at Cîteaux. During the late fifteenth century, because of a lawsuit between the two abbeys in 1483–86, copies of many of these documents were made for the abbey of Clairvaux. Much of the argument concerned the Collections and the endowments of the Chapter General. The monks of Clairvaux were anxious to gather as many documents as possible relating to finance. They pushed their researches as far as Edinburgh[29] and compiled a formidable dossier. In the seventeenth century, when the Order was again troubled by internal disputes, these documents were once again topical. They were copied out by a monk of Vauluisant. His manuscript is now MS 129 in the *bibliothèque municipale* in Sens. The original fifteenth-century compilation of which it is a copy has long since disappeared.[30]

There are other copies of financial documents made for the lawsuit, and now preserved in the *Archives départementales de l'Aube* at Troyes, where the records of Clairvaux are housed. Much material has thus been preserved which would otherwise have disappeared. It needs, however, to be used with caution. Copies at second or third hand present problems. A comparison of the Sens texts with earlier copies,[31] or with the originals,[32] shows that witness lists have been truncated, rhetorical phrases omitted, personal and place names misunderstood. This may have occurred in the fifteenth century, or the seventeenth, or both. The historical problems presented by these copies are even more baffling. They were originally made to provide ammunition for the abbot of Clairvaux at the *Parlement* of Paris. Polemical notes in the Sens manuscript show how the documents were to be used.[33] The litigants will also have decided, for their own immediate purposes, which texts should be presented, and which parts of them copied.

The financial organisation of the Order comes through most clearly from a study of two surviving lists of assessments: the Tax Books at Dijon and Modena. Of these, the one at Dijon is the most complete, though its interpretation is a matter of some difficulty. The original is lost, and it must be feared that when the fifteenth century copy, now in the *Archives de la Côte-d'Or,* was made, much historical information was destroyed. Were notes like *redemit anno* $M^o ccc^o liiij^o$ [34] added in a later hand in the original, or were they written at the same time as the rest of the manuscript? Were there any entries written in a different hand between the lines or at the bottom of the page, as in the Modena Tax Book? The original was clearly a complex document which included some thirteenth-century material.[35] A detailed study of the Accounts of 1337–47 shows, however, that it was not yet in use at that period.[36] Notes at the end of the Tax Book show that certain rents were redeemed in 1354–55.[37] If, in the original, these notes were made in a later hand, they would provide a convenient *terminus ad quem.* In that case the original, of which the present manuscript is a copy, was compiled some time during the years 1347–55, though no doubt older materials had been used. If the notes were in the same hand as the rest, one would have to assume that the book was compiled at a time when these redemptions were recent, and had to be kept in mind. In that case 1354 would be the starting point, the *terminus ad quem* a decade or so later.

The Dijon Tax Book shows the Cistercian Order at the height of its development. Houses are listed by generations, each with its assessments. Within each generation the houses are arranged, according to Cistercian tradition, in order of seniority. First come the immediate daughters of the original founding house, then the next line of descendants, and so on. Within each group, seniority is determined by the date of foundation. It is possible that the seating at the Chapter General was arranged in this way, and probably precedence at other meetings of abbots established as well. Lists or *tabulae* of Cistercian abbeys, which ranked them in order, were therefore a necessity for every house. Some of these *tabulae* have survived. A fifteenth-century list in the Royal Library in Copenhagen, based most probably on an earlier model, has much the same arrangement of houses as the Dijon Tax Book.[38] This method of establishing precedence within the Order was so complex however, that it invited muddles and, indeed, historical arguments. Quite often the order in Dijon and Copenhagen manuscripts is the same, but there are also divergences. It is clear at least that the Dijon Tax Book tried to arrange houses according to some traditional order of seniority though, at times, there were uncertainties and even omissions.[39]

A.O. Johnsen, who has examined the fifteenth-century copy most carefully, has followed older authorities in concluding that it was made '*circa* 1460—but with allowance for a margin of 20 to 30 years on either side'.[40] A statute of the Chapter General made in 1454 ordered a general tax throughout the Order in accordance with a list which was to be attached. There is no such list attached to the present statute, but Chapter's decision may have stimulated the copying of an ancient register of assessments.[41] There is some evidence that the copyist made 'a somewhat slavish copy of the original'.[42]

The arrangement of abbeys according to seniority was traditional, but hardly convenient in a document which was to be used for administrative purposes. Another fourteenth-century Tax Book now at Modena, MS Estense Latino 142, listed the abbeys within each generation in alphabetical order. The Cistercians, who were among the pioneers of alphabetization,[43] here put their skills to very practical use. Unlike the Dijon Tax Book, which is a fair copy, the one at Modena shows every sign of having been in working use, possibly at Cîteaux itself.[44] The text has been altered in a number of places and extra information added between the lines and at the bottom of pages. The manuscript begins with a *Provinciale*.[45] There follows a list of Cistercian abbeys

under generations, with their assessments.[46] Then come additions from the fifteenth century—first a decree of 1424 from
Jean de Martigny, abbot of Cîteaux, lowering the assessments of certain Spanish abbeys,[47] then an incomplete list of
Cistercian abbeys arranged by diocese,[48] finally a list of abbeys with new assessments, also unfinished and very difficult
to read.[49]

A study of the *Provinciale* gives a clue to the dating of the
first and fourteenth-century part of the manuscript. Dr Adriano Franceschini has pointed out that the *Provinciale*
includes the diocese of Montefiascone, created by pope
Urban V in 1369.[50] The later additions to the financial
section which follows can sometimes be dated. One records
the incorporation into the Order of the priory of St William
in Strasbourg in 1379.[51] Another concerns the abbey of
St Bernard in the suburbs of Valencia, founded in 1381.[52]
It seems likely, therefore, that the fourteenth-century part
of the Modena Tax Book was already in use when it was
found necessary to add this information. One may conclude
that it was being used in the early 1380s, and that it was compiled some time after 1369. It was written, therefore, around
the time of the Great Schism. Dr Franceschini has noted that
the *Provinciale* does not mention any of the changes made by
the Urbanist popes in the diocesan map of Italy.[53] On the
other hand, earlier changes made by pope John XXII are
recorded: his creation of the diocese of Cortone,[54] and the
final organisation of the archdiocese of Toulouse with its
suffragans.[55] It was obviously a *Provinciale* used at Avignon
which the Cistercians incorporated into their new register of
assessments.

If much of the Order's financial organisation can be reconstructed from a study of the Tax Books, the Accounts of
1337–47 show how it worked in practice. Three scribes
worked on them, one after the other. It was common
enough, in the fourteenth century, to employ professionals,
but in this case it is more likely that those who wrote up the

Accounts were Cistercian monks. If pope Benedict XII could take members of the Order to Avignon with him to help with papal administration,[56] it seems probable that in 1337–47 the Order still had all the personnel it required for the needs of its Chapter General.

The first scribe worked on the Accounts from 1337–40.[57] He had a beautiful hand. His letters were large and well-formed, his abbreviations clear, his work completely legible. He had an unerring instinct for spacing.[58] The Accounts consist mostly of lists of abbeys with the sums of money they paid. There is no doubt, in the pages written by scribe Number 1, about the sum of money which goes with any particular name, although he never found it necessary to link them by a line. The effect was achieved by perfect spacing between the lines, so that each entry formed a unity standing out on the page. There were ample headings over each of the different sections. These had the effect of breaking up the page so that the material was easy to use. Scribe Number 1, it must be admitted, was not economical with parchment. On f. 9b, for instance, he gave a whole page to arrears from three small generations. In fact he only put ten entries on the page. These, with separate headings for each generation, and a great heading for the whole page, still left plenty of empty space. It made a beautiful and restful page, but at this rate the parchment would have been used up quickly. Like other medieval scribes, this one enjoyed a rest from work. On two occasions he wrote 'time for a break'.[59] It must be presumed that his snack, whatever it was, was brought to him and was consumed on the spot. He wrote his comment when he was waiting for it. Had he been obliged to fetch it from somewhere, he would hardly have wasted valuable time.

The second scribe took over rather suddenly on f. 15a col. 1, halfway through the Accounts of 1340 and in the middle of a section. He began with an elaborate capital D on the top left hand corner but his exuberance was perhaps checked, for he started again with a more modest *De Salem.*

The new capital D was different from all his others, but fairly restrained.[60] Scribe Number 2 kept only a small portion of the Accounts, from f. 15a col. 1 to a little way down col. 1 of f. 16a. His letters were somewhat smaller than those of his predecessor. He was even more generous with parchment. He left, on the whole, more room between his lines than scribe Number 1 but he was less able to judge spacing. Sometimes his lines are too close together, sometimes very wide apart. He also, on occasion, failed conspicuously to keep his lines straight. His two and a quarter pages therefore do not look as tidy or as beautiful as do those of Scribe Number 1, whose virtues are enhanced by the comparison. Nevertheless, the new man was equally legible, tidy, at least in intention, and meticulous about his margins. He linked abbeys and the sums they paid with a line and, in spite of his generous spacing, this was clearly necessary. On the whole the writing in this part of the Accounts is less attractive, and it may be that the scribe's rather upright letters with their long strokes slowed him up. One may judge, from the appearance of his work, that he did his best, but that he was relatively inexperienced. Perhaps he was a 'stop-gap' scribe.

It was still 1340 when the third scribe took over, a little way down a column of receipts. It is impossible to guess at the circumstances under which these three succeeded one another in the course of a single operation. The fact that each change took place in the middle of work on a section implies, perhaps, that the Accounts were being drawn up under fairly leisurely conditions. It is difficult to imagine such replacements taking place under the stress of a busy Chapter General. That the scribes could follow each other at any moment is also, possibly, a sign that they were religious, acting under obedience.

Most of the surviving Accounts are the work of the third scribe. He recorded the Order's financial affairs for the rest of 1340 and to September 1347.[61] His work is very different from that of his two predecessors. The writing is very much smaller. He left little space between his lines. The line linking the name of an abbey to the sum it paid was thus, in his case, vital.[62] He was extremely economical with parchment. He sometimes wrote the headings of different sections in letters larger than the others, but he often began a new year with a heading so inconspicuous that it is difficult to find where one year ends and the new one begins.[63] Sometimes he left a space between sections,[64] sometimes sections were simply separated by lines.[65] Unlike scribe Number 1, he did not mind starting a new year half way down a column.[66] The pages for which he was responsible have a cramped appearance, although he maintained the traditions of legibility and neatness established by his predecessors. It is probably not his fault that the mix of ink he used has not lasted well. Only in a few places is it still as black as it was in the fourteenth century.[67] Altogether this scribe was clearly extremely professional and no doubt very quick, but his pages betray a lack of aesthetic sense, and a mean soul.

Scribe Number 3 also made particularly heavy weather of foreign place names. His confusions often make identifications difficult. *Saevenloberne* may possibly be Scharnebeck in Lower Saxony.[68] Dobrilugk in Brandenburg occurs as *de Dorbeleioliis*.[69] Raitenhaslach in Upper Bavaria is *Rathehaselay*,[70] *Rotenbascla*,[71] *Ragehuazerod* and *Ratenhanslach*. The latter two forms appear together on the same page of the Accounts of 1342.[72] For Hardehausen in Westphalia this scribe wrote *Hyrdehuseen*,[73] *Horsedewitohusen*,[74] *Haldehusen*,[75] *Hersedevanthusen*,[76] *Hermedhusen*,[77] *Hersedhinelssten*.[78] Foreign place names were, admittedly, a difficulty for the monks of Cîteaux, and a comparison of these forms with those in the Dijon Tax Book shows that others in the Mother House also stumbled over them.[79] It is difficult, nevertheless, to escape the conclusion that this scribe was not trying very hard. Perhaps he thought his absurdities were funny.[80]

Thus it is possible to detect certain scribal idiosyncracies

in the Accounts. Their layout, however, must have been decided by the *receptores*. The current rate of exchange between
livres tournois on the one hand, *florins* and occasionally *écus*
on the other, was written across the top of every two facing
pages.[81] The rest of the material was set out in two columns
on every page. In the years immediately following *Fulgens*
there seems to have been a little experimentation with the
way the material should be arranged. By 1341, however, the
receptores had hit upon a form which they found would
answer all their needs.

The first section of every set of annual Accounts was
headed *Recepta,* and recorded receipts. First came payments
from individual abbeys, grouped by generations. Within each
generation there were two lists of unequal length. The first
and longer consisted of *nova* or current payments. This was
followed by a shorter list of *antiqua* or arrears.[82] After these
lists there often followed an elaborate series of *summae* or
totals, sometimes as many as thirteen. Total receipts from
each of the generations were given twice over—once for
nova and once for *antiqua.* Then came the overall total of
current payments, and the same for arrears, finally the grand
total of all receipts.[83] No doubt the intermediary totals
helped the *receptores* to add up the final one, though, in
fact, the arithmetic was often faulty. There were years when
it was felt that only the last and final total need be recorded.[84] After receipts from individual houses came those
from rents and alms.[85] With these the first part of the
Accounts, concerned with the Order's income, was closed.

The next part of the Accounts was headed *Expensa,* and
recorded expenditure, losses, and debts. The lists of the
Order's expenses during the year included very miscellaneous
items. Some had involved the payment of large sums, others
were comparatively trivial.[86] On the whole, this hetero-
geneous material was arranged logically.[87] *Expensa* included
the Order's losses—from the depreciation of the coinage, for
instance.[88] The Order's unpaid debts were recorded immed-

iately above the final assessment of its financial position, as it had been declared to the diffinitors of St Lambert's day.[89]

The Accounts of 1345 and 1346 followed this general pattern but were made unusually brief. Individual abbeys were not listed. The *Recepta* section consisted only of the thirteen *summae*.[90] Separate items of expenditure were still listed,[91] but the Accounts of these years give an abbreviated impression. The whole set for 1345 is on a single page.[92]

The Accounts for 1347 returned to the older and fuller format. The amount paid by each abbey was not, however, always recorded. On one page the names of abbeys are crowded together in three or four columns, without sums against them or space to record them.[93] The Accounts for this year are the only ones which show signs of having been compiled in haste, as if the scribe had to meet some deadline, and was instructed not to bother about individual payments.

Before 1341 there was no standard format for the Accounts. The arrangement for 1340 is extremely elaborate. In this year the Order was making a special effort to solve its financial problems.[94] Contributions could be paid in two instalments—at Easter and September. For the Easter payments collecting centres were set up in Paris, Avignon, and Metz. The Easter Accounts move uncertainly between these centres and the Order's generations. First comes a list of payments made to abbot Jean of Jouy at Paris by abbeys in the generation of Cîteaux,[95] then follow abbot Pierre of Clairefontaine's receipts at Metz from the same generation.[96] The next section returns to abbot Jean at Paris for payments from the generations of La Ferté, Pontigny, and Clairvaux.[97] Then comes money collected by abbot Pierre at Metz from the generation of Clairvaux.[98] The next part of the Accounts is devoted to the generation of Morimond: first the few houses which paid at Paris,[99] then those which paid at Metz.[100] These sections are followed by a list of the houses which sent money to the Order's proctor at Avignon, arranged

under generations.[101] After this we move to the Chapter
General at Cîteaux in September, and the payments made
there, arranged under the five generations.[102] In all the lists
there is the usual division into *nova* and *antiqua.*

The Accounts of 1340 continue with a list of rents and
alms.[103] Then come the *Expensa,*[104] and the final balance
sheet for the year, as presented on St Lambert's day.[105]

In the financial history of the Order, the year 1340 was
an exceptional one.[106] This explains the complicated arrangement of the Accounts, but in that form they must have been
difficult to use. No doubt the simpler scheme of 1341 reflects
dissatisfaction with the previous format. In 1341 too, payments were made in two instalments and at different collecting centres.[107] The *receptores,* however, collated all the
material relating to each generation and presented it together.[108] This remained the practice. The 1340 Accounts,
nevertheless, provide a historian with valuable information,
making it possible to reconstruct in every detail a 'Collection
in the Cistercian Order. They also show clearly the raw
materials upon which the Accounts of later years were
based.

Each of the Accounts for the years 1337–39 has a character of its own. The set for 1337 is short and possibly incomplete. It is a list of backpayments divided into the five
generations. Nuns, who until 1339 were liable to contribute
to the Collections, figure prominently.[109] Receipts are followed by rents and alms.[110] Expenses for the year follow,[111]
then a list of defaulting abbeys,[112] and finally the total sum
for receipts and expenditure.[113] The contributions paid in
1338 are also presented according to generations. Within
each generation the abbeys which paid through the proctor at
Avignon are listed separately. There is also a separate list of
contributions from nuns.[114] Arrears come under a separate
section.[115] The year 1339 was set aside for collecting
arrears. The abbeys which paid up were once again arranged
according to their generations, but nuns were now omitted,

since they were no longer obliged to pay.[116] In both 1338
and 1339 receipts were followed by rents and alms. Then
came *Expensa* and finally a balance sheet for the year.[117]

Medieval administrative records were not usually provided
with lists of contents or alphabetical indices. The arrangement, therefore, was all important if information was to be
retrieved. To find a particular abbey, it would always be
necessary to know its generation. For the rest, the searcher
was guided by the headings and the marginalia. The first
scribe was generous in providing them. Payments which had
fallen short were marked in the margin with a *Nota* or a
Nota debet.[118] The iniquities of the bursar of Cîteaux
merited a marginal *furtum*.[119] If a payment had not been
made direct to the *receptores* but had come through someone else, this was marked by a sign, whether the agent was
the proctor of the Order,[120] or one of the five seniors.[121]
These marginalia and notes ceased when the first scribe
stopped working on the Accounts. At this point there was
probably a change of policy. No doubt the *receptores* felt
that the more logical and standardised arrangement adopted
for the Accounts from 1341[122] would make marginalia and
elaborate headings unnecessary.

None of the original statements presented at the Audit on
St Lambert's day have survived. The texts are known only
from later copies. Most of these are to be found in the
seventeenth-century Sens MS 129.[123] The statement presented in 1390 however, can be read from a copy made for
the lawsuit of 1483–86.[124] Indeed, all the Clairvaux documents now in the *Archives de l'Aube* at Troyes, and which
relate to the Order's financial affairs, were copied for the
lawsuit, as detailed notes on most of them show.

When an abbey paid money to the Chapter General,
whether for a rent or as a contribution to the Collections, a
receipt was issued. Sens MS 129 has the texts of some which
were issued to the abbot of Coupar Angus in Scotland during
the fourteenth century.[125] A receipt issued by one of the

Order's *receptores* to the abbey of Fürstenfeld in Bavaria has survived. It records the payment of a contribution in 1393.[126] It is at Munich, in the Bavarian archives which house several more such documents issued in the fifteenth century, some of them bearing the seals of the *receptores.*[127]

Compared to the rich documentation of Cistercian finance in the fifteenth century,[128] the materials for the fourteenth century are sparse, and there are many gaps. Enough survives, however, to show how the Order organised an increasingly elaborate financial system in the period of 1290–1400.

NOTES TO CHAPTER ONE

For full references, consult the Bibliographies.

1. *Répertoire numérique des . . . archives ecclésiastiques . . . abbaye de Cîteaux* [iii].
2. *Ibid.,* [iii] –[iv].
3. See P. King, 'Materials for a financial history of the Cistercian Order to 1486'.
4. See e.g. *Statuta* 1257, 7.
5. Sens MS 129, ff. 164–165a.
6. See below, p. 21.
7. *Fulgens* 18, *Statuta,* iii, pp. 421–2.
8. Accts., f. 4b, col. 1.
9. *Fulgens* 18, *Statuta,* iii, 421–2.
10. See below, p. 23.
11. See below, p. 167.
12. Accts., f. 11b, col. 2.
13. *Ibid.,* f. 17b, col. 2.
14. *Ibid.,* f. 29b, col. 2.
15. See below, p. 32.
16. *Ibid.*
17. See below, pp. 12 and 38.
18. See below, p. 62.
19. *Ibid.*
20. See below, pp. 65-71.
21. Information kindly supplied by Fr Edmond Mikkers OCSO, Achel, Belgium.
22. See below, p. 74.
23. See above, p. 8.
24. See below, p. 91.
25. See below, p. 80.
26. See below, p. 108.
27. See below, p. 107.
28. Accts., f. 32a.
29. See King, 'Coupar Angus and Cîteaux', 49-50; 66-9. On the lawsuit see Ganck, 'Les pouvoirs . . . ', 54-5; Telesca, 'Jean de Cirey and the Question of an Abbot General', 195-6.

30. See *Catalogue général des manuscrits des bibliothèques publiques de France—Départements* vi, 175-6.

31. E.g. Sens MS 129, ff. 174a-177 and Troyes MS 3 H 153 (Audit of 1390).

32. Sens MS 129, f. 99b and Easson, *Coupar Angus Charters*, i, 60-1.

33. Sens MS 129, ff. 1a-57a.

34. *TB*, 29b, 17, 18, 20.

35. *TB*, p. 19.

36. See below, p. 71.

37. *TB*, 29b, 17-21.

38. Copenhagen MS Thott 138, ff. 295b-298b. Discussed by Janauschek, *Orig.*, xviii.

39. See *TB*, pp. 13-14.

40. A.O. Johnsen, *TB*, p. 9.

41. Johnsen, *TB*, p. 9.

42. Johnsen, *TB*, p. 14.

43. Rouse, 'Cistercian aids to study', 125-132.

44. Franceschini, 'Un registro cisterciense della fine del sec. XIV', 123.

45. MTB, ff. 1a-10b.

46. *Ibid.*, ff. 11a-28b.

47. *Ibid.*, ff. 29a-b.

48. *Ibid.*, ff. 30a-33a.

49. *Ibid.*, ff. 34a-37a.

50. *Ibid.*, f. 1b, col. 2. Franceschini, 123.

51. MTB, f. 12a.

52. *Ibid.*, f. 20b. On the abbey see *Orig.*, 273.

53. Franceschini, 123-4.

54. MTB, f. 1b, col. 2; Franceschini, 123.

55. MTB, f. 5a, col. 2.

56. Schäfer, *Die Ausgaben der apostolischen Kammer unter Benedikt XII*, 23.

57. Accts., ff. 1a-14b.

58. See plate 1.

59. *Ibid.*, ff. 12a, col. 2; 14b, col. 1.

60. See plate 2.

61. Accts., ff. 16a, col. 1-29b, col. 2.

62. See plate 3.

63. E.g. heading for 1345, *ibid.*, f. 27b, col. 1.

64. E.g. *ibid.*, f. 26b.

65. E.g. *ibid.*, f. 26a.

66. *Ibid.*, f. 25b, col. 1 (1344); f. 27b, col. 2 (1346); f. 28a, col. 1

(1347). Cf. scribe No. 1, *ibid.,* f. 1a (1337—start of the whole book); f. 12a (1340).

67. *Ibid.,* f. 22a, col. 2; f. 22b, cols. 1, 2.
68. *Ibid.,* f. 27a, col. 1.
69. *Ibid.,* f. 17a, col. 2.
70. *Ibid.*
71. *Ibid.,* f. 20a, col. 2.
72. *Ibid.,* f. 22b, col. 2.
73. *Ibid.,* f. 20a, col. 2.
74. *Ibid.,* f. 22b, col. 1.
75. *Ibid.,* f. 24b, col. 2.
76. *Ibid.,* f. 27a, col. 1.
77. *Ibid.,* f. 29a, col. 2.
78. *Ibid.,* f. 29b, col. 1.
79. *TB,* 23b, 23; 24b, 7.
80. The author, whose name was once Königsberger, has some experience of this kind of joke.
81. See table below, p. 159.
82. Accts., ff. 18a, col. 1—20b, col. 1 (1341).
83. E.g. *ibid.,* f. 20b, cols. 1, 2 (1341).
84. *Ibid.,* f. 25b, col. 1 (1343); f. 27a, col. 2 (1344); f. 29b, col. 2 (1347).
85. E.g. *ibid.,* f. 20b, col. 2 (1341).
86. E.g. Accts., ff. 20b, col. 2—21a, col. 1 (1341).
87. See below, p. 173.
88. See below, p. 167.
89. E.g. Accts., f. 21a, col. 1 (1341).
90. *Ibid.,* f. 27b, col. 1 (1345); f. 27b, col. 2 (1346).
91. *Ibid.,* f. 27b, cols. 1, 2 (1345); ff. 27b, col. 2—28a, col. 1 (1346).
92. *Ibid.,* f. 27b, cols. 1-2.
93. *Ibid.,* f. 28a, col. 2.
94. See below, pp. 78 and 100.
95. Accts., f. 12a, cols. 1-2.
96. *Ibid.,* f. 13a, col. 1.
97. *Ibid.,* ff. 13a, col. 1—14a, col. 1.
98. Accts., ff. 14a, col. 2—14b, col. 2.
99. *Ibid.,* f. 14b, col. 2.
100. *Ibid.,* ff. 14b, col. 2—15b, col. 1.
101. *Ibid.,* ff. 15b, col. 1—16a, col. 2.
102. *Ibid.,* ff. 16a, col. 2—17b, col. 1.
103. *Ibid.,* f. 17b, col. 1.
104. *Ibid.,* f. 17b, col. 2.

105. *Ibid.,* f. 17b, col. 2.
106. See below, p. 100.
107. *Statuta* 1340, 14.
108. See above, p. 20.
109. Accts., ff. 1a, col. 1–1b, col. 2.
110. *Ibid.,* f. 1b, col. 2.
111. *Ibid.,* f. 2a, col. 1.
112. *Ibid.,* f. 2a, cols. 1–2.
113. *Ibid.,* f. 2a, col. 2.
114. *Ibid.,* ff. 2b, col. 1–7b, col. 1.
115. *Ibid.,* ff. 7b col. 1–8a, col. 2.
116. *Ibid.,* ff. 9b, col. 1–10b, col. 2. On nuns see below, p. 143f.
117. Accts., ff. 8a, col. 2–9a, col. 2 (1338); ff. 10b, col. 2–11b, col. 2 (1339).
118. *Ibid.,* ff. 5a, col. 1, 6a, col. 2; 6b, col. 2; 7b, col. 2; 10a, col. 1; 11b, col. 2; 12a, col. 1; 12a, col. 2; 13b, col. 2; 14a, col. 1; 14a, col. 2.
119. *Ibid.,* ff. 3b, col. 1; 3b, col. 2; 4b, col. 1.
120. *Ibid.,* ff. 2b, col. 2; 3a, cols. 1, 2; 6b, cols. 1, 2; 8a, col. 1.
121. *Ibid.,* ff. 4a, col. 2; 8a, cols. 1, 2; 10a, col. 1.
122. See above, p. 20.
123. Sens MS 129, ff. 169b-177a.
124. *Archives de l'Aube* 3 H 153.
125. See King, 'Coupar Angus and Cîteaux', 58-63, docts. 5, 6, 7, 8, 11, 13, 14, 15.
126. Krausen, 'Generalkapitel ausserhalb Cîteaux während des grossen Schismas', 7.
127. *Ibid.,* 8-10.
128. See King, 'Materials for a financial History of the Cistercian Order', 28-29. The Modena Tax Book should be included in any such survey, see above, p. 15.

CHAPTER TWO

The Endowments of the Chapter General and the Beginnings of the Collections.

LIKE ALL REFORMERS of the religious life in the Middle Ages, the founders of the Cistercian Order stressed the importance of poverty. Some twenty years after the event, a short history of the exodus from Molesmes thus described the motives of the seceders: 'Because possessions and virtues are not usually steady companions, several members of that holy community, men truly wise and filled with higher aspirations, decided to pursue heavenly studies rather than to be entangled in earthly affairs. Accordingly, these lovers of virtue soon came to think about that poverty which is fruitful to man'.[1]

The Cistercians did not, indeed, display the total aversion to money which was later to characterise St Francis and his companions. One of the Order's early statutes allowed monks to receive a fair price for their produce, in gold, silver, or base metal.[2] Cistercian abbeys were, however, to be, as far as possible, self-sufficient. Monks were to live from the work of their hands, the cultivation of the soil, and the care of flocks.[3] They were not to enjoy revenues from churches and tithes, from feudal rights, mills, furnaces, and other properties which would yield an income for which the community had not worked.[4] In the first chapter of the *Carta Caritatis* abbot Stephen and his community promised never to exact a tax from other abbeys in the new Order.[5] At meetings of the Chapter General the abbots present, inspired by the charity which had been the mark of their movement, were to come to the aid of any house which was in financial difficulties.[6]

In the early days, when the Chapter General was an annual gathering of a handful of Burgundian abbots, the meetings cannot have been a heavy charge on the Mother House. An early statute has been preserved, probably from 1119, when the number of abbots present was ten.[7] At this time the visitors would have been outnumbered by the community of Cîteaux which, together with abbot Stephen, formed an integral part of the early Chapters General. Some statutes from the first half of the twelfth century, however, show a certain anxiety about costs, as an increasing number of abbots had to be accommodated. It was decreed that an abbot going to the Chapter General could not take one of his monks with him. He must content himself with one lay-brother, and he was to have only two horses.[8] No guests were to be received at Cîteaux during this period. If it proved absolutely impossible to turn someone away, the abbey was on no account to feed his horses.[9] Whilst the Chapter General was meeting there were to be no visiting monks at the Mother House or one of its granges. If any were found they were to be whipped.[10] Some of these enactments may also have been intended to ensure secrecy during Chapter's deliberations.[11]

The Order spread quickly. Once its abbeys were to be found throughout Christendom it is unlikely that there was ever a Chapter General attended by all the abbots.[12] Those who did come, however, were a heavy charge upon the Mother House. Cîteaux was obliged to build a large hall which could accommodate three hundred persons.[13] By the end of the twelfth century it had become necessary to find ways to meet the expenses. In 1189 king Richard I of England gave the church of Scarborough to provide 'procurations'[14] for all the abbots at Cîteaux during the three days of the Chapter General.[15] Other endowments followed, from kings and magnates.[16] Eventually the more prosperous abbeys of the Order were prevailed upon to set aside estates, or make other arrangements, which would provide an annual income to lighten the burden of the Mother House in September, when the Chapter General met.

It is tempting to moralise about the way financial considerations intruded themselves upon an Order intent on poverty. A distinguished historian of the Order has written of the acquisition of Scarborough that 'the story . . . points a strong moral lesson . . . It is the story of the breach of one small item in the *Carta Caritatis,* and of the consequences that followed from it'.[17] The incident is here seen as the decisive step on the Order's road to perdition. It was like

> Man's First Disobedience, and the Fruit
> Of that Forbidden Tree, whose mortal taste
> Brought Death into the World, and all our Woe.[18]

In fact Scarborough was given to Cîteaux in order to lighten burdens wholly unforeseen in the early days. Throughout the Middle Ages the Mother House had to grapple with the consequences of the Order's too rapid growth during the twelfth century. Cistercian abbeys were forbidden to own churches, not by the *Carta Caritatis,* but by an early statute of the Chapter General.[19] The enactment may have been forgotten by 1189, or thought out of date. It is more likely that the authorities at Cîteaux were aware that chapter one of the *Carta Caritatis* forbade the raising of a tax within the Order.[20] Faced with expenses which no other abbey had to bear, Cîteaux may have found it more acceptable to disregard an early statute than to defy the *Carta Caritatis.* During the thirteenth century the Order's increasing indebtedness made even more drastic remedies necessary. As they foundered in a financial morass, the Cistercians of the late Middle Ages may be forgiven if they did not search the annals of their Order for a moral lapse to explain their difficulties.

By 1300 there were a number of rents and endowments from various sources, sometimes known as 'procurations', which had been given to the Mother House to cover the

expenses of the Chapter General. At some time in the early
fourteenth century it seems to have been thought necessary
to assign some of them to the abbey of Cîteaux, and others
directly to the Chapter General itself. This division had been
made at least by 1321. A statute of that year clearly dis-
tinguishes the two kinds of endowments.[21] Three documents
illustrate the process of division. One is a loose sheet of
parchment of the fifteenth century now in the *Archives
de l'Aube* at Troyes.[22] It is headed, 'Annual Rents of the
Chapter General'. There are signs that it was once part of a
book, and it appears to be a copy of a fourteenth-century
list.[23] Another document is the list of the Chapter General's
rents which comes at the end of the Order's fourteenth-
century Tax Book at Dijon.[24] This too is a copy of a
fourteenth-century original,[25] probably drawn up slightly
later than the list at Troyes, to which it is closely related.
Finally there is a small book made at the time of the lawsuit
of 1483-86, and also preserved in the *Archives de l'Aube*.[26]
It gives an inventory, and in some cases abstracts of documents relating to procurations.

The little book was polemical in intention and was to
provide evidence against Cîteaux in the lawsuit. The Troyes
list and that in the Dijon Tax Book are almost identical in
arrangement and wording, but there are a few significant
differences between them. The Troyes list begins with the
church of Scarborough, which the Tax Book list omits. At
some time in the fourteenth century, therefore, there seems
to have been disagreement about this prestigious property. In
the end it was assigned to the Mother House. An annual rent
from the abbey of Clairefontaine occurs only on the list in
the Tax Book. The two documents disagree about the size of
the rent owed by the abbey of Isle-de-Ré.

During the lawsuit of 1483-6, the monks of Clairvaux
claimed that none of these properties should ever have been
assigned to Cîteaux. They were intended for the upkeep of
the Chapter General and should have been absolutely at the

disposal of that body at all times. It was also claimed that the money from them had been misappropriated by the Mother House. In the *dossier* drawn up for use at the Parlement of Paris, the documents were accompanied by polemical notes. Some of those which gloss the Coupar Angus material will give an impression of the general style: 'Here they begin to claim that this rent belongs to themselves, and make no mention of the Order or the Chapter General' (about a receipt of 1287).[27] 'Another receipt from the abbot of Cîteaux . . . for payment due in 1324 and for past arrears, in which receipt he mentions only Cîteaux and not the Order'.[28] 'Another receipt from Jean abbot of Cîteaux . . . for the years 1346 and 1347, in which only Cîteaux and not the Chapter General is mentioned'.[29]

No historian today can investigate the charge of mis-appropriation of funds. It should be noted, however, that the fifteenth-century lawyers claimed no inside knowledge of the procedures at Cîteaux during previous centuries. They used the *argumentum e silentio,* assuming that if a receipt or other document did not expressly mention the Chapter General, the money had been misapplied. As for the division of properties between the Chapter and the Mother House, the decisions upon which it was based have not been recorded. There is sufficient doubt to make a detailed discussion of all endowments for the upkeep of the Chapter General necessary, whatever the fisc into which the revenues were paid.

The earliest of these endowments, and the most prestigious, was the church of Scarborough in Yorkshire, England.[30] Shortly after his coronation in 1189 king Richard I gave this church, over which he had patronage, to the abbey of Cîteaux. Twenty marks *sterling* out of its revenues were to be set aside for the vicar. The rest would provide for the abbots of the Order during the three days of the Chapter General. It was a generous gift intended to defray the entire costs. The king added, therefore, that what remained after

the expenses of hospitality had been met could be spent on
the other needs of the Mother House. At the beginning the
abbot of Cîteaux had some difficulty in establishing his
rights. He was involved in lawsuits with other claimants to
the patronage. There were disputes over parish rights with
the citizens of Scarborough, and later with the friars. Although the church was a royal gift, the most serious threat
came from the English Crown. Whenever there was a war with
France, the flow of revenues was interrupted. In 1294, for
instance, Edward I confiscated the church in order to prevent
money going across the sea to his enemies. The Order
appealed to the pope,[31] and its Accounts show that 1,550
livres tournois were spent on litigation over Scarborough.[32]

Most profit from the church seems to have come to
Cîteaux during the early fourteenth century. From the end
of the thirteenth century until 1311, Jacques Duport, one of
the monks of the Mother House, was its proctor in Scarborough. He was a man of energy and ability. He brought the
various lawsuits about the church to a successful conclusion.
He redecorated the building and added a fine new chapel. He
erected a house for the vicar and chaplains, and on some vacant
ground put up houses to let. Altogether he so improved the
properties that Cîteaux's revenues from them were greatly
increased. This prosperous period was brought to a halt by
the outbreak of the Hundred Years' War. The revenues of
Scarborough were again seized by the English Crown. For a
time they were assigned to the abbey of St Mary Graces, near
the Tower of London. In 1400 they were handed to the
abbey of Bridlington, which had long claimed the church.
Cîteaux tried until the eve of the Reformation to assert its
ancient claim, but to no avail.[33]

The annual revenue from Scarborough is nowhere clearly
stated. It may have depended upon circumstances and the
energy of the proctor. Jacques Duport was said to have
increased the annual profits by 18 marks 6 *s.* (*sterling*).[34]
As we have seen, the Chapter General at some time laid claim

to the church, but Cîteaux held on to it.[35] The documents show clearly that, until its seizure by the English Crown, the revenues were always paid directly to the Mother House. The Chapter General's claims were revived in 1483-6.[36]

Cîteaux obtained other English benefactions for the upkeep of the Chapter General. Earl Richard of Cornwall, brother of king Henry III, presented the church of Stainley in Yorkshire.[37] In the early fourteenth century Jacques Duport was engaged in litigation about this church.[38] In 1240 Richard of Cornwall gave Cîteaux an annual rent of 20 marks *sterling* to be levied on his mill at Boroughbridge. If for some reason the money could not be obtained from the mill, it was to be paid out of the earl's manor at Knaresborough.[39] It is likely that, as a result of the Barons' Wars in England, Cîteaux was never able to make use of these gifts.

In 1220 king Alexander II of Scotland gave the church of Airlie in Angus to the cistercian abbey of Coupar Angus.[40] The sum of 20 *l. sterling* out of the revenues was to be paid annually to Cîteaux for the upkeep of the Chapter General on its fourth day. It was a heavy charge on Airlie, and in order to get some profit out of it themselves, the monks of Coupar never established a vicarage for the church, which was served until the Reformation by a chaplain. In the thirteenth century the rent seems to have been paid regularly, but there were difficulties in the fourteenth. By 1344 Coupar Angus owed a large sum to Cîteaux for rents unpaid in former years. In the years which followed the abbey suffered heavily from the ravages of English invaders. Payments were excused for a time, and in 1350 a reduced rate was agreed. Things had improved sufficiently for full payment to be resumed in 1367. Some years later it was even possible to make up arrears. In the fifteenth century, however, it was usually necessary to send someone to Scotland to collect the money. The expense for the Order was hardly justified. In 1448 Coupar Angus redeemed the pension by paying a lump sum.

No rent had been due from this source for thirty-eight years, therefore, when the partisans of Clairvaux made their accusations of malversation.[41] It is impossible to tell what was done with all the money when it was paid, but the records show clearly that the Coupar Angus pension was never one of those which had been assigned to the Chapter General.

Benefactions also came from the French royal family. In 1225 Louis VIII celebrated the reconciliation of Raymond, count of Toulouse, with the Church by giving 2,000 marks of silver, which would cover all the costs of the Chapter General for that year.[42] In 1244 St Louis granted 40 *livres parisis.* from the prévôté of Sens.[43] In the same year his mother Blanche also granted an annual 40 *l.p.* from the prévôté of Melun,[44] and his brother Robert of Artois the same sum annually from his prévôté of Bapaume.[45] Philip IV continued the tradition by giving 30 *l.t.* to the Cistercian Chapter General in 1305.[46] It was one of a number of such gifts during that year to the General or Provincial Chapters of various religious Orders.[47] There were also benefactions from French magnates,[48] which occasionally led to arguments. Guy, count of Foix, had, at some time, left 100 *l.t.* to the Chapter General at Cîteaux. His heir refused to hand over the money and in September 1252 the abbot of Sept-Fons was empowered to write to him on the Chapter's behalf.[49] The vicomte of Thouars, who had pledged an annual 100 *s.t.,* had not, by 1252, paid for many years.[50] Chapter eventually appealed to his suzerain, Alphonse of Poitiers.[51]

From further afield came the rents from royal salt mines given by Alfonso IX of Leon in 1211, and confirmed in 1223 by Ferdinand III of Castile.[52] In 1246 king Bela of Hungary gave the revenues of four royal chapels in Transylvania.[53] No more seems to have been heard of these royal gifts, though the Hungarian document was brought up in the arguments of 1483-6.[54] Equally abortive was a gift from the king of Portugal in 1206. He sent it to some abbots (presumably from his kingdom) who were on their way to the Chapter General. Unfortunately he did not make his wishes at all clear, and Chapter was obliged to send two abbots to enquire politely what the money was for and what were his intentions.[55]

Help also came from the wealthier abbeys in the Order. Some time before 1200 the abbey of L'Arrivour in France (*dep.* Aube) granted a rent from one of its granges. It was later assigned to the Chapter General and will be discussed in its place.[56] In 1277 the abbey of Balerne in France (*dep.* Jura) settled a debt to the Mother House by promising an annual rent of 20 *l.t.* as procurations for the Chapter General. The abbot of Clairvaux, father abbot of Balerne, was to use his powers to ensure regular payments.[57] Some time in the fourteenth century *florins* were substituted for *livres tournois,* and later *francs* for *florins.*[58] The 20 *fr.* rent from Balerne appears in the Accounts of the bursar of Cîteaux for the years 1378-9,[59] and 1382-3.[60] Although this was one of the rents claimed in 1483-6 for the Chapter General,[61] it does not appear on the lists of its endowments,[62] and it is clear that the revenues were always paid to Cîteaux.

In 1277 the abbey of La Bénissons-Dieu in France (*dep.* Loire) promised an annual rent of 60 *l.t.* for the Chapter General, to be levied on its grange of Poant.[63] The sum (expressed as 60 *fr.*) was still coming in regularly in the late fourteenth century. It was paid in two instalments in the summer of 1379,[64] and at the time of the Chapter General in 1382.[65] In 1298 the abbey of Fontenay in France (*dep.* Côte d'Or) granted an annual 10 *l.t.* to be levied on some town property in Dijon.[66] The rent occurs in the Accounts of the bursar of Cîteaux in 1378-9.[67] There is no evidence, on the other hand, that a rent granted in 1316 by the abbey of Chassagne in France (*dep.* Ain)[68] was ever paid. It is the only one of those listed above which was not claimed for the Chapter General in 1483-6. All the others were demanded back from the Mother House.[69]

Cîteaux's policies in the last decades of the fourteenth century provided some ammunition for later critics. After the papal schism of 1378, the abbots who gathered at the Mother House for Chapters General were those who recognised the popes at Avignon. The power and prestige of this rump were much reduced, and it was over-shadowed by the great and famous abbey which provided the meeting place. The obedientiaries of Cîteaux took over the administration of the rents which survived. The Chapter General ceased to have separate endowments, and its financial officers accepted a subordinate position under the bursar of Cîteaux.[70] It was an urgent task to improve finances. One way of doing this was to increase the number of abbeys which promised to pay rents. In the period of 1378-83, eight such arrangements were made[71] and in November 1383 it was possible to draw up a list of fourteen abbeys which were paying rents to the Mother House.[72] There were houses like Balerne and La Bénissons-Dieu who had been paying for many years, but also new names like Auberive (Haute-Marne), Buillon (Doubs), Cherlieu (Haute-Saône), Royaumont (Seine-et-Oise), and the nunnery of Espagne (Somme). All were in France. Most of them seem to have paid about 30 *fr.* a year.[73] Payments were made directly to Cîteaux. They were far from regular and most of these arrangements do not seem to have lasted for more than a few years. Only the annual rent from Boulancourt (Haute-Marne), which began to be paid in 1378,[74] appears to have survived into the fifteenth century.[75] Thus by the time the papal schism had ended, Cîteaux had taken over all the rents, and the Chapter General had no endowments of its own.

As for the rents which, during the fourteenth century, were assigned to the Chapter General, they appear in two lists,[76] the older of which, possibly compiled in the 1340s and now in the *Archives de l'Aube*,[77] runs as follows:

Annual rents of the Chapter General

Scarborough	
The abbot of Rievaulx	50 *l.*
The abbess of Verguines	25 *l.*
The abbot of Val St. Lambert	50 *l.*
The abbot of Heisterbach	50 *l.*
The abbot of Bithaine	25 *l.*
The abbot of Disibodenberg	10 *l.*
The abbess of Épinlieu	15 *l.*
The abbot of Valdieu	100 *l.*
The abbot of Quincy	25 *l.*
The abbess of Groeninghe	15 *l.*
The abbot of l'Arrivour	50 *l.*
The abbot of St. Léonard	20 *l.*
The abbot of Isle-de-Ré	150 *l.*
The abbot of La Charité, whom the Chapter lent 600 *l.,* will pay, at a rate of 20 *s.* to the *florin*	30 *l.*

Sum total of the annual revenues of the Chapter General, with Scarborough and the rents of La Charité: 526 *l.* [78]

The list in the Dijon Tax Book is almost identical to that at Troyes. The abbeys are in the same order; the wording of the entry about La Charité is the same. The two lists must have been compiled from the same materials, and at dates very close to one another. In the Dijon list, however, Scarborough is omitted. The annual rent from Isle-de-Ré is lower. An annual rent from Clairefontaine is recorded. The latter arrangement may have been made to compensate for the loss of Scarborough. There is no sum total in the Dijon Tax Book, but there are notes about the redemption of many of the rents.[79]

It is now possible to consider individually each of the Chapter General's endowments:

Rievaulx, England, Yorkshire

Letters relating to a rent of 50 *l.t.* a year from Rievaulx were listed for use in the lawsuit of 1483-6.[80] Unfortunately they were not quoted. The origins of this rent cannot, therefore, be traced. During the fourteenth century payments were irregular, and only made under difficulties. The abbey was able to send 37 *l.t.* in 1337.[81] This was a backpayment. By then the abbey owed 601 *l.t.* for unpaid rents. A further 100 *l.t.* were owed for 1336 and 1337.[82] The Hundred Years' War made it almost impossible for English abbeys to send money to France. Rievaulx was one of those which, in 1343, made token payments to the Order in acknowledgement of arrears. In that year the abbey sent 40 *écus* for money owed in 1335, and 20 *écus* for 1337.[83] It is not clear whether this was for past rents, or for failure to contribute to Collections in the Order. In any case the amount paid, equivalent to 180 *l.t.*, was only a small proportion of the debt recorded in 1337. Nevertheless, as is clear from the Dijon list, at some time and in some way unrecorded, Rievaulx made an amicable agreement with the Order whereby the rent was redeemed.[84]

Verguines, Belgium

It is not easy to identify this abbey. In the Troyes list it is called *Vallis Celi*. In the Dijon list someone has written against this name, *Varguines*.[85] Canivez identified *Vallis Coeli* as Verguines or Vivegnis.[86] The nunnery of Vivegnis was in the province of Liège in modern Belgium.[87] The documents about this rent used for the lawsuit of 1483-6, however, speak of the abbess and convent of *Vallis Celi* in Brabant.[88] No monastery of that name in the province is recorded in *Monasticon Belge,* though there were two Cistercian nunneries in Brabant sometimes known as *Vallis virginum*—Val St Bernard at Diest, and Val Virginal at Oplinten.[89]

Although abstracts from documents relating to this rent were produced in 1483-6, none bears a date. There was often disagreement about the amount to be paid. The original grant seems to have promised 20 *l.* of Flemish silver.[90] In the Troyes and Dijon lists Verguines is down for 25 *l.*[91] There were certainly misunderstandings about the currency to be used. The Accounts of the Order record that in 1337 the nuns paid 20 *l.* for the previous year.[92] This payment may have been made in Flemish silver, as the original grant demanded. Elsewhere in the Accounts for that year, however, it is stated that the nuns' debt for 1336 was 25 *l.t.* and that they owed 100 *l.t.* for rents unpaid in the past.[93] In 1338 they were trounced for paying 25 *l.* in Flemish silver, worth only 21 *l.* in the money of Tours.[94] In 1341 they paid 50 *l.t.* for the current and previous years, as well as 48 *l.* 6 *s.t.* in arrears.[95] In 1342 they paid 25 *l.t.*,[96] and in the next year 20 *l.t.*[97] Some time in the fifteenth century the abbess of Verguines, owing to poverty, was allowed to pay a lump sum which freed her of having to pay the rent.[98]

Val St Lambert, Belgium, Liège

The rent, its origins unknown, was worth 50 *l.t.* a year. There were considerable difficulties about payment. In 1337 Val St Lambert owed 800 *l.t.* for unpaid rents in past years, and 100 *l.t.* for 1336 and the current year.[99] In 1343 the abbey paid 155 *l.t.* in arrears of rents for the last three years.[100] No more rents are recorded after this, though the abbey contributed regularly when Collections were made in the Order. In 1354 the rent was redeemed for a lump sum.[101]

Heisterbach, German Federal Republic, Nordrhein-Westfalen

The famous Rhineland abbey pledged itself, at some date unknown, to pay an annual rent of 50 *l.t.* In 1337 it owed 100 *l.t.* for the current and the previous years.[102] In 1341 it paid 50 *l.t.* for the current year and another 250 *l.t.* in arrears.[103] A payment of 50 *l.t.* duly came in 1342,[104] but only half that amount in the next year.[105] Since Heisterbach, like Val St Lambert, contributed regularly to the Collections in the Order, its financial support of the Chapter General in the middle years of the fourteenth century was very generous. It was allowed to redeem the rent with a lump sum in 1354.[106]

Bithaine, France, Haute-Saône

The abbey of Bithaine owed a yearly rent of 25 *l.t.* It was duly paid in 1337 and 1338.[107] Nothing came in 1339. In 1340 Bithaine paid 25 *l.t.* for the previous year and 11 *l.t.* for the current year.[108] The balance came in as 17 *l.t.* in 1341, in which year the abbey also paid the current rent which was due.[109] The apparent overpayment in 1340 may have been justified by the devaluation of French silver.[110] The abbey paid the rent it owed in 1343.[111]

Bithaine regularly contributed to the Collections in the Order during the years 1337-47, but its assessment was rather low.[112] The annual rent may have been considered a juster estimate of its obligations. Although there is no mention of redemption in the 1350s, Bithaine does not come into the Accounts of the bursar of Cîteaux some thirty years later. The rent from this abbey was still remembered in the fifteenth century, however, and it was claimed for the Chapter General in 1483-6.[113]

Disibodenberg, German Federal Republic, Rheinland-Pfalz

This abbey was pledged to pay a yearly rent of 10 *l.t.* In 1339 it paid 30 *l.t.* for the three years 1337-39.[114] After that, and up to 1344, it paid its rent in full, regularly and punctually.[115] The abbey also contributed faithfully to Collections. It was thus a valuable support to the Chapter General at this period. In 1354 it redeemed its rent with the payment of a lump sum.[116] Documents relating to the rent from Disibodenberg were used in the lawsuit of 1483-6.[117]

Épinlieu, Belgium, Hainault

The nunnery was founded some time in the thirteenth century.[118] At some time the community promised the Chapter General an annual rent of 15 *l.t.* It was duly paid in 1337.[119] Past payments were, however, outstanding—the nuns owed 30 *l.t.* for 1333 and 1335.[120] When the abbess paid 15 *l.t.* in 1338, the sum was recorded, confusingly, 'for last year'.[121] The next payment came in 1341—15 *l.t.* for the current year, and 30 *l.t.* for the previous two.[122] The nuns also made a modest contribution to the Collections in 1338.[123] In 1355 they made a composition relieving them from the annual rent.[124] Documents relating to the Épinlieu rent were used in the lawsuit of 1483-6.[125]

Valdieu, Belgium, Liège

The very valuable rent of 100 *l.t.* a year from this rich

abbey in the diocese and principality of Liège was pledged in 1294.[126] It was potentially the largest of all the rents, but it seems never to have been paid during the fourteenth century. In 1337 the abbey's debt to the Order for unpaid rents stood at 2,344 *l.t.* The rent for 1336 had not been paid, nor the one for the current year, adding a further 200 *l.t.*[127] There are no further references to Valdieu in the Order's Accounts for 1337-47, nor does it figure in the slightly later ones of the bursar of Cîteaux. The 100 *l.t.* rent from Valdieu was not forgotten, however, and was listed among the assets of the Chapter General in 1483-6.[128]

Quincy, France, Yonne

The rent from this abbey was worth 25 *l.t.* a year. In 1338, 50 *l.t.* were paid for the current year and the previous one.[129] The rent was paid in 1339,[130] 1342,[131] and 1343.[132] Quincy contributed frequently to the Collections in the Order during the period 1337-47, and contributions from the abbey were expected in 1378.[133] In 1381 it negotiated a new agreement under which it agreed to pay an annual rent of 30 *fl.* in procurations for the Chapter General.[134] In 1450 this rent was redeemed by the gift to Cîteaux of a small estate.[135]

Groeninghe à Courtrai, Belgium, Flandre occidentale

The abbey, founded on another site in 1236, moved, after a boundary dispute with another nunnery, to Groeninghe near the walls of Courtrai.[136] At some time the nuns pledged themselves to pay the Chapter General an annual rent of 15 *l.* in the silver of Flanders.[137] In the Order's Accounts for 1337 it was noted that they owed 15 *l.t.* for 1334.[138] For the current year they paid 13 *l.* 5s. 5½ *d.t.*[139]

The odd sum is almost certainly the result of reckoning up in terms of money of Tours a payment made in that of Flanders. In 1338 the abbess was again caught out; the 12 *écus* she had paid were worth 15 *l.* in Flemish money, but only 12 *l.* in the silver of Tours.[140]

As is clear from the fifteenth-century abstracts, the nuns had originally promised payments in their own currency.[141] Pressure upon them to pay in money of Tours, however, or at least have their payments calculated in terms of that currency, were irresistible. After 1338 Groeninghe seems to have surrendered, and thus acquiesced in an increase of its rent. In 1341 the abbey's payment was 15 *l.t.* for the current rent, and 28 *l.* 15 *s.t.* in arrears.[142] In 1342 the payment was 15 *l.t.* and another 25 *s.t.* in arrears.[143] The nuns were now considered up to date, and paid their due rent of 15 *l.t.* in 1343.[144] They had been heavily penalised for their temerity in adhering strictly to the terms of their original agreement with the Order.

No further payments from them are recorded, and in the fifteenth century they were able to redeem the rent with the payment of a lump sum.[145]

L'Arrivour, France, Aube

The rent from L'Arrivour was for 50 *l.t.* a year. It had been granted some time before 1200 from the profits of the abbey's grange of Le Don l'Evesque which L'Arrivour held from the Chapter General in farm.[146] Thus some ten years after the grant of Scarborough, its rents were no longer sufficient to cover all the costs to the Mother House in September. In 1321 the Chapter General confiscated the grange, because the pension had not been paid for some time,[147] but the matter appears to have been settled. By 1337 the abbey was again in possession of Le Don l'Evesque and paid the 50 *l.t.* due for that year, as well as 10 *l.t.* in arrears.[148] It still owed 80 *l.t.,* however.[149] From 1338-44 the abbey faithfully paid its annual rent.[150] The 80 *l.t.* arrears were also paid off: 10 *l.t.* in 1338;[151] another 10 *l.t.* in the following year;[152] and 60 *l.t.* in 1340.[153] The abbey contributed regularly to the Collections in the years 1337-47.

In the last decades of the fourteenth century the Mother House took over the rent, and raised it to 100 *l.t.* a year.[154] It proved extremely difficult to pay. In 1377 L'Arrivour sent 50 *fr.* towards what was owed in that year.[155] In April 1378 the abbey sent 25 *fr.* and in May 16 *fr.*[156] In 1392 L'Arrivour owed Cîteaux 1,300 *l.t.* for unpaid rents. The 100 *l.t.* due for the current year showed no sign of appearing. The abbey therefore offered its grange of Champigny to clear the debt and redeem the rent for all time.[157]

There may have been some justification in this case for the complaints, made in 1483-6, that Cîteaux had usurped rents set aside for the Chapter General.[158]

St Léonard-des-Chaumes, France, Charente Maritime

This rent is only mentioned in the two lists of the endowments of the Chapter General,[159] according to which it was worth 20 *l.t.* a year. It does not figure in the Accounts, or in the lawsuit of 1483-6.

Isle-de-Ré, France, Charente Maritime

The amount of rent owed by this abbey is uncertain. In the Troyes list it is 150 *l.t.* a year;[160] in the Dijon Tax Book the sum is 110 *l.t.*[161] During the period 1337-47, the abbey contributed fairly regularly to Collections in the Order, but paid no rent for some years. Then, in 1340, 10 *l.t.* were sent towards what was owed in the current year. For the years 1337, 1338, and 1339, the abbey paid 465 *l.t.*—155 *l.t.* for each.[162] In 1342 the sum was 10 *l.t.* towards what was owed in the current year.[163] In 1343 Isle-de-Ré paid 25 *l.t.* and 155 *l.t.* as backpayment for 1341.[164]

There is some evidence, therefore, that during this period the rent was 155 *l.t.* a year. In any case the rent owed was the highest of all those recorded, and was clearly a heavy burden for a house which was neither rich nor famous. Even so, this abbey was more conscientious than the prosperous abbey of Valdieu.[165] Isle-de-Ré does not figure in the Accounts of the bursars of Cîteaux, and was not mentioned in the lawsuit of 1483-6.

La Charité, France, Haute-Saône

The annual payment of 30 *l.t.* from the abbey of La Charité was interest (at 5%) on a loan of 600 *l.t.*[166] The abbey was protected from fluctuations in the value of French silver by the promise that, for the purposes of this transaction, a rate of 20 *s.t.* to the *florin* would always be used. Payments came in punctually from 1336-9.[167] In 1340 the capital sum was repaid in full.[168] The abbey also contributed to the Collections throughout the period of 1337-47.

It is not easy to understand why the Dijon Tax Book, which recorded the redemption of so many rents, should not mention the settlement of this debt. Since in 1483-6 the monks of Clairvaux were in possession of an ancient list which mentioned it,[169] they included La Charité among the rents they claimed for the Chapter General.[170]

Clairefontaine, France, Haute-Saône

The annual rent of 50 *l.t.* from the abbey is listed only in the Dijon Tax Book.[171] A note records that at some time it had been redeemed.[172] Though the abbey contributed to the

Collections in the period 1337-47, the rent is not mentioned in any of the Order's Accounts, nor does it occur in the arguments of 1483-6.

It is clear that some of the abbeys listed above, especially those which paid rents and contributed to the Collections, were generous in their support of the Chapter General. For some time during the fourteenth century Chapter also received a handsome annual gift of 100 *l.t.* in alms from Philip VI's queen, Jeanne of Burgundy, who took a personal interest in the famous meeting of abbots which took place every year in the land of her birth. She had a special affection for Cîteaux where, after her death, her heart was buried.[173]

Her alms were regularly paid in the years 1337-41,[174] except in 1338 when the queen sent 98 *l.* 40 *s.* 2 *d.t.*[175] In 1342 the expected sum failed to arrive,[176] but 200 *l.t.* came in the next year.[177] The Accounts of 1345 are so sketchy that it is impossible to tell what was received from the queen. She seems to have sent something, since the Order later had to count up its losses from her depreciated silver.[178] No alms came from her in 1346 and 1347.[179] She died of the plague in September 1348.[180] When the pension from the queen was paid in 1349,[181] it may have come from Blanche, daughter of King Philip of Navarre, whom King Philip VI married very quickly after the death of his first wife.[182]

Queen Jeanne must have made some kind of promise, since the Order regarded her alms as a regular source of income, and noted when they did not arrive. On the other hand, these payments were a free gift and there could be no question of arrears. No doubt the benefactions were temporarily interrupted by the troubles which overwhelmed Philip VI and his court after the battle of Crécy.

The financial requirements of Cîteaux and the Cistercian Order could not, however, always be met by fixed rents and alms. The need for something more showed itself quite early. In 1235 Cîteaux was in serious difficulties because of storms, crop failures, mortality among its animals, and 'other afflictions'.[183] The last, it has been suggested,[184] were the attacks on the Order by bishops and magnates. It looks, however, as if, in the opinion of the Chapter General, Cîteaux had, through its improvidence, brought its troubles upon itself. It was decided that the whole Order must help, and that a Collection from all constituent abbeys should be organised. The money was to be handed over to three abbots, who had the responsibility of settling Cîteaux's debts. The Mother House was to undertake no more building, either at home or on its groups, until the debt was reduced to 1,000 marks.[184a] Until that time, its economic activities were to be strictly supervised. The three abbots were to give a financial report to the four seniors when these latter carried out their annual visitation of the Mother House.[185]

The raising of the subvention from the Order was organised in some detail. The total to be raised was 4,000 marks. Father abbots were to raise a certain sum from their daughter houses. These in turn would take part of it from the houses dependent upon themselves, and so on down the Cistercian hierarchy, until every house had a quota.[186] These arrangements foreshadowed exactly the organisation of the later Collections. The fixing of a global sum which was handed down the ranks of abbeys in the Order, the appointment of two or three abbots to supervise the whole process, were expedients used again and again after 1250. On this, the first occasion, however, there was considerable opposition. The decision of 1235 was based upon the chapter of the *Carta Caritatis* which urged abbots to come to the aid of any house which was in difficulties.[187] In 1235 there seems, however, to have been an element of compulsion. Three years later the Chapter General admitted that there had been complaints that the subvention to Cîteaux was against the spirit of the *Carta Caritatis*.[188] Chapter promised therefore that nothing of this kind would ever be done again, and that in future, if any abbey required help, all should freely decide how much they wished to give.[189] The subvention of 1235 was not, however, remitted. In 1241 those who had not yet paid were reminded of their obligations.[190] In 1246 laggards were threatened with suspension, though Chapter added that all this was without prejudice, and that the promises made in 1238 were still valid.[191] These promises, like all those made by public authorities, were soon forgotten. In 1250 the Chapter General decided upon a mandatory Collection throughout the Order.[192]

The heavy financial burdens which made it necessary to take so grave a step, and go back on undertakings so recently made, resulted mainly from papal taxation.[193] In theory the Cistercian Order was exempt from all financial demands. Innocent III and his successors, however, had thought it wrong that the White Monks should stand aside when the needs of the Christians in the Holy Land, or of the Holy See, were pressing. In the thirteenth century the Cistercians were the subjects of much criticism, and they were finally induced to placate their detractors by paying large lump sums to the popes. In this way they hoped to avoid the assessments for property taxes to which other clergy were subject. The kings of France also felt that exempt Orders should contribute to the defense of the realm. In fact, it was not always easy to distinguish between the demands for money for the Holy Land, for the pope, or for the king of France. The reason given for the Collection of 1250 in the Cistercian Order was that 'the Order is liable for many debts which are accumulating interest, and is engaged in affairs of great difficulty'.[194] It was an official explanation, statesmanlike in its dignified vagueness. Later in the thirteenth century the Chapter General was more explicit when it ordered Collections. Statutes referred to the papal campaigns in Sicily, Crusading tenths, and the demands of papal legates for procurations.[195]

In deciding to raise what was, in all but name, a tax from the Order, the Cistercian Chapter General may have been encouraged by the fact that many other religious Orders did the same. The provinces of the Order of Knights Hospitaller were obliged, by their Rule, to give financial support to the convent in Jerusalem. Each priory of the Order sent an annual sum equivalent to one third of all the profits from its properties. These payments were known as 'responsions', and by the middle of the thirteenth century the amount expected from each priory seems to have been fixed.[196] There is evidence that by the end of the thirteenth century the Premonstratensians had worked out a system for taxing all their houses for the benefit of the Order. Each circary was assessed for a particular sum when a 'great collection' was held.[197]

It was soon apparent that a system of Collections must be flexible so that it could be adapted to varying situations. Because responsions in the Order of St John were based on fixed payments, extra imposts were devised to meet growing financial needs.[198] The Premonstratensians had two kinds of subvention: there was the 'Great Collection' which was to bring in altogether 8,000 *l.t.;* and the 'Half Collection', presumably to raise 4,000 *l.t.,* approved by the Chapter General in 1300.[199] Individual circaries were also assessed for Collections at these two levels.[200] These Premonstratensian arrangements were, as will be seen, very similar to those devised for the Cistercians. Details of the financial organisation of other religious Orders remain to be uncovered. When all the research has been done and the comparisons made, however, it will probably be found that all these systems were based upon, or greatly influenced by, the elaborate financial organisation of the papal *Camera.* With its army of experts, its searching methods of assessment, and its sophisticated accounting system, it left no ecclesiastical body or individual untouched. The regulars could not, in the end, escape its exactions; but they tried, on a smaller scale, to emulate some of its successes.

In 1238, those who objected to a compulsory Collection in the Cistercian Order could claim that it was against the spirit of the *Carta Caritatis*. It would have been difficult to use this argument later. In 1265 the Cistercians were given new fundamental legislation by Pope Clement IV. The *Carta Caritatis* was not, indeed, revoked. Clement IV was not as brutal with the primitive documents of the Order as Gregory IX had once been with the Testament of St Francis. Only on one point was the *Carta* expressly modified.[201] For the rest, the ancient document remained the classic expression of the Cistercian spirit, and was read out in its entirety at every meeting of the Chapter General.[202] In fact, however, the bull *Parvus Fons* of 1265 covered much the same ground and became the governing instrument of the Order. It too was read out at Chapters General.[203] After the bull *Fulgens* was added in 1335, Cistercians had a consistent body of papal legislation which catered for all their needs. The bulls were known together as 'the papal statutes', and it was to them that appeal was made in the fourteenth century and later.[204] Both these bulls sanctioned the collection of money from the whole Order for common purposes. *Parvus Fons* did so rather vaguely,[205] *Fulgens* approved the organisation of Collections in detail, and added papal sanctions to the punishments for non-payment.[206] It is otiose, therefore, to accuse the Cistercians of the later Middle Ages of falling away from their primitive ideals when they raised money from the Order. They dealt, as best they could, with new and disturbing developments. Above all, these men have a right to be judged by the rules which they themselves felt bound to obey.

NOTES TO CHAPTER TWO

1. *Exordium Cistercii*, trans. in Lekai, *The Cistercians*, 443.
2. *Instituta Generalis Capituli*, LI, *Statuta*, i, p. 24.
3. *Capitula* XV, *Les plus anciens textes de Cîteaux*, 123.
4. *Capitula* XXIII, *Les plus anciens textes*, 124.
5. *Carta Caritatis prior* I, *Les plus anciens textes*, 91; *Carta Caritatis posterior* I, *Statuta* i, p. xxvi.
6. *Carta Caritatis prior* VII, *Les plus anciens textes*, 95; *Carta Caritatis posterior* XX, *Statuta* i, p. xxix.
7. *Les plus anciens textes*, 105.
8. *Instituta Generalis Capituli* XLII, *Statuta* i, p. 23.
9. *Instituta Generalis Capituli* LV, *Statuta* i, pp. 25-6.
10. *Instituta* LXXVI, *Statuta* i, p. 30.
11. See Mahn, *L'ordre cistercien*, 177.
12. Lekai, *The Cistercians*, 69.
13. Mahn, *L'ordre cistercien*, 174.
14. 'ad procurandos omnes abbates'.
15. See below, p. 33f.
16. See below, p. 36f.
17. Talbot, 'Cîteaux and Scarborough', 95.
18. *Paradise Lost*, i, 1-3.
19. See above, p. 29.
20. *Ibid.*
21. *Statuta* 1321, 16.
22. 3 H 148.
23. See discussion in TB, p. 33.
24. *TB* 29b, 15-29.
25. See above, p. 14.
26. 3 H 157.
27. King, 'Coupar Angus and Cîteaux', 58.
28. *Ibid.*
29. *Ibid.*, 61.
30. For what follows see complete account with all the documents in Talbot, 'Cîteaux and Scarborough'.

31. Sens MS. 129, f. 24b.
32. See below, p. 93.
33. Talbot, 'Cîteaux and Scarborough', 106-116.
34. *Ibid.,* 142.
35. See above, p. 32.
36. Sens MS 129, ff. 69b-80b.
37. Talbot, 128.
38. *Ibid.,* 141.
39. *Ibid.,* 128.
40. For what follows, see complete account with all the documents in King, 'Coupar Angus and Cîteaux'.
41. See above, p. 33
42. Sens MS 129, ff. 155b-156a. In this, as in many of the other documents copied into Sens MS 129, the currency is not specified.
43. *Archives de la Côte d'Or* 11 H 157.
44. Mahn, *L'ordre cistercien,* 272-3.
45. *Ibid.,* 274.
46. *Comptes royaux (1285-1314)* ii, No. 16338.
47. *Ibid.,* Nos. 16339-16348.
48. *Archives de la Côte d'Or* 11 H 151-160.
49. *Statuta* 1252, 46.
50. *Statuta* 1252, 47.
51. *Statuta* 1253, 36.
52. *Archives de la Côte d'Or* 11 H 161.
53. Mahn, *L'ordre cistercien,* 274-6.
54. Sens MS 129, f. 81b.
55. *Statuta* 1206, 76.
56. See below, p. 45.
57. *Archives de l'Aube* 3 H 148; 3 H 157; Sens MS 129, ff. 114b-117a.
58. *Archives de l'Aube* 3 H 148.
59. Accts., f. 49b, col. 2.
60. *Ibid.,* f. 94b, col. 1.
61. *Archives de l'Aube* 3 H 157.
62. See below, p. 39.
63. *Archives de la Côte d'Or* 11 H 163; Sens MS 129, ff. 117a-119a.
64. Accts., f. 49b, col. 2.
65. *Ibid.,* f. 94b, col. 1.
66. *Archives de la Côte d'Or* 11 H 166; *Archives de l'Aube* 3 H 157.
67. Accts., f. 49b, col. 2.
68. *Archives de la Côte d'Or* 11 H 165.
69. *Archives de l'Aube* 3 H 157.
70. See below, p. 111.

71. Accts., ff. 49b, cols. 1-2; 94b, col. 1.
72. *Ibid.,* f. 94b, col. 1.
73. *Ibid.*
74. Accts., f. 49b, col. 1.
75. *Archives de l'Aube* 3 H 157.
76. See above, p. 32.
77. 3 H 148.
78. Without Scarborough it comes to 515 *l.* but 11 *l.* a year seems too low for the church. See above, p. 34.
79. *TB* 29b, 15-29.
80. *Archives de l'Aube* 3 H 157.
81. Accts., f. 1b, col. 2.
82. *Ibid.,* f. 2a, col. 2.
83. *Ibid.,* f. 24b, col. 1. See below, p. 000.
84. *TB* 29b, 15.
85. *TB* 29b, 15.
86. *Statuta* viii, pp. 512, 526.
87. *Monasticon Belge* II, i, 212-7.
88. *Archives de l'Aube* 3 H 157.
89. *Monasticon Belge* IV, 549-84.
90. *Archives de l'Aube* 3 H 157.
91. See above, p. 39 and *TB* 29b, 16.
92. Accts., f. 1b, col. 2.
93. *Ibid.,* f. 2a, col. 1.
94. *Ibid.,* f. 8a, col. 2.
95. *Ibid.,* f. 20b, col. 2.
96. *Ibid.,* f. 23a, col. 1.
97. *Ibid.,* f. 25a, col. 2.
98. *Archives de l'Aube* 3 H 157.
99. Accts., f. 2a, col. 2.
100. *Ibid.,* f. 25a, col. 2.
101. *TB* 29b, 17.
102. Accts., f. 2a, col. 1.
103. *Ibid.,* f. 20b, col. 2.
104. *Ibid.,* f. 23a, col. 1.
105. *Ibid.,* f. 25a, col. 2.
106. *TB* 29b, 18.
107. Accts., ff. 1b, col. 2; 8a, col. 2.
108. *Ibid.,* f. 17b, col. 1.
109. *Ibid.,* f. 20b, col. 2.
110. See below, p. 159.
111. Accts., f. 25a, col. 2.

112. *TB,* f. 22b, 6.
113. *Archives de l'Aube* 3 H 157.
114. Accts., f. 10b, col. 2.
115. *Ibid.,* f. 17b, col. 1 (1340); 20b, col. 2 (1341); 23a, col. 1 (1342); 25a, col. 2 (1343); 27a, col. 1 (1344).
116. *TB* 29b, 20.
117. *Archives de l'Aube* 3 H 157.
118. *Monasticon Belge* I, ii, 364-71.
119. Accts., f. 1b, col. 2.
120. *Ibid.,* f. 2a, col. 1.
121. *Ibid.,* f. 8a, col. 2.
122. *Ibid.,* f. 20b, col. 2.
123. *Ibid.,* f. 5b, col. 2.
124. *TB* 29b, 21.
125. *Archives de l'Aube* 3 H 157.
126. Sens MS 129, ff. 137a-b.
127. Accts., f. 2a, col. 1.
128. *Archives de l'Aube* 3 H 157.
129. Accts., f. 8a, col. 2.
130. *Ibid.,* f. 10b, col. 2.
131. *Ibid.,* f. 23a, col. 1.
132. *Ibid.,* f. 25a, col. 2.
133. Accts., f. 50b, col. 1.
134. Sens MS 129, f. 137b; *Archives de l'Aube* 3 H 157.
135. *Archives de l'Aube* 3 H 157.
136. *Monasticon Belge* III, i, 513-44.
137. *Archives de l'Aube* 3 H 157.
138. Accts., f. 2a, col. 1.
139. *Ibid.,* f. 1b, col. 2.
140. *Ibid.,* f. 8a, col. 2.
141. *Archives de l'Aube* 3 H 157.
142. Accts., f. 20b, col. 2.
143. *Ibid.,* f. 23a, col. 1.
144. *Ibid.,* f. 25a, col. 2.
145. *Archives de l'Aube* 3 H 157.
146. Sens MS 129, ff. 150b-155; *Archives de l'Aube* 3 H 157; *Statuta* 1268, 59.
147. *Statuta* 1321, 16.
148. Accts., f. 1b, col. 2.
149. *Ibid.,* f. 2a, col. 2.
150. *Ibid.,* ff. 8a, col. 2 (1338); 10b, col. 2 (1339); 17b, col. 1 (1340); 20b, col. 2 (1341); 23a, col. 1 (1342); 25a, col. 2 (1343); 27a, col. 1 (1344).

151. *Ibid.,* f. 8a, col. 2.
152. *Ibid.,* f. 10b, col. 2.
153. *Ibid.,* f. 17b, col. 1.
154. *Ibid.,* f. 45b, col. 1.
155. *Ibid.*
156. *Ibid.*
157. *Statuta* 1392, 5, 6, 7.
158. *Archives de l'Aube* 3 H 157.
159. See above, p. 39.
160. *Ibid.*
161. *TB* 30a, 27.
162. Accts., f. 17b, col. 1.
163. *Ibid.,* f. 23a, col. 1.
164. *Ibid.,* f. 25a, col. 2.
165. See above, p. 43.
166. See above, p. 39.
167. Accts., ff. 1b, col. 2 (1336, 1337); 8a, col. 2 (1338); 10b, col. 2 (1339).
168. *Ibid.,* f. 17b, col. 1.
169. See above, p. 39.
170. *Archives de l'Aube* 3 H 157.
171. *TB* 30a, 29.
172. *Ibid.*
173. Anselme, *Histoire Généalogique et Chronologique de la Maison royale de France,* i, 103.
174. Accts., ff. 1b, col. 2 (1337); 11a, col. 1 (1339); 17b, col. 1 (1340); 20b, col. 2 (1341).
175. *Ibid.,* f. 8a, col. 2.
176. *Ibid.,* f. 23a, col. 1.
177. *Ibid.,* f. 25a, col. 2.
178. See below, p. 167.
179. 'Nihil', Accts., ff. 27b, col. 2; 29b, col. 1.
180. Anselme, *Histoire Généalogique,* i, 103.
181. *Les journaux du Trésor de Philippe VI de Valois,* No. 2534.
182. Anselme, i, 105.
183. *Statuta* 1235, 20.
184a. The marks were probably of Troyes, but are not specified in text.
184. Buczek, 'Pro defendendis Ordinis', 104.
185. *Statuta* 1235, 20.
186. *Statuta* 1236, 35.
187. *Carta Caritatis posterior* XX; *Statuta,* i, p. xxix.
188. *Statuta* 1238, 6.
189. *Ibid.*
190. *Statuta* 1241, 7.

191. *Statuta* 1246, 6.
192. *Statuta* 1250, 21.
193. For what follows see D.S. Buczek, 'Medieval Taxation, the French Crown, the Papacy, and the Cistercian Order', 42-106.
194. *Statuta* 1250, 21.
195. *Statuta* 1268, 7; 1269, 10, 11; 1270, 7; 1277, 9; 1278, 18: 1279, 76.
196. See J. Riley-Smith, *The Knights of St. John,* 344-47; T.H. Olsen, *Dacia og Rhodos,* 20, 72 n. 34.
197. *Monasticon Praemonstratense,* iii, 374, 417-51. For administrative purposes Premonstratensian houses were grouped, according to their geographical locations, into 'circaries'.
198. Riley-Smith, *op. cit.* 344; Olsen, *op. cit.,* 73 n. 34.
199. *Monasticon Praemonstratense,* 417.
200. *Ibid.,* 417-51.
201. *Parvus Fons* 2, *Statuta,* iii, p. 24.
202. Mahn, *L'ordre cistercien,* 194.
203. *Statuta* 1272, 9.
204. See e.g. *Statuta* 1340, 6; 1341, 6; 1343, 6; 1346, 2; etc.
205. *Parvus Fons* 4, *Statuta,* iii, p. 27.
206. *Fulgens* 17, 18; *Statuta,* iii, pp. 420-2.

CHAPTER THREE

The Organisation of the Collections

FROM THE OFFICIAL RECORDS it is clear that the responsibility for organising Collections within the Order lay with the abbot of Cîteaux and the four senior abbots. The Accounts and the Tax Book arrange their material according to the five 'generations'. The main lines of the organisation can already be discerned in the Collection of 1235.[1] They become even clearer in 1250. In that year payment was made mandatory. Chapter General used the words 'has decided and commands'. One thousand marks were to be raised from the whole Order. The abbot of Clairvaux would collect 500 within his generation, the abbot of Morimond 250 in his; the other 250 were to be divided among the generations of Cîteaux, La Ferté, and Pontigny.[2] In the fourteenth century the five seniors continued to be regarded as the chief executors of the Order's financial policies. Although the abbot of Cîteaux was mentioned first, statutes about finance made it clear from their wording that the five were equal.[3]

The total sum to be raised was probably divided up among the generations as a result of bargaining. There were naturally complaints about unfairness. Chapter stated in 1326, 'In future each abbot shall answer for his contributions directly to the Chapter General alone. Thus it will be clear, when contributions are levied in future, whether any generation has been prejudiced.'[4] Whilst the Chapter General stepped in, on occasions, to make sure that burdens were fairly distributed, the sanctions which enforced payment

59

were the responsibility of the five seniors. The *Libellus Diffinitionum* of 1340 laid down that, in remote areas, the five seniors must, each in his own generation, appoint abbots who would report back about unpaid contributions.[5] The five seniors pronounced sentences of excommunication and deposition upon those who did not pay.[6] Their ultimate responsibility in financial matters was stressed as early as 1314, 'In order to avoid controversy, the Chapter General commands and decrees that whenever there are Collections in the Order, the *receptores* must present an account of a meeting of the abbot of Cîteaux, the four seniors, and the diffinitors of the Chapter General or their representatives. Father abbots who had the responsibility of imposing quotas must give an account in writing to the abbot of Cîteaux, stating what they have done.'[7]

After a generation had been allocated its collective quota, each of the five seniors divided it up among the abbots of his immediate daughter houses. Some information about the way this was done comes from the *Codex Dunensis*. In 1284, when a tithe was demanded for the French king's Aragonese Crusade, the abbot of Clairvaux held consultations with all his dependent abbots. He then allocated a sum which an abbot would either pay alone, or, if he had daughter houses himself, would subdivide in the same way. As much as possible was done through consultation and agreement, and after a conscientious calculation of the resources of each abbey and its daughters.[8] In an undated letter, probably of the late thirteenth century, the abbot of Clairvaux told the abbots of his daughter houses, 'Out of the sum allocated to us and our generation, we have thought it right to assign to you and to your daughter houses certain sums, which we hereby send to you under our seal, according to the list below. We have done this on the advice of wise men, and guided by our conscience, as faithfully, exactly, and justly, as possible.'[9] On 21 September 1311 the abbot of Clairvaux addressed a letter to fifteen of his abbots in the kingdom of France, with whom he had probably discussed matters immediately after the Chapter General of that year. He declared that he sympathised with their financial difficulties. He felt considerable reluctance in asking them for money. The Chapter General had decided, however, that a subsidy must be raised. The list of Clairvaux's immediate daughter houses in the kingdom, and of the sums which they and the abbeys below them must pay, was appended.[10] The abbot of Morimond, who was sometimes given special responsibility for collecting money in Germany,[11] no doubt dealt with the abbots immediately below him in much the same way.

The next stage was for father abbots to summon the abbots below them and impose sums, until each house had its quota.[12] In making the assessment of an individual abbey they were to take into account its wealth and revenues, and to consult all the other abbots of daughter houses. They were entitled to be paid reasonable expenses, but could make no extra charge. They were also to impose a fair quota upon their own abbey, and to make sure that it was paid.[13] When holding meetings to assess quotas, they must account for the payment of their own contribution and for their handling of the other abbots' money. The whole procedure was to be under the supervision of the Chapter General, to which appeals could be made.[14]

All this implied that accurate information about the economic state of each abbey was available. In 1285 father abbots were asked to declare exactly how many monks each daughter house could support. Once the limits were fixed according to the revenues of each house, they were not to be exceeded.[15] In 1310 the obedientiaries of every Cistercian abbey were told that during a visitation they must supply an accurate account of revenues and expenditures.[16] The election of an abbot was another occasion for such enquiries. When the father abbot came to supervise the proceedings he was instructed to have a written survey of the abbey's

properties and debts compiled.[17] All this information should
have been available to father abbots when they had to impose quotas during Collections. In the latter half of the
fourteenth century, however, the statutes of the Chapter
General until he had been named by his father abbot or one
of the Chapter's commissaries.[18] In 1353 it was necessary,
When the Chapter General excommunicated and deposed
abbots in general terms for non-payment, it was left to the
father abbots to single out the culprits and apply the sentences. In 1338 it was decreed that no abbot was to consider
himself deposed by reason of a sentence of the Chapter
General until he had been named by his father abbot or one
of the Chapter's commisssaries.[18] In 1353 it was necessary,
because of the disorders caused by the Hundred Years' War,
to state that if an abbot found it too dangerous to go to a
particular abbey, he could summon its superior to a safe
place.[19]

In the meantime the assessment of quotas had been somewhat simplified by appeals to precedent. In 1350 father
abbots were warned not to be arbitrary in imposing quotas
but to be guided by amounts due in the past.[20] The best way
to ensure this was to compile a central register of assessments.
In 1318 father abbots and visitors were asked to inform the
Chapter General fully about the economic state of the
houses they had visited.[21] They were also to make known the
quotas they had imposed during Collections. All this material
was to be recorded in a book, and thus there would be no
further reason for complaints about unfairness.[22] The statute
was repeated in greater detail in 1320,[23] and in 1326 an elaborate system for recording assessments was devised. In every
ecclesiastical province the abbots would elect two of their
number to make detailed enquiries about the sum paid by
each house during the last Collections, the value of its revenues and of its immovable property. All this information,
recorded on rolls in which the abbeys were distinguished by
generations, was to be forwarded to Cîteaux.[24] A similar

survey was ordered in 1329.[25] In 1330 father abbots were once more urged to forward details of assessments to the bursar of Cîteaux, who would compile a book.[26]

It is reasonable to doubt the efficacy of statutes which had to be so often repeated. Chapter was asking for a great deal of detailed information to be ready by the time it met again. It seems to have wanted in these years, not only a register of assessments, but an elaborate survey of the wealth of every house in the Order. Even the compilation of a more modest book of quotas or Tax Book was attended by formidable difficulties. Assessments were often the subject of arguments, and frequently changed. Moreover, the Cistercian tradition of using every possible place-name variation in any catalogue of abbeys in order to emphasise the extent of the Order[27] will surely often have led to muddles. It is also clear, from a study of the two surviving Tax Books that local research for them had been very haphazard. In the one at Modena, for instance, the abbey of Himmelpfort in Brandenburg (German Democratic Republic) was at first omitted, although the abbey, founded in 1299,[28] had been in existence for at least seventy years when the book was compiled. A later hand inserted the name *Celi Porta* between two lines and, in order to help with identification, wrote in the margin, 'in the diocese of Meissen'.[29] In fact, the abbey was in the diocese of Brandenburg. Himmelpfort does not occur in the Tax Book at Dijon at all. It was by no means an obscure house. It paid its contributions to Collections regularly in the period 1337-47, as the Accounts of the Order show. It must have been in regular touch with the Mother House during this period.

The fourteenth-century records show that the Chapter General imposed assessments on each Cistercian house at several levels. It has been seen that by 1300 the Premonstratensians had a 'Great Collection' and a 'Half Collection' to raise, as circumstances required, 8,000 *l.t.* or 4,000 *l.t.*, and each house had two assessments accordingly.[30] The Cistercians also had, by the beginning of the fourteenth century, two levels of Collections, known as *contributio moderata* and *contributio mediocris,* which are first mentioned in statutes of the Chapter General for 1314 and 1316.[31] A *contributio mediocris,* as is clear from the Accounts of 1338,[32] was designed to bring in 12,000 *l.t.* In September 1339 the Chapter General felt impelled to ask the Order for twice this amount, and in 1340 for twice the *contributio moderata.*[33] Thus by the time the Dijon Tax Book was compiled there were four levels of assessment. The lowest was the *contributio moderata* designed to raise 9,000 *l.t.* The *contributio mediocris* was for 12,000 *l.t.,* the *contributio duplex* for 18,000 *l.t.,* and the *contributio excessiva* for 24,000 *l.t. Duplex* and *excessiva* were twice *moderata* and *mediocris* respectively,[34] and usually paid in two instalments.

It is thus reasonably clear that a twofold system of assessments was in use by 1314, and that a fourfold system came as a result of the financial demands of 1340-1. In the Dijon Tax Book, however, there are three abbeys which had long ceased to exist in the fourteenth century but which have a fourfold assessment. They are the abbey of S. Trinità della Magione in Palermo,[35] which was suppressed by the emperor Henry VI in 1197;[36] the abbey of St Angelus in Constantinople,[37] which must have disappeared after the fall of Latin Constantinople in 1261; and the abbey of Belmont in Syria,[38] which cannot have survived the fall of Tripoli in 1289. The historical evidence is so strongly against a fourfold assessment having been used in the thirteenth century that these entries must either be mistakes or fantasy. It is noteworthy that other houses in the Latin East—Salvatio, St John in Nemore, S. Trinitas de Refech, and the 'abbey in Greece'—all occur in the Dijon Tax Book, but the assessments are blank.[39]

In the *Coucher Book of Furness Abbey* there is a list of all the Cistercian abbeys of the province of York, assessed according to a six-fold system, for raising totals of 10*l.,*

10 *marks,* 5 *marks,* 7 *l.,* 100 *s.,* 40 *s. sterling.*[40] The sums involved are much smaller than those in the Tax Books, even allowing for the higher value of English silver. The statutes of the Order had laid down that when an individual abbey was in trouble, all the abbots of the province must come to its aid.[41] It was an extension of an earlier enactment of the *Carta Caritatis.*[42] It looks as if the abbots of the province of York had adapted to their local needs a system familiar to their Order.

A comparative study of the Tax Books shows how difficult and controversial was the task of fixing assessments. Some very rich houses were given suspiciously low quotas.[43] In the Dijon Tax Book many houses occur several times, each time differently assessed. Quotas seem to have been changed often, either because it was felt that earlier arrangements had been unfair, or because of altered circumstances. Another list in the *Coucher Book of Furness Abbey* throws some light upon the process of negotiation and change.[44] It is headed 'For contributions of 12,000 pounds'. It contains the Cistercian abbeys of England, Wales, Scotland, and Ireland, with their assessments for the *contributio mediocris.* The original from which the list is copied was almost certainly drawn up before the Hundred Years' War. Although financial relations between the Order and its houses across the English Channel were not completely severed after 1337, it is unlikely that such a list could have been drawn up after the War had begun. In its present form it is probably based upon the rolls, which the proctor of Cîteaux at Scarborough is known to have had, recording the taxes owed by all abbeys in the kingdom to the Order.[45] If the entries on this English list are compared with those in the Dijon Tax Book a picture will emerge of changes in assessment over about twenty years in the fourteenth century.[46] The overwhelming number of entries are the same. For that reason it is assumed that the English list are in *livres tournois* and not in *sterling.*

A number of abbeys are assessed more highly in the *Coucher Book:*

Abbey	CB Quota	TB Quota
Abbeyknockmoy	24 *l.t.*	14 *l.t.*[47]
Abbeymahon	20 *l.t.*	11 *l.* 6 *s.* 8 *d.t.*[48]
Inch	12 *l.t.*	10 *l.* 14 *s.* 4 *d.t.*[49]
Kirkstead	54 *l.t.*	44 *l.t.*[50]
Llantarnam	34 *l.t.*	24 *l.t.*[51]
Newenham	10 *l.* 7 *s.* 4 *d.t.*	5 *l.* 7 *s.* 4 *d.t.*[52]
Sibton	10 *l.t.*	5 *l.* 6 *s.* 8 *d.t.*[53]
Warden	24 *l.t.*	23 *l.t.*[54]

A number of houses occur more than once in the Dijon Tax Book. The *Coucher Book* records only the highest assessment:

Buckland	12 *l.t.*	12 *l.t.*[55]
		10 *l.* 13 *s.* 4 *d.t.*[56]
Coggeshall	24 *l.* 10 *s.* 8 *d.t.*	
		24 *l.* 10 *s.* 8 *d.t.*[57]
		14 *l.* 13 *s.* 4 *d.t.*[58]
Cymmer	17 *l.t.*	17 *l.t.*[59]
		5 *l.t.*[60]
Meaux	34 *l.t.*	34 *l.t.*[61]
		24 *l.t.*[62]
Netley	13 *l.* 13 *s.* 4 *d.t.*	
		13 *l.* 16 *s.* 8 *d.t.*[63]
		8 *l.t.*[64]
Revesby	23 *l.t.*	23 *l.t.*[65]
		13 *l.* 6 *s.* 8 *d.t.*[66]

In one case the assessment in the *Coucher Book* is considerably lower than at Dijon:

Grace Dieu	4 *l.t.*	13 *l.* 5 *s.t.*[67]

There are four Irish abbeys with multiple assessments in the Dijon Tax Book, only the lowest of which, or an even lower one, occurs in the *Coucher Book:*

Abbey	*CB* Quota	*TB* Quota
Abbeylara	8 *l.t.*	16 *l.t.*[68]
		10 *l.t.*[69]
		8 *l.t.*[70]
Bective	5 *l.t.*	14 *l.t.*[71]
		5 *l.t.*[72]
Boyle	16 *l.* 16 *s.* 8 *d.t.*	
		26 *l.* 13 *s.* 4 *d.t.*[73]
		16 *l.* 16 *s.* 8 *d.t.*[74]
Monasteranenagh	10 *l.t.*	30 *l.t.*[75]
		20 *l.t.*[76]

Of the three assessments of Assaroe in the Dijon Tax Book, the middle one appears in the *Coucher Book:*

Assaroe	25 *l.t.*	58 *l.t.*[77]
		25 *l.t.*[78]
		8 *l.t.*[79]

From the comparison of these assessments one may therefore conclude that over about twenty years, eight of the abbeys listed above had managed to get their quotas reduced. Six were negotiating a reduction. The Order had raised one assessment. It was trying to raise four more. One Irish house was arguing for a lower assessment, and the Order for a higher one.

A comparison of actual payments made in the period 1337-47 with the assessments in the Tax Books can also be fruitful. Care must be taken, however, in interpreting the figures. In theory, abbeys which sent in payments late were liable to be charged interest.[80] The abbot of Cîteaux's rate could be as high as 20%.[81] In practice it was not often possible to charge interest on arrears, but some abbeys found it advisable to slip in a small backpayment with the current quota. The abbot of Balerne, for instance, who was 6 *s.* 8 *d.t.* short on a payment in 1339,[82] added it on to his payment due in 1340.[83] In this part of the Accounts it would escape notice and he would not be charged interest. Whoever wishes to compare the Accounts with the Tax Books must keep such tricks in mind. In some cases, however, it is possible to uncover the story of the way assessments were altered. The abbey of Marienfeld, in the modern German Federal Republic (Nordrhein-Westfalen), provides a good illustration. It made the following payments in 1340 and 1341:

1340 *(Excessiva)*	52 *l.t.*[84]
1341 *(Duplex)*	36 *l.t.*[85]

Since each payment was made in exactly equal instalments, the abbey's fourfold assessment in these years was almost certainly

18 *l.t.* / 26 *l.t.* / 36 *l.t.* / 52 *l.t.*

After 1341 the abbey made the following payments:

1342 *(Mediocris)*	16 *l.t.*[86]
1343 *(Duplex)*	24 *fl.*[87]
1344 *(Mediocris)*	16 *fl.*[88]
1347 *(Moderata)*	12 *fl.*[89]

From 1343 Florentine *florins* were simply substituted for *livres tournois.*[90] The abbey's payments in the years 1342-47 correspond exactly to its assessment in the Dijon Tax Book:

12 *l.t.* / 16 *l.t.* / 24 *l.t.* / 32 *l.t.*[91]

In the period covered by the Order's Accounts, therefore, the abbey's assessments were reduced. Those recorded in the Dijon Tax Book date from 1341-42.

———

A similar story emerges from an analysis of the payments made by the abbey of Monthéron in modern Switzerland (Vaud):

1340 *(Excessiva)*	10 *l.t.*[92]
1341 *(Duplex)*	9 *l.t.*[93]

The assessments in those years must therefore have been
4 l. 10 s.t. / 5 l.t. / 9 l.t. / 10 l.t.
After 1341 the abbey made the following payments:

1342 *(Mediocris)*	3 *l.t.*[94]
1343 *(Duplex)*	4½ *fl.*[95]
1344 *(Mediocris)*	3 *fl.*[96]
1347 *(Moderata)*	2 *fl.*[97]

These payments correspond more or less to the assessments
in the Dijon Tax Book:
2 l. 5 s.t. / 3 l.t. / 4 l. 10 s.t. / 6 l.t.[98]
This abbey, too, must have had its assessments reduced to
the level recorded at Dijon around 1341-42.

The abbey of Bonmont in modern Switzerland (Vaud)
appears to have had its assessments reduced to the levels in
the Dijon Tax Book around 1346-47. Payments recorded in
the Accounts between the years 1338 and 1343 were:
9 l.t.[99] / 12 l.t.[100] / 18 l.t.[101] / 24 l.t.[102]
In 1347 the abbey paid a *moderata* of 8 *fl.* which corresponds
to its assessment at that level in the Dijon Tax Book.[103]

During the period 1337-47, many abbeys paid at rates
higher than those of the Tax Books. The following will serve
as examples:

Altofonte, Italy, Sicily.

Payments	9 *l.t.*[104] / 12 *l.t.*[105] / 18 *l.t.*[106]
	24 *l.t.*[107]
Tax Books:	7 *fl.* 10 *s.* / 10 *fl.* / 15 *fl.* / 20 *fl.*[108]

Raitenhaslach, German Federal Republic, Oberbayern

Payments:	16 *l.* 10 *s.t.*[109] / 22 *l.t.*[110] / 33 *l.t.*[111]
	42 *l.t.*[112] [sic]
Tax Books:	12 *l.t.* / 16 *l.t.* / 24 *l.t.* / 32 *l.t.*[113]

Sellières, France, Aube.

Payments: 9 *l.t.*[114] / 12 *l.t.*[115] / 18 *l.t.*[116]
                 24 *l.t.*[117]
Tax Books: 4 *l.* 10 *s.t.* / 6 *l.t.* / 9 *l.t.* / 12 *l.t.*[118]

Light is also thrown on some of the multiple assessments in the Dijon Tax Book by a comparison with payments actually made in 1337-47.

The abbey of Le Valasse in France (Seine-Inférieure) seems to have been roughly in accord with the authorities in the Order about the size of its quota, but there were disagreements about very small sums. Monetary uncertainties may have complicated matters:

Payments:
        1347 *(Moderata)*   47 *fl.* 3 *gr.*[119]
        1338, 42, 44 *(Mediocris)* 63 *l.* 6 *s.* 8 *d.t.*[120]
        1341, 43 *(Duplex)*   95 *l.* 2 *s.* 6 *d.t.*[121]
                                  94 *fl.* 9 *gr.*[122]
        1340 *(Excessiva)*   126 *l.* 13 *s.t.*[123]

Assessments in the Dijon Tax Book are:
                47 *l.* 16 *s.* 8 *d.t.* / 64 *l.* 6 *s.* 8 *d.t.* /
                95 *l.* 13 *s.* 4 *d.t.* / 128 *l.* 13 *s.* 4 *d.t.*[124]
                47 *l.t.* / 62 *l.* 13 *s.* 10 *d.t.* / 94 *l.t.* /
                125 *l.* 7 *s.* 4 *d.t.*[125]

To judge by its payments, Morimondo Coronato in Italy (Lombardia), was rated as follows in the years 1337-47:
                9 *l.t.*[126] / 12 *l.t.*[127] / 18 *l.t.*[128] / 24 *l.t.*[129]
This corresponds to one of its assessments in Dijon.[130] There is, however, another:
                6 *l.t.* / 8 *l.t.* / 12 *l.t.* / 16 *l.t.*[131]
When the Dijon book was compiled, therefore, Morimondo was claiming that its assessments should be reduced.

A more complicated story is revealed by a study of the payments and assessments of Schöntal in the German Federal Republic (Baden-Würtemberg). Until 1342, to judge by the payments it made, its assessment seems to have been as follows:

16 *l*. 10 *s.t.*[132] / 22 *l.t.*[133] / 33 *l.t.*[134] / 44 *l.t.*[135]

In 1344 the abbey made a *mediocris* payment of 20 *fl.*[136] This corresponds to one of its assessments at that level in the Dijon Tax Book:

15 *l.t.* / 20 *l.t.* / 30 *l.t.* / 40 *l.t.*[137]

The abbey occurs twice more in the Dijon Tax Book, each time differently assessed:

10 *l.t.* / 13 *l.t.* 13 *s*. 4 *d.t.* / 20 *l.t.* /
27 *l*. 6 *s*. 8 *d.t.*[138]
9 *l.t.* / 12 *l.t.* / 18 *l.t.* / 24 *l.t.*[139]

There are obvious signs here of pressure from this abbey to have its quotas reduced from the levels at which it was paying in 1340-42.

No Tax Book survives for the years 1337-47. Assessments have to be deduced from a study of payments in the accounts for those years. This can most easily be done when an abbey consistently paid in round numbers, and did not figure among those which paid arrears. It is clear from the evidence available (most of it indirect) that many assessments were reduced in the middle decades of the fourteenth century. It may well be that the Dijon Tax Book was compiled because there had been so many changes.

Abbeys whose assessments were increased by the time the Dijon Tax Book was written are less easy to detect. There are many reasons why payments could be less than the quotas later recorded. The evidence is clear, however, for the abbey of Villeneuve in France (Loire-Inférieure). In 1338 it made a *Mediocris* payment of 21 *l*. 10 *s.t.*[140] In 1340, as a first instalment for an *Excessiva,* it paid 19 *l*. 10 *s.t.* 'He owes 40 *s*.', commented the scribe,[141] who clearly expected half of what was owed. In 1338-40, therefore, Villeneuve's *Mediocris* quota was 21 *l.* 10 *s.t.* In the Dijon Tax Book it is 24 *l.t.*[142] This abbey's assessment was therefore raised in the 1350s.

A comparison of the two Tax Books in Dijon and Modena shows that a revision of assessments went on into the 1360s and 70s. The Modena book gives only *Moderata* and *Mediocris* assessments. The other two had passed out of use, but in any case could easily be calculated. The compilers of the book at Modena clearly worked on the same material as those who made up the lists at Dijon. The resemblances are striking, but there are about one hundred instances of altered assessments in the later compilation. It is noteworthy that in the decades preceding the papal schism, the Order still attempted to raise assessments. A spectacular example is provided by the abbey of S. Michele a Quarto in Italy (Toscana). This house had the lowest quotas in the Dijon Tax Book.[143] The authorities in the Order must have felt that it could afford to pay much more, for much higher rates are recorded in the Modena book:

	Dijon	Modena
Moderata	15 *s.t.*	15 *fl.*
Mediocris	1 *l.t.*[144]	20 *fl.*[145]

Most increases were more restrained:

Zdár, Czechoslovakia (Jihlava)

	Dijon	Modena
Moderata	6 *l.t.*	8 *fl.*
Mediocris	8 *l.t.*[146]	12 *fl.*[147]

Examples of the reduction of assessments are, however, far more numerous, and are most interesting when they show the progress of negotiations. Volkerode in the German Democratic Republic (Thüringen) occurs once in the

Dijon book and twice at Modena:

	Dijon	Modena (i)	Modena (ii)
Moderata	20 *l.* 10 *s.t.*	15 *fl.* 10 *s.t.*	8 *fl.*
Mediocris	27 *l.t.*[148]	17 *fl.*[149]	12 *fl.*[150]

Here it is clear that the quotas were gradually reduced, no doubt as a result of continued pressure by the abbey in the 1360s and 70s.

Comparison of the available material shows that assessments were never regarded as final. The Order might decide, on the basis of more accurate information, that a house could afford more. It was probably more common for abbeys which thought themselves overburdened to persuade the authorities to lower the quotas. Either way, books of assessments had to be compiled whilst these discussions were in progress.

Pleas for reductions had, in the long run, some chance of success. A petition to be excused payment altogether was very seldom entertained. In 1338 the abbot of Faleri in Italy (Lazio) paid 15 *l.t.* arrears for the previous year. The scribe commented, 'Note that he still owes 10 *fl.*, but owing to poverty he cannot pay, so he says'.[151] The Order was inexorable, and the missing 10 *fl.* were paid, at last, in 1342.[152] The abbot of Brondolo in Italy (Veneto) was more fortunate. In 1338 he paid his current quota and some arrears. A note adds, 'The diffinitors excused the said abbot from the rest of the arrears until such time as he is sufficiently prosperous to pay them'.[153] In the same year the abbot of Arabona in Italy (Abruzzi) paid 30 *l.t.* in back-payments. It is clear that more was owed, but the abbot of Cîteaux agreed to declare him quit.[154] In the Accounts of 1337-47 there are only two more examples of such indulgence. The abbey of Buillon in France (Doubs) was excused payment in 1342 'as a favour'.[155] The payment due from

La Trappe in France (Orne) was remitted, without explanation, in 1344.[156]

More often laggards were vigorously pursued. In 1338, for
instance, the Chapter General was collecting a *Mediocris*
subsidy. The abbot of Balerne owed, as the Dijon Tax Book
shows, 16 *l.* 6 *s.* 8 *d.t.*[157] He paid 10 *l.t.* 'He owes 6 *l.t.*',
stated the scribe, adding in the margin, 'Note what is
owed'.[158] The sum of 6 *l.t.* was paid in 1339. 'He owes
6 *s.* 8 *d.t.*', stated the scribe.[159] The missing sum was slipped
in, as has been seen, with a current payment in 1340.[160] The
collection of an *Excessiva* subsidy in 1340 proved a heavy
burden for some houses. There were many like Quincy and
Villers-en-Brabant, which could pay only one instalment,[161]
and were obliged to pay the remainder, together with their
current quota, during the next year.[162]

In the period 1337-47 campaigns to collect backpayments
were a feature of the Order's financial policy. In 1339, for
instance, an enquiry was ordered in every area to find out
who had not paid contributions since 1330. Abbots and monks
were to be put on oath. Those who were found to owe the Order money were either to make suitable arrangements to pay,
or have their names sent to the Chapter General so that they
could be deposed from office.[163] The results can be seen in
the Accounts for that year.[164] The abbot of Candeil in
France (Tarn) settled debts going back seven years.[165] For
the rest, however, few payments went back further than
1335, and most referred to 1337.[166] A special effort was
made to reach abbeys remote from Cîteaux; contributions
came in from Denmark,[167] Norway,[168] and Livonia.[169] At
times the pace was frantic. During the Chapter General
the abbot of Clairefontaine took money from 'several foreign
abbots whose names he does not know. They will receive
receipts as soon as the *receptores* know their names'.[170] In
1340 the Order seems to have made a special effort to bring
in money from eastern Europe. Contributions came from
Polish abbeys whose names had hardly ever before appeared

in Cistercian financial records. They included Gemelnice, Jedrzejów, Koprzywníca, Obra, Rudy, and Sulejów.[171] Payments also came in, for the first time, from Daphni in Greece, Szepes in Hungary, and Kostanjevica in modern Jugoslavia.[172] Further backpayments came from Denmark,[173] and several Portuguese abbots paid a large lump sum to cover future contributions.[174]

There was another campaign in 1347. The subsidy was to be a *contributio moderata,* the lowest of the four assessments.[175] Once again it was possible to reach abbeys which had not paid before: La Baix in Spain,[176] Eldena in Mecklenburg,[177] San Michele alla Verruca and Buonsolazzo in Tuscany,[178] Corazzo in Calabria and Michaelstein in Thuringia.[179] There were also backpayments from Irish abbeys which because of the Hundred Years' War had made no previous contributions.[180] The sums sent probably bore little relation to what was owed, but it is clear that the Order's collectors had made a considerable effort to involve as many houses as possible. The long lists of abbeys paying arrears in 1347 are a further indication of this.[181] There was, however, something unsystematic about all these campaigns. None of the eastern European abbeys whose support had been whipped up in 1340 paid anything in the years which followed.

Abbeys which contributed nothing to the Collections were threatened with heavy penalties. A statute of 1257 laid down that the abbot of such a house must be suspended from the altar, and that the obedientiaries should be removed from office and fast twice a week on bread and water until the quota had been paid.[182] In 1268 the abbots and obedientiaries of houses which had not contributed to the Collections were excommunicated.[183] Later statutes emphasised deposition rather than excommunication.[184] In *Fulgens* Benedict XII gave the abbot of Cîteaux and the four seniors the right to pronounce sentence in such cases by apostolic authority, and to proceed to excommunication, suspension, or interdict, without appeal.[185] The fact that threats of punishment had to be made so often makes it likely that they were little heeded. Occasionally, however, the Order hit upon effective methods. In 1338 the abbot of Morimond and the *receptores* enforced the payment of arrears from three Austrian and one Spanish abbot by seizing their goods at the Chapter General.[186]

Abbots actually attending the Chapter General brought their money with them. For those who were, for reasons good or bad, absent from Cîteaux, there was a variety of arrangements. In 1341 five Spanish abbots banded together and sent, presumably through one of their number, a collective quota.[187] The abbots of Adwert, Bloemkamp, Klaarkamp, Gerkeskleaster, and Ihlo, often called 'the abbots of Frisia', always sent a joint contribution in this way.[188] In 1338 contributions from three Danish abbeys were sent through one of their monks.[189] Since father abbots were often responsible for collecting money, they sometimes brought it all together to Cîteaux. In 1342 the abbot of Himmerod came with his own contribution and that of his 'generation' (Heisterbach and Marienthal).[190] At the same Chapter General the abbot of Lubiaź paid for himself and his daughters Henrykow and Kamieniec.[191] In 1339 the abbot of Otterberg brought payments from his own abbey and his daughter Disibodenberg.[192] The abbot of La Grâce Dieu also frequently brought his own contributions and those of his daughter Charon.[193]

The task of collecting from abbots who were not coming to the Chapter General was usually in the hands of the father abbots, but sometimes special 'collectors' were appointed. In *Fulgens* Benedict XII authorised the appointment of reliable persons for this work. They were empowered to use their personal seals to issue receipts, and had to render an account at the Chapter General following their appointment.[194] The pope was not always satisfied with their conduct. He had, on various occasions, to forbid them to enrich themselves, and to threaten to suspend those who did not hand over the money within two months of their return to Cîteaux.[195]

Unlike the papacy, the Cistercian Order had no professional financial agents. The collectors mentioned in the records were almost always abbots, and probably indistinguishable, most of the time, from the father abbots. A statute of 1334, for instance, forbade the collectors to use their duties as an excuse for staying away from the Chapter General.[196] The campaign of 1339, which involved detailed enquiries about money owed to the Order, was also entrusted to abbots.[197] In 1378 two visitors were appointed by the Chapter General to visit the abbeys of Spain and Portugal and collect arrears.[198] Their names are known, but not their status. It is most likely that they were abbots also. Indeed it is difficult to imagine, in a rather conservative Order, how any monk could have exercised authority without the rank which alone would win him the necessary respect.

In 1317 the Chapter General decreed that the money which was brought to Cîteaux must be stored in a chest to which each of the four senior abbots and the Order's *receptor* had a key.[199] Benedict XII laid down that the chest was to have three locks and three keys; each of the three *receptores* was to have one.[200] In 1338 the Chapter General spent 22 *d.t.* on 'the keys and locks for the chest of the *receptores*'.[201] In 1384 the chest was provided with five locks, each of which had two keys.[202]

Abbots, designated *receptores,* supervised the actual gathering in of the money, payments at the Chapter General, the accounting and the calculation of the totals. Their office goes back at least to 1235 when, as we have seen, three abbots were appointed to supervise the Collection which was to save the Mother House from bankruptcy.[203] In the bull *Parvus Fons* Clement IV had decreed that two abbots should be appointed to take charge of alms brought to the Chapter General. One was to be appointed by the abbot of Cîteaux and the other by each of the four seniors in turn.[204] Benedict XII laid down that every year the Chapter General or the

diffinitors should appoint three abbots to receive the Collections and take responsibility for spending the money as the
Chapter and the diffinitors should direct.[205] The abbots
appointed in 1336 were Jean, abbot of Jouy, Guy, abbot of
Vauluisant, and Pierre, abbot of Clairefontaine.[206] Although
their appointment was for one year only, they must have
given satisfaction, for their names appear continually in the
Accounts until 1340.[207]

The importance of the *receptores* in supervising and
coordinating the cumbersome machinery of the Collections
can be gauged from the heading of the first page of the
Order's Accounts: 'The contributions of the Cistercian Order,
received by brothers Jean of Jouy, Guy of Vauluisant, and
Pierre of Clairefontaine in the year 1337 at the time of the
Chapter General'.[208] The arrangements for spending the money turned out to be far more complicated than Benedict XII
had envisaged. Some was disbursed by the *receptores*[209]
some by the Order's proctor at Avignon,[210] some by
the bursar of Cîteaux.[211] The work of the *receptores* stands
out most clearly from the Accounts of 1340. In that year the
Chapter General had ordered a *contributio excessiva*. It was
to be paid in two instalments. The first was due at Easter and
could be brought or sent to the Order's proctor at Avignon,
to St Bernard's College in Paris, or to the Cistercian House of
Studies in Metz. The second instalment was to be paid in
September at the Chapter General.[212] At Easter Jean of
Jouy went to Paris[213] and Pierre of Clairefontaine to
Metz.[214] At their respective collecting centres they received
the money, recorded the payments, and added up the
totals.[215] Jean of Jouy worked out the interest due on
arrears,[216] and Pierre of Clairefontaine took responsibility
for calculating the sum of all that had been collected to
date.[217] Abbot Jean made the arrangements for sending some
of the money to the Curia.[218] Nothing is known about the
division of responsibility at the September Chapter General,
but no doubt all three abbots shared the labour. In all this

the work of abbot Guy of Vauluisant stands out less clearly. He is usually mentioned in conjunction with the other two.[219]

Abbot Jean made it very clear that he was personally responsible for the Order's Accounts in the years 1337-40.[220] From 1341 they were arranged according to a new plan,[221] and this may mean that he had ceased to be one of the *receptores*. Neither he nor abbot Guy mentioned again in the Accounts from that year onwards. In 1341 the financial work during the Chapter General was supervised by the abbots of Morimond and La Creste.[222] The Easter payments at Metz had been received by the latter, assisted by Pierre of Clairefontaine.[223] Scattered references to the abbot of La Creste give the impression that he took the lead in organising the Collections,[224] whilst Pierre of Clairefontaine, though still involved as late as 1343,[225] had a subordinate rôle. In 1350 the Collections were organised by the abbots of La Ferté and San Galgano, with the help of the bursar of Cîteaux.[226] In 1342 the *receptores* were provided by the Chapter with wax, paper, and other necessities,[227] and small payments for their expenses figure frequently in the Accounts.[228]

Apart from the *receptores* there were other senior members of the Order to whom, by tradition, contributions could be paid. Some abbots preferred to deal directly with the abbot of Cîteaux. In 1338 the abbot of Arabona in Italy settled his debts to the Order by making a payment to the abbot of the Mother House, who issued a receipt declaring him quit.[229] At Easter 1340 the abbot of Reigny in France (Yonne) did not find it convenient to go to any of the collecting centres. Instead he sent his money directly to the abbot of Cîteaux, who informed abbot Jean of Jouy by letter.[230] The Abbot of Cîteaux, indeed, was meticulous in supplying information about such payments.

The bursar of Cîteaux was less scrupulous in this matter, and relations between him and the *receptores* were often strained. As chief financial officer of the Mother House, the bursar of Cîteaux had probably taken the lead in organising many of the Collections during the thirteenth century. It was the bursar of Cîteaux who waited at the Troyes Fair for contributions from the abbeys during the Collections of 1290 and 1294.[231] In 1330 this official had been charged with the responsibility of compiling a book of assessments.[232] Benedict XII had ordered that the money from Collections should be kept 'in a secure monastery'.[233] There was little alternative to keeping it at Cîteaux where the Chapter General met, or perhaps at the Mother House's town property at Dijon, where the annual Audit was held. The physical security of the money must have been the bursar's responsibility most of the time. It is also likely that arrears and other payments sent to Cîteaux when the Chapter General was not sitting were put under his charge. Individual abbots also, on occasion, paid their contributions at the Chapter General to him. Whenever this happened he was expected, not only to hand over the money, but also to give an account. Failure to provide the necessary details made it impossible to keep the records in order, as abbot Jean of Jouy complained in 1338: 'From Sept-Fons in Burgundy, 20 *livres* paid in by the bursar of Cîteaux. Note that the bursar did not give an account. I, Jean, abbot of Jouy, have put the 20 *livres* in at this point, but now the addition at the end is wrong.[234] There had been a similar argument already, recorded in an earlier part of the Accounts for that year.[235] On both occasions the scribe, surely acting under instructions, had written in the margin, 'Theft!'[236]

Since the balance sheet had to be ready for 17 September, there were only a few days in which to get all the figures for income and expenditure. Abbot Jean's exasperation can easily be understood. As it was, the *receptores* could sometimes be overcome by pressure of business. It has been seen that Pierre of Clairefontaine himself had no record of the foreign abbots who had given him money in 1340.[237] He was caught out again in 1343, when he handed over 10 *l.* 19 *s.t.* 'from someone'.[238] The Order had no financial experts of its own, and did not admit help from outsiders. The larger the sum that needed to be raised, the greater were the problems. This may in itself explain why *Duplex* and *Excessiva* ceased to be levied in the later fourteenth century. There was always something haphazard about the financial organisation of the Chapter General. The Cistercians were monks, and their primary function was not to raise money. Their amateurishness in this respect is entirely to their credit.

NOTES TO CHAPTER THREE

1. See above, p. 49.
2. *Statuta* 1250, 21. The marks are not specified in the text.
3. See e.g. *Statuta,* iii, pp. 420-21; also *Statuta* 1328, 13; 1336, 7; 1348, 6.
4. *Statuta* 1326, 4.
5. *Nomasticon Cisterciense,* 519.
6. See e.g. *Statuta* 1390, 6.
7. P.B. Griesser, 'Unbekannte Generalkapitelstatuten', 47.
8. *Codex Dunensis* No. 79.
9. *Ibid.,* No. 296.
10. *Ibid.,* No. 372. The document quotes the statute in *Statuta* 1311, 3.
11. See e.g. *Statuta* 1356, 2.
12. *Statuta* 1319, 3.
13. *Statuta* 1262, 1.
14. *Nomasticon Cisterciense,* 415-16.
15. Griesser, 'Unbekannte Generalkapitelstatuten', 60.
16. *Statuta* 1310, 1.
17. *Statuta* 1329, 4.
18. *Statuta* 1338, 4.
19. Griesser, 'Unbekannte Generalkapitelstatuten', 8-9.
20. *Statuta* 1350, 6.
21. *Statuta* 1318, 11.
22. *Statuta* 1318, 8.
23. *Statuta* 1320, 10.
24. *Statuta* 1326, 4.
25. *Statuta* 1329, 7.
26. *Statuta* 1330, 10.
27. See below, p. 128.
28. *Orig.,* 266-67.
29. MTB, f. 24b.
30. See above, p. 51.
31. *Statuta* 1314, 7; 1316, 1.
32. Accts., ff. 2b, col. 1-9a, col. 2. Cf. assessments in *TB.*

33. See below, p. 100.
34. *TB*, pp. 28-30.
35. *TB*, 18b, 16.
36. White, *Latin Monasticism in Norman Sicily*, 180-1.
37. *TB*, 16b, 23.
38. *TB*, 22b, 22.
39. *TB*, 22b, 23; 23b, 3; 27b, 20, 21.
40. *CB*, iii, 637-8.
41. *Statuta* 1261, 5; 1276, 10.
42. See above, p. 29.
43. See *TB*, pp. 30-1.
44. *CB*, iii, 639-42.
45. Talbot, 'Cîteaux and Scarborough', 108.
46. For the dating of *TB* see above, p. 14.
47. *TB*, 10b, 8.
48. *TB*, 18b, 2.
49. *TB*, 14b, 15.
50. *TB*, 17b, 7.
51. *TB*, 19b, 20.
52. *TB*, 4b, 6.
53. *TB*, 16b, 9.
54. *TB*, 15b, 27.
55. *TB*, 15b, 19.
56. *TB*, 14b, 17.
57. *TB*, 11b, 1.
58. *TB*, 13b, 5.
59. *TB*, 19b, 18.
60. *TB*, 21b, 22.
61. *TB*, 17b, 14.
62. *TB*, 9b, 2.
63. *TB*, 4b, 5.
64. *TB*, 15b, 10.
65. *TB*, 15b, 29.
66. *TB*, 13b, 8.
67. *TB*, 3b, 27.
68. *TB*, 15b, 4.
69. *TB*, 15b, 5.
70. *TB*, 11b, 24.
71. *TB*, 10b, 7.
72. *TB*, 18b, 25.
73. *TB*, 9b, 17.
74. *TB*, 18b, 23.

75. *TB,* 18b, 21.
76. *TB,* 20b, 27.
77. *TB,* 20b, 28.
78. *TB,* 19b, 12.
79. *TB,* 14b, 1.
80. *Statuta* 1310, 3.
81. Accts., f. 11b, col. 2.
82. *Ibid.,* f. 10a, col. 1.
83. *Ibid.,* f. 16b, col. 2.
84. *Ibid.,* ff. 15a, col. 1; 17b, col. 1.
85. *Ibid.,* f. 20a, cols. 1, 2.
86. *Ibid.,* f. 22b, col. 1.
87. *Ibid.,* f. 24b, col. 2.
88. *Ibid.,* f. 26b, col. 2.
89. *Ibid.,* f. 29b, col. 2.
90. See below, p. 166.
91. *TB,* 24b, 28.
92. Accts., ff. 15a, col. 2; 17a, col. 1.
93. *Ibid.,* ff. 19b, col. 2; 20a, col. 2.
94. *Ibid.,* f. 22b, col. 1.
95. *Ibid.,* f. 24b, col. 2.
96. *Ibid.,* f. 26b, col. 2.
97. *Ibid.,* f. 29a, col. 2.
98. *TB,* 23b, 15.
99. Calculated from *duplex.*
100. Accts., f. 5a, col. 1.
101. *Ibid.,* f. 19a, cols. 1, 2.
102. *Ibid.,* f. 16a, cols. 1, 2.
103. *Ibid.,* f. 28b, col. 1; *TB,* 7b, 16.
104. Accts., f. 28b, col. 1.
105. *Ibid.,* ff. 4a, col. 1; 22a, col. 1.
106. *Ibid.,* ff. 19a, cols. 1, 2; 24a, col. 2.
107. *Ibid.,* f. 17a, col. 1.
108. *MTB,* f. 14a, *Duplex* and *excessiva* calculated from first two.
109. Calculated from *duplex.*
110. Accts., ff. 7a, col. 2; 22b, col. 1; 27a, col. 2.
111. *Ibid.,* f. 25a, col. 1.
112. *Ibid.,* f. 17a, col. 2.
113. *TB,* 23b, 23.
114. Accts., f. 28a, col. 2.
115. *Ibid.,* ff. 3b, col. 1; 21b, col. 1.
116. *Ibid.,* ff. 18b, col. 1; 23b, col. 2.

117. *Ibid.,* ff. 13a, col. 2; 16b, col. 2.
118. *TB,* 6b, 30.
119. Accts., f. 28b, col. 1.
120. *Ibid.,* ff. 4a, col. 1; 21b, col. 2; 26a, col. 2.
121. *Ibid.,* ff. 18b, col. 2; 19b, col. 1.
122. *Ibid.,* f. 24a, col. 2.
123. *Ibid.,* ff. 14a, col. 1; 16b, col. 2. There should almost certainly be another 4 *d.t.* Cf. *Mediocris.*
124. *TB,* 12b, 23.
125. *TB,* 11b, 8.
126. Calculated from *duplex.*
127. Accts., ff. 7a, col. 1; 22b, col. 1; 27a, col. 1.
128. *Ibid.,* f. 20a, cols. 1, 2.
129. Calculated from *mediocris.* The abbey's *excessiva* payment in 1340 was 23 *l.t.*: Accts., ff. 16a, col. 2; 17a, col. 2.
130. *TB,* 27b, 17.
131. *TB,* 22b, 10.
132. Calculated from *duplex.*
133. Accts., f. 22b, col. 1.
134. *Ibid.,* ff. 19b, col. 2; 20b, col. 1.
135. *Ibid.,* ff. 14b, col. 2; 17a, col. 2.
136. *Ibid.,* f. 26b, col. 2.
137. *TB,* 27b, 2.
138. *TB,* 23b, 22.
139. *TB,* 13b, 21.
140. Accts., f. 4b, col. 2.
141. *Ibid.,* f. 13b, col. 2.
142. *TB,* 17b, 4.
143. *TB,* p. 31.
144. *TB,* 21b, 18.
145. *MTB,* f. 20a.
146. *TB,* 27b, 4.
147. *MTB,* f. 27b. The identical assessment as in Dijon is on f. 28b.
148. *TB,* 24b, 5.
149. *MTB,* f. 28b.
150. *Ibid.*
151. Accts., f. 3b, col. 2.
152. *Ibid.,* f. 22a, col. 2.
153. Accts., f. 5b, col. 1.
154. *Ibid.,* f. 7b, col. 2.
155. *Ibid.,* f. 22a, col. 1.
156. *Ibid.,* f. 26b, col. 1.

157. *TB,* 8b, 13.
158. Accts., f. 5a, col. 1.
159. *Ibid.,* f. 10a, col. 1.
160. See above, p. 68.
161. *Ibid.,* ff. 14a, col. 2; 16b, col. 2.
162. *Ibid.,* ff. 18b, cols. 1, 2; 19b, col. 2. Cf. *TB,* 5b, 14; 9b, 12.
163. *Statuta* 1339, 4. The statute was almost certainly passed in the previous year.
164. Accts., ff. 9b-10b.
165. *Ibid.,* f. 9b, col. 2.
166. *Ibid.,* ff. 10a-b.
167. *Ibid.,* f. 10a, col. 1.
168. *Ibid.,* f. 10a, col. 2.
169. *Ibid.,* f. 10b, col. 2.
170. *Ibid.,* f. 10b, col. 1.
171. *Ibid.,* f. 17b, cols. 1, 2.
172. *Ibid.,* f. 17b, col. 1.
173. *Ibid.,* f. 17a, col. 2.
174. *Ibid.,* f. 17b, col. 1.
175. *Ibid.,* f. 28a, col. 1. Not in *Statuta.*
176. Accts., f. 28b, col. 2.
177. *Ibid.*
178. *Ibid.*
179. *Ibid.,* ff. 29a, col. 1; 29b, col. 1.
180. *Ibid.,* f. 29a, col. 1. See below, p. 141.
181. *Ibid.,* ff. 28a, col. 2; 28b, col. 1; 29a, cols. 1, 2; 29b, col. 1.
182. *Statuta* 1257, 7.
183. *Statuta* 1268, 7.
184. *Statuta* 1295, 13; 1296, 4; 1297, 2; 1298, 2.
185. *Fulgens,* 17; *Statuta,* iii, pp. 420-21.
186. Accts., f. 8a, cols. 1-2.
187. *Ibid.,* f. 20b, col. 1.
188. *Ibid.,* ff. 19a, col. 2; 22a, col. 2; 26a, col. 1.
189. *Ibid.,* f. 10a, col. 1.
190. *Ibid.,* f. 22a, col. 1.
191. *Ibid.,* f. 22b, col. 1.
192. *Ibid.,* f. 10a, col. 1.
193. *Ibid.,* ff. 22a, col. 2; 24a, col. 2.
194. *Fulgens,* 18; *Statuta,* iii, p. 422.
195. Benoît XII, *Lettres communes,* Nos. 7406, 9536.
196. *Statuta* 1334, 1.
197. *Statuta* 1339, 4. See also *Statuta* 1342, 2.

198. Accts., f. 45b, col. 2.
199. *Statuta* 1317, 7.
200. *Fulgens,* 18; *Statuta,* iii, p. 421.
201. Accts., f. 8b, col. 1.
202. See below, p. 196.
203. See above, p. 49.
204. *Parvus Fons,* 4; *Statuta,* iii, p. 27.
205. *Fulgens,* 18; *Statuta,* iii, p. 421.
206. *Statuta* 1336, 6.
207. Accts., ff. 12a, col. 1; 13a, col. 1.
208. Accts., f. 1a, col. 1.
209. *Ibid.,* f. 8b, col. 1.
210. *Ibid.,* f. 8b, cols. 1, 2.
211. *Ibid.,* f. 9a, col. 1.
212. *Statuta* 1339, 9.
213. Accts., ff. 12a, cols. 1, 2; 13a, cols. 1,2; 13b, cols. 1, 2; 14a, col. 1; 14b, col. 2.
214. *Ibid.,* ff. 13a, col. 1; 14a, col. 2; 14b, cols. 1, 2; 15a, col. 1; 15b, col. 1.
215. *Ibid.,* ff. 14b, col. 2; 15b, col. 1.
216. *Ibid.,* f. 15b, col. 1.
217. *Ibid.*
218. *Ibid.,* f. 17b, col. 2.
219. *Ibid.,* ff. 1a, col. 1; 9b, col. 1.
220. See above, p. 8.
221. See above, p. 20.
222. Accts., f. 20b, col. 1.
223. *Ibid.,* f. 20b, col. 2.
224. *Ibid.,* ff. 20b, col. 1; 21a, col. 1.
225. Accts., f. 23b, col. 1.
226. Sens MS. 129, f. 169a.
227. Accts., f. 23a, col. 2.
228. E.g. *Ibid.,* ff. 9a, col. 1; 17b, col. 2; 27b, col. 1; 28a, col. 1.
229. *Ibid.,* f. 7b, col. 2. See above, p. 73.
230. Accts., f. 13b, col. 2.
231. See below, p. 91.
232. *Statuta* 1330, 10.
233. *Fulgens,* 81; *Statuta,* iii, p. 421.
234. Accts., f. 4b, col. 1.
235. *Ibid.,* f. 3b, cols. 1-2.
236. 'Furtum', *ibid.,* ff. 3b, col. 1; 4b, col. 1.
237. See above, p. 74.

238. Accts., f. 23b, col. 1.

CHAPTER FOUR

The Collections in the Fourteenth Century

THE SOURCES for a financial history of the Order during the fourteenth century are somewhat unevenly distributed.[1] For the period before 1337 it is necessary to rely mainly upon the statutes of the Chapter General. These show when the Order decided upon a Collection, and usually (though not always) how much was to be raised. The statutes also occasionally comment, in a somewhat generalised way, on the financial situation. Accounts survive, in a fragmentary form, only for three years during this period. After 1337 the picture changes. The financial story can be reconstructed in some detail because of the survival of the Order's Accounts for every year to 1347. They can be studied together with the statutes for the period. The two surviving Tax Books, though compiled after 1347 can, with due caution, be used retrospectively. For the period 1347-78 it is again necessary to rely mainly upon the statutes, supplemented by some statements drawn up for the Chapter General's Audit on St Lambert's day. After the papal schism of 1378 the houses of the Order were divided according to Roman or Avignonese loyalties. Financial information for this period comes from the statutes of the two rival Cistercian Chapters General, the Accounts of the Bursar of Cîteaux, and some more statements for the Audit.

Only for the period 1337-47, therefore, is the documentation relatively full. The Accounts need, however, to be interpreted with subtlety. It took some time before a standard arrangement for them emerged.[1a] It is impossible, therefore, to compare one year with another before 1341. Money borrowed by the Order was imperfectly recorded and was, indeed, a matter for secrecy. Expectations of revenue, goods, services, even spiritual benefits, could all be regarded as the equivalent of money in the Middle Ages. Items therefore sometimes 'disappeared' and credits turned into deficits in ways disconcerting to the modern student of these records.

The Accounts were also affected by the proceedings on St Lambert's day. The Audit on 17 September was an innovation introduced by pope Benedict XII. In the bull *Fulgens* he had decreed that the three *receptores* must give an annual account of receipts and expenditure to the diffinitors.[2] In the few days available to them the *receptores* could not present the Accounts in detail, but they had obtained accurate figures of the totals which they presented at the Audit. They were the executors, however, not the initiators of the Order's financial policies. Responsibility lay with the five seniors, and the Audit was the occasion for revealing only what these men wanted the others to know. Careful study shows that the figures were manipulated in 1339, and that certain information was suppressed in 1346 and 1347.[3] The intention was always to highlight the financial needs of the Order, and justify the policies of the inner circle which directed its affairs. The *summae* in the annual Accounts faithfully reproduce the statements made on St Lambert's day. They must be regarded as part of the campaign to persuade the diffinitors and others that there were sound reasons for the financial demands made at the Chapters General.

In the last decades of the thirteenth century the Order was being hard-pressed by the pope, and, with papal connivance, the king of France.[4] In 1289 a tenth had to be paid to the king,[5] and the earliest surviving Accounts of the Order consist of a fragment giving some details of the way the money was collected. It is likely that contributions came only from the Cistercians of France. The fragment in Sens

MS 129 records the proceedings from 21 September to Christmas 1290.[6] During that time the bursar of Cîteaux was at the Fair of Troyes in charge of the organisation, whilst a subordinate waited at Provins for payments which could be transferred, from time to time, to his superior.

Collected at Troyes from the feast of St Matthew to Christmas 1290:

From the generation of Cîteaux	4,997 *l.t.*
From the generation of Pontigny	3,900 *l.t.*
From the generation of Clairvaux	27,500 *l.t.* or
	28,100 *l.t.*
From the generation of Morimond	1,000 *l.t.*

Collected at Provins:

From the abbot of Bellebranche	5,220 *l.t.*
From the abbot of Cherlieu	2,100 *l.t.*
From the abbot of Jouy	200 *l.t.*
From the abbot of La Noë ⎱	6,000 *l.t.*
From the abbot of Sellières ⎰	
Total	40,410 *l.t.* [sic]

Only four of the five generations are mentioned at Troyes. It may be that contributions from La Ferté came in at another time. The five abbots who paid at Provins must have been collecting money on the Order's behalf, perhaps from daughter houses. Because Philip IV had increased the official value of the French gold coinage in 1290, two alternative totals were given for money from the generation of Clairvaux. It was difficult to decide what rate should be used in the calculations of totals.[7]

After the receipts came the expenses. For the eighth time in the year payments were made to the representatives of Italian banking houses:

To Giovanni Marguto and his companions from Florence	5,240 *l.t.*
To Michele Daniel and his companions from Florence	7,240 *l.t.*
To Dante Producio and his companions from Florence	5,200 *l.t.*
To Landuccio Margoti and his companions from Florence	17,906 *l.* 13 *s.* 4 *d.t.*
Total payments	36,626 *l.* 13 *s.* 4 *d.t.* [sic]

The balance for these months was stated to be 3,784 *l.* 6*s.* 8 *d.t.* out of which 2,160 *l.t.* were sent to the Order's bankers in Provins. The bursar of Cîteaux was left with 1,623 *l.* 6 *s.* 8 *d.t.*

Even by medieval standards the arithmetic in this fragment is exceptionally faulty. It has to be remembered that in a year of exceptional monetary mutations, confusion in adding up totals was to be expected.[8] There were other difficulties. Some of the abbots who were appointed to act as collectors were slow to hand in what they had obtained. As late as September 1291 the Chapter General had to threaten with deposition abbots who had borrowed sums out of the tenth and were holding on to the money.[9]

Another subsidy was ordered in 1292. It was to be organised by the abbot of Cîteaux and the four seniors. Abbots in the kingdom of France were to pay the quotas imposed upon them by Easter at a place later to be determined. For abbots outside the kingdom both the time and the place of payment were undecided when the statute was issued.[10] It seems likely that this subsidy was being collected over a long period, and that the fragment of 1294[11] relates to it.

The intention of the Chapter General was to raise 15,000 *l.t.*

From the generation of Cîteaux	1,768 *l.* 7 *s.t.*
From the generation of La Ferté	100 *l.t.*
From the generation of Pontigny	1,250 *l.t.*
From the generation of Clairvaux	6,000 *l.t.*
From the generation of Morimond	2,470 *l.t.*
Total	11,588 *l.* 8 *s.t.*

The sum, by modern reckoning, is almost correct—only 1 *s.t.* out.

Expenses:

'For the Roman Curia, Biche and Mouche, at Provins'	9,600 *l.t.*
For the church of Scarborough	1,500 *l.t.*
For the abbot of Pontigny	80 *l.t.*
For the abbot of Jouy	105 *l.t.*
Total	11,435 *l.t.*

The total was only 150 *l.t.* out by modern reckoning. It was calculated that the bursar had 153 *l.* 6 *s.t.* in hand.

The presence at Provins of Albizzo Guidi and Musciatto Guidi ('Biche' and 'Mouche'), the financial agents of Philip IV of France, shows that, although the money was being collected by papal authority, the king was being given direct access to it. Since contributions had come from the entire Order, there had to be an agreement about a division. The larger share, 9,600 *l.t.*, went to Philip; 1,685 *l.t.* could be used for the purposes of the Chapter General. It may be that in 1294, as often in the fourteenth century, most of the contributions had come from abbeys in France,[12] but 'Biche' and 'Mouche' will have known how to apply pressure so that their master got the lion's share.

In the last decades of the thirteenth century the exemptions and immunities from royal taxation enjoyed, at least in theory, by all clergy, were battered down.[13] Henceforth the clergy, regular and secular, paid taxes to their kings. The anomalous arrangement of 1294, however, when the king of France took money which had been collected from Cistercians outside, as well as inside his kingdom, was very unusual. It is possible that something like it occurred in 1315. In that year Louis X was paid 5,800 *l.t.* 'by the whole Cistercian Order'.[14] This was one of the payments made for a six year tenth voted at the Council of Vienne for crusading purposes,[15] and Cistercian abbeys outside France may have felt obliged to contribute. Usually, however, kings could only raise money from abbeys within their own dominions. In 1298, for instance, Philip IV was paid a tenth 'by the Cistercian Order in all the kingdom of France'.[16] During most of the fourteenth century the Collections within the Order were quite independent of royal taxation, though certainly the ability of abbeys to contribute was affected by demands from their own rulers and the kings of England tried to sever all financial connections between Cistercian abbeys under their jurisdiction and the Chapter General.

The surviving statutes record eighteen Collections in the Order between 1294 and 1335.[17] In the time of pope John XXII their aim was often to support his wars in Italy.[18] The burden on the Cistercians was a heavy one. In a remarkable memorandum written in 1317-18, and addressed to the pope, Jacques de Thérines, abbot of Chaalis, discussed the Order's financial problems with his customary eloquence.[19] He was writing in the aftermath of the great European famine of 1315-17,[20] the impressions of which were still vivid in his mind. 'For the last seven years, and most particularly in the last three, there has been a famine in that kingdom [France] in which the houses of the Order are most numerous, such as has not been heard of in history. During the period of hunger and dearth many more persons than in prosperous times flocked to the abbeys of the Order for alms and shelter. The abbeys did not have sufficient income from their lands and vineyards, and lost the profits of their labour and expense. Although they did not have the revenue to pay interest on loans, they had to borrow large sums in order to maintain themselves, keep up an increased burden of hospitality, and give more alms to the poor.'[21]

A number of other factors, according to abbot Jacques, coincided. The abbeys of France had been taxed for Philip IV's wars in Gascony; 60,000 *l.t.* had been expected from them. The sum had since risen, with interest, to 100,000 *l.t.* and it was still increasing. During the king's wars in Flanders, abbeys in the theatre of war were either completely destroyed or heavily burdened by the army. Abbot Jacques must have been uneasily aware that he might be criticised for placing too much emphasis on French grievances, for he added, 'and just as the abbeys of the kingdom of France are heavily afflicted because of wars and other misfortunes, so in general, all the other abbeys of the Order are troubled for similar reasons. In every area to which the Order has spread there have been wars, and they are increasing more than ever.'[22] To these difficulties must be added the papal crusading tenths, and the oppressions of nobles.[23] Altogether the Cistercian Order was in debt to the amount of over 500,000 *l.t.,* apart from the pensions it had to pay. Abbot Jacques knew of five abbeys, four of them in France, which owed more than 100,000 *l.t.* each.[24]

These complaints form part of a long and able *apologia* for the Cistercian Order, only a part of which is concerned with economic matters. Its author was the most prominent Cistercian of his time, and had been the spokesman for the exempt Orders at the Council of Vienne.[25] His views undoubtedly reflected authoritative opinion among the White Monks, and the broad lines of the picture he presents must be accepted. Some of his facts can be corroborated. There is ample evidence that in 1298 supplies were requisitioned from certain Cistercian abbeys for French troops in Flanders.[26] The pensions of the cardinal protectors were a heavy burden, and subsidies had to be raised from the whole Order so that they could be paid.[27] Nevertheless certain portions of Jacques' memorandum must be treated with scepticism. He seems to have been aware himself that he sometimes assumed that the experience of the French Cistercians applied to the whole Order. He did not really know what wars had occurred outside France. He was seemingly unaware that the famine of 1315-17 had afflicted the whole of Europe from England to the Slavic lands.[28] For Jacques it was 'the famine in the kingdom of France'. Above all his statistics cannot be treated seriously. He wrote of five abbeys (four, naturally, in France) which owed more than 100,000 *l.t.* each. When he wrote of the Order's total debt of over 500,000 *l.t.* he had probably done no more than add the five sums together. Otherwise one would have to conclude that the Order's total debt came to 1,000,000 *l.t.*

In any case, the figures are fantastic. They bear no relation to any known debt of the Order in its surviving Accounts. The sum of 500,000 *l.t.* is equivalent to two or three times the entire annual revenue of pope John XXII, and roughly the same as the reserve fund he handed to his successor.[29] It must be remembered that in modern times the use of arabic numerals has made it easy to understand high numbers, so that billions, millions, and thousands present no difficulties, even to children. In the Middle Ages, when such quantities were usually expressed through cumbrous roman numerals, many people, even among the learned, had difficulty in conceiving them. This was undoubtedly the case with Jacques de Thérines, or his copyist.

In the early years of the fourteenth century the main lines of the Order's financial organisation emerged ever more clearly. In 1316 the abbots living in the province of Bordeaux were instructed to bring contributions to Montpellier; those living on the French side of the Alps, the Rhine and the sea should go to St Bernard's College in Paris. The rest should bring their payments to Cîteaux at the time of the Chapter General.[30] There is less information about the size of subsidies during this period. The contribution of 1300, raised only from abbeys in France, was described as a tenth.[31] It must be presumed that father abbots calculated the actual amount to be paid by each house. In 1316 *Mediocris* and *Moderata* were demanded,[32] possibly to be paid in two unequal instalments. On four occasions the subsidy was described as a *Moderata*.[33] There is no mention of *Duplex* and *Excessiva* in these years. The latter rates seem to have been levied for the first time in 1340 and 1341.[34] At the beginning of the fourteenth century the Cistercians, like the Praemonstratensians,[35] seem to have managed with two rates for their Collections.

In the years immediately preceding *Fulgens* the Order's financial activities were largely undertaken to satisfy pope John XXII. In 1322 and 1327 the aim was to raise 10,000 *fl.* for his needs, and especially for fighting his enemies in Italy.[36] There is some evidence that many abbots were slow to pay, leaving the Order in an embarassed position.[37] In 1331 the Chapter General ordered a *contributio moderata*.[38] In 1333 there was a drive to collect arrears. Abbeys in France were to send their payments to Cîteaux by Easter, the rest by the next Chapter General.[39] At the same time, as a fragment of the Order's Accounts for 1334 shows, another subsidy was being raised. The fragment was used as part of the *dossier* compiled against Cîteaux in 1483-86. It does not even pretend to be a complete transcription as the heading shows: 'The following articles were extracted from an ancient Account of the monastery of Cîteaux'.[40] The picture of the Order's finances on the eve of Benedict XII's reforms is therefore incomplete. In what follows the material has been rearranged, and an interpretation of some of the items attempted.[41]

The Order expected 2 or 3,000 *l.t.* from backpayments, and the Collections of 1333-4 were to raise another 3,000 *l.t.* Out of this 600 *l.t.* had been promised to the

Mother House to help it redeem an annual rent which was paid to the Benedictine abbey of St Germain-des-Prés near Paris. The rent was for a priory, formerly belonging to St Germain, which Cîteaux had acquired in 1300.[42]

Much less money came in than had been expected. Back-payments amounted to 775 *l.* 4 *s.* 4 *d.t.* The Collections realised only 693 *l.* 17 *s.* 4 *d.t.*

Out of this various debts had to be paid:

400 *l.t.* were owed to the abbot of St Germain, of which only 40 *l.t.* had been paid so far.

284 *l.* 21 *d.t.* were paid to the abbot of Cîteaux on St Juliana's day (23 February). It must be presumed that this payment had nothing to do with the 600 *l.t.* promised above.

200 *l.* 15 *s.* went to cover the general expenses of the Order.

180 *l.t.* were spent on Scarborough.

135 *l.* 42 *s.t.* was for the castle of Longecourt,[43] of which 85 *l.* 15 *s.t.* had already been paid. Perhaps these last two items were for repairs.

There were some minor payments:

72 *gr.t.* to merchants of Sorgues.

14 *l.t.* to the proctor of the Order, of which 13 *s.t.* were already paid.

Payments to the obedientiaries of Cîteaux closely resemble similar lists in later Accounts:[44]

22 *l.t.* to the prior of Cîteaux.

20 *l.t.* to the cellarer.

10 *l.t.* to the bursar.

60 *l.t.* to the sub-bursar.

Two payments were made to individuals whose connection
with the Order is unknown:

10 *l.t.* to Anthony.

100 *fl.* to Matthew Succar'.

The balance, stated to be 82 *l.* 18 *s.t.,* was handed
over to the abbot of Cîteaux. The hope that the
Mother House would be cleared of a debt arising
from the acquisition of a property was not
realised.

Benedict XII's bull *Fulgens* is a landmark in the history of
the White Monks during this period. The pope wanted all
Cistercians to shoulder the Order's financial burdens, and he
insisted on efficiency in financial organisation. The intro-
duction of the annual audit was a spur to proper accounting.[45] The excellent order and arrangement of the Accounts
from 1337-47 are a tribute to the zeal of the White Monks in
obeying the wishes of the pontiff.[46]

The first of the Collections held after the promulgation of
the bull was in 1337. Chapter decided that a thorough campaign to bring in arrears should be undertaken. According to
the statute authorising it, some of the debts went back as far
as 1320.[47] In fact, enquiries were pushed back no further
than 1335.[48] By September 1337 the authorities could
report that 4,751 *l.* 5 *s.t.* had been collected.[49]

For 1338 the Order decided on a *contributio mediocris*
to raise 12,000 *l.t.*[50] The total collected came to 8,964 *l.*
10 *s.* 8 *d.t.*[51] Expenses for the year were 9,092 *l.* 18 *d.t.*[52]
The bursar of the Mother House also had a debt of 626 *l.*
16 *d.t.,* which could not be paid in the current year and
therefore had to be held over.[53] It is possible that this was
the debt to St Germain-des-Prés, mentioned in 1334.[54] Debts
to Italian merchants also had to be cleared.[55] The five
seniors were therefore empowered to negotiate a loan.[56]
They entrusted the detailed arrangements to the Order's

proctor,[57] who borrowed an unspecified sum at the Fairs of Champagne.[58] In all these details, reproduced in the Accounts from the statement made on St Lambert's day, there is no reference to the money that had been collected in back-payments in the previous year. No doubt the five seniors relied on the fact that the diffinitors would not keep the figures in their heads from one year to the other.

To clear the Order's debts, another campaign to bring in arrears was undertaken 1339, since, it was suggested, the Order's difficulties arose from the fact that so many abbots failed to pay their contributions.[59] The total collected, after the bursar's debt for the previous year had been deducted,[60] came to 2,371 *l*. 3 *s*. 8 *d.t.*[61] The expenses of the year were added up, rather improbably, to exactly the same sum.[62] The intention here seems to have been to show that the Order had the resources to meet day-to-day running costs, but that there were enormous extra debts which could only be met by exceptional measures. Loans from Italian merchants were accumulating interest.[63] No money was available for the two cardinals who received pensions from the Order,[64] for the pension regularly paid to the proctor at Avignon,[65] or to defray the cost of the previous year's Chapter General.[66] It followed that the very special subsidy which had just been approved by the Chapter General was absolutely necessary.[67]

Thus an atmosphere of urgency was created to warrant a Collection to bring in 24,000 *l.t.*, decreed by the Chapter General in September 1339. The rate, known in the Dijon Tax Book as the *contributio excessiva*, may have been invented for this occasion. There is, at least, no evidence in the statutes that it had ever been levied previously. It was justified by 'the pressing debts of the Order which are running at interest, to pay pensions and services at the Roman Curia, and to forward the Order's business where necessary'.[68] The bulky Accounts of 1340 are evidence of the gigantic effort made.[69] It has already been noted that the

Order was successful in bringing in contributions from Polish, Hungarian, Dalmatian, and Portuguese abbeys.[70] Yet at the Audit on St Lambert's day, the whole elaborate operation was depicted as a disappointment. The total brought in from current payments, arrears, and other sources of revenue was stated to be 15,929 *l.* 6 *d.t.*[71] Expenses for the year amounted to 18,367 *l.* 11 *s.* 8 *d.t.*[72] The deficit was given as 3,438 *l.* 11 *s.* 2 *d.t.*[73] The debt to the Italians had only been slightly reduced,[74] and the cardinals were still unpaid.[75]

At the Chapter General of September 1340, the authorities tried another financial experiment. Demands had hitherto been made in *livres tournois.* Chapter now asked for 12,000 Florentine *florins.*[76] At the current rate of exchange this was really worth 18,000 *l.t.* or twice the *contributio moderata.* In the Dijon Tax Book it was to be called a *contributio duplex,* but perhaps, by using different money of account, the Order had somewhat disguised the nature of what was being done.[77] The authorities justified the new subsidy in the familiar way: the Order was heavily in debt and had to pay interest; it was liable for services in the Curia; the pensions of the cardinals were unpaid.[78] Another enquiry into arrears was to accompany the Collection.[79] According to the Accounts of 1341, the sum brought in amounted to 9,643 *fl.* 8 *gr.* 28½ *d.t.*[80] The sum total of current expenses was reported to be 9,643 *fl.* 8 *gr.* 22½ *d.t.*; 'the same as the receipts',[81] wrote the scribe, ignoring a profit of 6 *d.t.* The Italians were paid off,[82] and some progress was made towards satisfying the cardinals and the proctor,[83] although they had to wait a little longer before receiving everything due to them.[84] Remaining debts to the cardinals and other were expressed as 5,478 *fl.* 11 *gr.*[85]

For the Collections of 1342 the Order returned once more to *livres tournois* as its money of account. The sum of 12,000 *l.t.* was to be raised, the *contributio mediocris.*[86] There was considerable confusion about currencies. Because the contribution of the previous year had been expressed in *florins* abbeys which owed money for 1341 had their arrears recorded in that currency, and reckoned their current payment in *livres tournois.* The abbey of Sobrado in Spain (La Coruña), for instance, had its payment for 1342 entered as 26 *l.* 13 *s.* 4 *d.t.,*[87] and its backpayment as 13 *fl.*[88] Some abbeys seem to have preferred *florins* for all their payments.[89] Adding up at the end of the Accounts presented great difficulties. Totals were expressed in *livres tournois,* but the equivalent in *florins* was sometimes added.[90] Backpayments were reckoned in both currencies,[91] except for those from the generation of Morimond which, for some reason, were added up in *florins* only.[92] For the Audit on 17 September the authorities clearly wanted the final totals presented in both currencies. It looks as if the operation ended in disaster. In the Accounts for 1342 the final sums have been cancelled and done a second time.[93] There must have been a general feeling that the figures as presented on 17 September had been wrong.

The final and corrected result was expressed as a total receipt of 8,897 *l.* 15 *s.* 8 *d.t.* or 3,559 *fl.*[94] Expenses came to 8,911 *l.* 14 *s.* 2 *d.t.* or 3,564 *fl.* 8 *gr.t.* Thus there was a small deficit, expressed as 13 *l.* 19 *s.* 2 *d.t.*[95] Much was left unpaid, however. There were still arrears on the pension of one of the cardinals (the other was now dead); the Order owed 4,000 *fl.* to the abbot of Clairvaux, and 6,000 *fl.* to the pope. The total debt was said to be 13,275 *fl.*[96] Once again it seems that the figures, in spite of the confusions caused by the two currencies, were carefully marshalled. They showed that the Order was still capable of meeting its ordinary expenses, but that Collections were justified because of the wholly exceptional extra burdens placed upon it.

After 1342 the relatively stable Florentine *florin* was always used as money of account. The old assessments were retained. Florins were simply substituted for *livres tournois,* regardless of rates of exchange.[97] For 1343 the Chapter

General demanded 18,000 *fl.*[98] This was twice the lowest rate, and was to be known in the Dijon Tax Book as a *contributio duplex.* The total receipt was 10,586 *fl.* 2 *gr.t.*[99] Expenses were 10,662½ *fl.* The deficit was 76 *fl.* 4 *gr.t.*[100] The Order's debts, which had been given such prominence in the previous year, were not mentioned.

For 1344 the Order decided upon a *contributio mediocris,* which was intended to raise 12,000 *fl.*[101] It brought in 8,430 *fl.* 8 *gr.t.*[102] Expenses came to 8,624 *fl.* 5 *s.t.,*[103] the greater part of which was spent on paying everything that was owed to the cardinal.[104] There was a small deficit of 93 *fl.* 9 *gr.t.*[105] Altogether the five seniors will not have been able quite to disguise the fact that, from a financial point of view, the years 1340-4 had been rather successful. For the first time since 1339, the Order was free from debt. Although income from Collections always fell below the nominal totals expected, a large amount of money had been raised in five years, and it was clear that the abbeys were well able to bear the exceptionally high rates imposed.

There are many puzzling features about the Accounts of 1345. The Chapter General decided upon a *contributio moderata* to raise 9,000 *fl.*[106] The lowest rate for a subsidy was justified because of the more buoyant state of the Order's finances. The total collected came to 7,934½ *fl.* 22 *d.t.* 1 *poitevin.*[107] Expenses totalled 4,209 *fl.* 2 *d.t.*[108] The Order stated its balance to be 3,644½ *fl.* 20 *d.t.* 1 *poitevin.*[109] It must be presumed that money was therefore available to pay the pension of the cardinal, which amounted to 3,000 *fl.* a year.[110] In fact he only received 279 *fl.* 4 *s.* 8 *d.t.,*[111] and, as the Accounts of the succeeding years show, his pension was again allowed to fall behind. It is impossible to avoid the conclusion that the full facts were not revealed on 17 September 1345.

For 1346 the Chapter General decreed a Collection to raise 18,000 *fl.*[112] The total gathered in came to more than one-third of the target: 6,789 *fl.*[113] Expenses amounted to

4,418 *fl.* 5 *s.* 1 *d.t.*[114] so that a balance of 2,371 *fl.* could be declared.[115] Since the cardinal had hardly been paid in the previous year, however, there was now a considerable debt to him, and in the current year he received only half of his pension.[116] The Order was again negotiating a loan from merchants. The new company came from Savoy. The amount they lent is not recorded, but they took 250 *fl.* for their services.[117] The balance for the previous year was not mentioned.

The year 1347 is the last in the fourteenth century for which full Accounts are preserved. The Collections for that year were intended to raise 9,000 *fl.*[118] Receipts were stated to be 9,292 *fl.* 5½ *gr.t.*,[119] but this satisfactory total was only reached by adding on the balance of the two previous years, which suddenly made their appearance at this point. The balance of 1345 was introduced somewhat covertly as 'the balance of the aforesaid year'.[120] It requires some reflection before the meaning of the words becomes clear. The 1345 profit was stated to be 2,360 *fl.* 10 *s.t.*[121] Over 1,200 *fl.* of it had thus been spent in some mysterious way, before the rest appeared in the Order's Accounts again.[122] The balance of 1346 was stated to be 41 *fl.*;[123] 2,330 *fl.* had 'disappeared'. The rest had been brought into the current Account to give the impression that the Collections for 1347 had been quite successful. Expenses in 1347 were stated to be 10,660 *fl.* 3 *gr.* 19 *d.t.* There was thus a deficit of 1,367 *fl.* 10 *gr.* 6½ *d.t.* to be declared. Moreover the debt to the cardinal stood at 1,700 *fl.* 1,500 *fl.* were owed to the merchants of Savoy. The Order's total debt was 4,567 *fl.* 10 *gr.* 6 *d.t.*[124]

Altogether the sum of 3,530 *l.t.* was 'lost' in 1345-7. One can only speculate here, but it may be noted that at this period the clergy of France were paying a three-year tenth granted by pope Clement VI to Philip VI in 1344.[125] To use money contributed by the whole Order for this purpose was a delicate matter and it would be impossible to admit that it had been done. It is just possible, however, that the money was used to help the French Cistercians during these years.

The statutes of the Chapter General are an important source of information about the Order's financial situation in the period 1348-78. They can be supplemented by a few surviving statements issued for the St Lambert's day Audit. In 1348 the Chapter decided to raise 18,000 *fl.*[126] The figures presented at the Audit of 1347 had no doubt been intended to justify a *contributio duplex*. At the Audit of 1350 the diffinitors could reflect upon the success of recent attempts to raise money:[127]

Receipts:

With the bursar of Cîteaux	435 *fl.*
With the abbot of La Ferté	100 *fl.*
With the proctor	106 *fl.*
With the abbot of San Galgano	146 *fl.*
(The total would be	787 *fl.*)

Debits:

To the cardinal for 1349	3,082 *fl.*
To the cardinal for 1350	3,000 *fl.*
To Nicholas Francisci	2,000 *fl.*
To Cîteaux for the expenses of the Chapter General	1,500 *fl.*
To Cîteaux for the expenses of St Lambert's day	50 *fl.*
(The total would be	9,632 *fl.*)

The abbot of Cîteaux was authorised to borrow money until the Chapter met again.

A comparison with the Accounts of 1347 shows some constant features. Involvement with the Savoyard banking family of Nicholas Francisci had begun, as we have seen, in 1346,[128] and the debt had steadily increased. The cardinal's pension had begun to run behind in 1345[129] and was now once again the Order's heaviest financial burden. If receipts were candidly reported in this extract, they had never been so low. It is possible that the dislocation caused by the Black Death was to blame.

The Order's financial organisation continued to function in the 1350s, as the statutes of the Chapter General show. The traditional sanctions against those who did not pay were renewed on a number of occasions.[130] Financial assistance was promised to father abbots and others who, because of excommunications and other punishments which they had meted out to offenders, were cited to the Curia.[131] On occasions a more conciliatory note was to be discerned. In 1350, for instance, it was stated that father abbots should not be arbitrary in imposing quotas. Houses were to be liable only for what was anciently owed and an abbot who refused to pay a sum in excess of the traditional assessment incurred no penalties.[132] This statute may have inspired the compilation of the Dijon Tax Book, which is itself eloquent witness that Collections were alive and well in the years after 1347. Because of wars and other misfortunes, however, the Chapter General was readier than it had once been to grant delays for payments and to allow individual abbeys to make special arrangements.[133] Threats to punish father abbots who did not impose the traditional penalties for non-payment,[134] are probably also a sign that at the local level there was some unwillingness to endanger unity because of the financial demands of the Chapter General.

In 1351 it was decided that the Order would be asked for 6,000 *fl.* every year until further notice.[135] Only two years later this was not considered enough, and a collection of 12,000 *fl.* was decreed for one year only.[136] In 1354 the demand was for 9,000 *fl.*[137] In 1356 there was another Collection. The sum to be raised cannot, because of the corrupt state of the text, be determined.[138] By this time the Order was preoccupied with the financial demands of pope Innocent VI. The money he obtained from the Order had to be raised by borrowing from the abbots of Cîteaux, La Ferté, and Clairvaux. The annual repayments, made out of the Collections, were still being made in 1390.[139]

A brief statement, issued for St Lambert's day, 1363, gives some information about the Order's finances in that year. The debt to Cîteaux was expressed as 3,045 *fl.* 6½ *gr.* 8 *d.t.* To pay it with the interest due, the bursar or cellarer of Cîteaux or the proctor of the Order were authorised to borrow up to 1,055 *fl.* 6½ *gr.* 8 *d.t.*[140] The rest, presumably, was to be made up out of revenue. A similar document of 1377 declared a debt of 18,590 *fl.* 7 *gr.t.* The money was owed 'for many Chapters General of our Cistercian Order'. The Mother House was authorised to negotiate a loan.[141] These figures are perhaps best understood if they are put into the context of the Order's income in the 1340s. In 1343, a good year, Collections and other sources of income brought in 10,568 *fl.* After that, income declined: 8,430 *fl.* (1344); 7,934 *fl.* (1345); 6,789 *fl.* (1346). The Order used its reserves to boost the 1347 figures—the actual income for that year was more or less the same as for 1346.[142]

No doubt the Chapter General always had some money in hand which did not appear in the Accounts. Although it is likely that income had greatly declined in the 1360s, it is possible that the debt in 1363 was manageable. By any available standards of comparison, however, the sum of 1377 seems immense. The statements for the Audits of 1363 and 1377 do not, in fact, refer to the Collections. No statute mentions them between the years 1356 and 1382, though it should be noted that Canivez had few manuscripts available when compiling his series of Cistercian statutes for the second half of the fourteenth century.[143] It is possible that the decision of

1351, ordering an annual Collection of 6,000 *fl.*,[144] was still
in force twenty years later. In any case, evidence that Collections in some form were still taking place in the 1370s comes
from the Modena Tax Book. It was thought worthwhile to
alter it and keep it up to date in 1379 and 1381.[145] Con-
firmatory evidence comes from the Accounts of the bursar
of Cîteaux. This dignitary had always been one of those to
whom contributions could be paid. When this happened he
entered the payments in his own Accounts. They are there,
interspersed with revenue from Cîteaux's saltworks, orchards, vineyards, farms, and other possessions. The bursar
clearly now regarded these payments as absolutely the property of the Mother House.

A number of entries made in the Spring of 1378 give a
little information about the Collections in previous years:[146]

Receipts from Contributions:

First, from the abbot of Buillon on 13 January, for
the contribution imposed upon him in the year
1377, and to be paid in 1378—3 *fl.*
From the abbot of Chambons on 16 April for the
contribution imposed upon him in the year 1377,
and to be paid in the year 1378—14 *fl.* 4 gr.t.,
worth 12 *fr.*

These entries give the impression that contributions had
become a matter of individual bargaining. The payment from
Chambons is a near equivalent of its *moderata* assessments in
the Tax Books.[147] The Buillon payment is the equivalent of
its *mediocris* quota.[148] There was clearly no question of a
uniform rate for all abbeys in 1377-8. The abbey of Buillon
was persuaded, shortly afterwards, to pay an annual rent to
Cîteaux.[149]

In 1377 the Order also decided to send two dignitaries—
perhaps abbots—on visitation to Spain and Portugal. One of

their tasks was to collect contributions:[150]

Further, on 17 April [1378] from Father[151] John de Bacco and Father John de Chesiaco, the visitors in Spain, the payments which follow.

First, from the abbot of Valmagne near Montpellier, for the contributions imposed upon him in the year 1376 and payable in the year 1377—32 *fl.*
From the abbot of Villelongue for the contribution imposed upon him in the year 1371 and payable in 1372—2½ *fl.*
From the same abbot for the contribution imposed upon him in the year 1374 and payable in the year 1375—2½ *fl.*
From the same abbot for the contribution imposed upon him in the year 1375 and payable in the year 1376—4 *fl.*
From the abbot of St Christopher[152]—4 *fl.* He still has to pay 14 *fl.* arrears for past years.
From the abbot of St Paul[153] for the contribution imposed upon him in the year 1376 and payable in the year 1377—8 *fl.*
From the abbot of Fiães, for many years back— 18 *fl.*
From the abbot of Oya—9 *fl.* He still owes, as he himself admits, arrears for past years amounting to 62 *fl.*
From the abbot of Melón, for many years back— 11 *fl.*
From the abbot of Junqueira, for the subsidy for the lord pope—8 *fl.*
From the abbot of Carracedo, for past contributions—19 *fl.*

The list gives some information about the route taken by

the visitors. In the journey through southern France they
travelled, at least partly, along the way to be followed by a
much more famous Cistercian visitor in the sixteenth century. Dom Edme de Saulieu's journey in 1531 from Clairvaux
to the Iberian peninsula was also to take him *via* Valmagne
and Villelongue.[154] The fourteenth-century visitors, no
doubt, had started from Cîteaux. Like Dom Edme, they had
probably travelled south through Lyon and Vienne, making
towards the coast. Dom Edme had turned westwards at
Nîmes.[155] In 1377 the visitors, as can be seen, made for
Montpellier, from which they visited Valmagne. Villelongue,
further along the road towards Spain, could be reached from
Carcassone.[156]

The visitors are lost to view in the next part of their
journey. They clearly collected no money as they travelled
through Aragon and Castile. They re-emerge in Portugal.
São Paulo de Almaziva could be reached from Coimbra.
São Cristovão de Lafões was a little further North. Both
abbeys were visited by Dom Edme in 1533.[157] The other
monasteries mentioned in 1377 were to the north, in the
mountains, on either side of the Portuguese border: the
Portuguese ones in the province of Ninho, the Spanish ones
in Galicia and León.

Those portions of the bursar's Accounts which deal with
Collections are quite different in appearance from the Order's
Accounts of 1337-47. In the earlier period a decision of the
Chapter General had set off a complex but unified exercise.
Collecting centres had been established, and payments had
been expected at Easter or the September Chapter General.
This ordered process was reflected in the logical arrangement
of the Accounts. In the 1370s the size of a contribution and
the timetable of payments was a matter for bargaining between
each abbey and the Order. Some of the traditional organisation still survived, however. The two visitors sent to Spain
were not the only collectors at work during the period. In
May 1378 the abbot of Vauclair came to Cîteaux with

money 'from several abbots'.[158] In the autumn the abbots of Grandselve and Bellebranche brought a large sum collected from various houses.[159] Abbots still came to Cîteaux with money from colleagues, as did the abbot of Savigny, who arrived in May 1378 with the contribution of the abbey of Barbeaux.[160] St Bernard's College in Paris was still being used as a collecting centre, and payments from there were forwarded to the bursar of Cîteaux by its provisor and cellarer.[161] *Receptores* continued to be appointed. In the Bursar's Accounts they are now seen from his point of view: 'Also at the time of the Chapter General [1378], I received from the abbot of Grandselve the contributions of various abbots to the value of 45 *fr.* 7½ *gr.* and I gave an account of the money this year to the *receptores'*.[162]

In September 1378, whilst the Chapter General was meeting in Cîteaux, dramatic events took place in Rome which led eventually to the Great Schism. The setting up of rival obediences within the Western Church caused, in the end, the division of the great religious Orders. For the Cistercians this meant two Chapters General, and therefore two financial systems.

Because J.M. Canivez was unable to find any statutes of Chapters General held at Cîteaux between 1377 and 1387, the story cannot be reconstructed from the viewpoint of the Mother House. The five senior abbeys were in the territory of the king of France, and went over to the side of Clement VII. After 1380, however, Conrad, the German abbot of Morimond, changed over to Urban VI and left his abbey. For a time the abbot of Bellevaux took his place at the Chapter General,[163] but at least from 1388 a Frenchman who supported the Avignon line of popes was abbot of Morimond.[164] The Chapters General which met at Cîteaux during this period were gatherings of abbots, probably French for the most part, of the Avignon obedience.

As for abbots who recognised Urban VI, that pope was organising them into provincial Chapters as early as May

1379.[165] In 1382 a Chapter General of all Cistercian abbots of this obedience could be held in Rome.[166] It is noteworthy that financial matters ranked high on its agenda. This was also the case with all the other Chapters General which assembled under Urbanist auspices. The popes of the Roman line seem to have been aware that the Cistercians had a well-tried system of raising money from their Order. Urban VI was the first to recognise its potential for helping his cause. The Chapter General of 1382 granted him a subsidy. Abbot Conrad of Morimond was to collect it in Germany. The abbot of Esrom in Denmark was given the same duties in Scandinavia, Scotland, Russia, and the Slavic lands.[167] Urban was granted another subsidy by the Chapter General which met in Rome in 1383.[168] By February of the next year abbot Conrad was busy collecting it in Germany and could report a certain amount of success.[169] Boniface IX also relied on the help of his Cistercians. He personally summoned a Chapter General to Rome in September 1390. It agreed to make a Collection for him. Abbot Peter of Ebrach was put in charge of operations in Germany, the abbot of Esrom was assigned to Northern Europe.[170] All the statutes passed at a Chapter General held in Vienna in 1393 have survived and are in print.[171] A contribution of 6,000 *fl.* was decreed. No doubt the pope was to be the chief beneficiary. Half was to be paid by Easter, the rest by the next Chapter General. Collectors were appointed for the various regions: the abbots of Boxley and Sibton for England and Wales; the abbot of St Mary's Dublin for Ireland and Scotland; the abbot of Kamp for the Low Countries, the archbishopric of Cologne, Picardy, and the areas round about; the abbot of Eberbach for Westphalia, Saxony, and those parts of the Rhineland not in the archbishopric of Cologne; the abbot of Morimond for southern Germany, the March of Meissen, Bohemia, and Austria; the abbot of Pilis for Hungary; the abbot of Mogila for Poland and the East.[172] *Receptores* were also appointed, one of whom was the abbot of Kaisheim, and a chance reference shows that financial business was still done on St Lambert's day.[173] There is some evidence here of a desire to revive the ancient financial system, though the organisation was probably more impressive on parchment than on the ground. Collections continued to be organised by Cistercians of this obedience in the fifteenth century.[174]

The activities, financial and other, of the Chapter General which met at Cîteaux in these years are exceedingly obscure. A statement presented at the Audit of 1380 has survived. Four of the senior abbots were present. The abbot of Belle-vaux took the place of Conrad of Morimond, who had gone over to Urban VI.[175] The Order acknowledged a recent debt to the Mother House of 1,737 *fl.* 6 *gr.t.,* for the cost of the Chapter General and expenses at the Curia. Older debts, still unpaid, were recorded at the same time. The debt of 1377 — 18,590 *fl.* 7 *gr.t.*[176] — was still unpaid. The Order also owed Cîteaux 1,132 *fl.* The total debt to the Mother House in 1382 was 22,742½ *fl.*[177]

A generation earlier debts were attributed to the Order as a whole. The Accounts of 1347 ended with the words 'total sum of the debts which the Order owes altogether'.[178] Simi-lar language was used at the Audit of 1350.[179] The debt was a collective burden on the entire Order, for which all consti-tuent abbeys were responsible. A change of attitude may have come after 1357, when some of the Order's senior abbots had to bail it out to meet the financial demands of Innocent VI. These abbots had to be repaid, out of the income from Collections, over a number of years.[180] It may have been from this that the idea of Cîteaux as the sole creditor of the Order developed. The Mother House had always expected to be reimbursed for the expenses of hospitality at the Chapter General, but was content, in the 1340s, to rank among the others to whom money was owed. After 1363 debts were expressed at the Audit as money owed to Cîteaux alone. Whilst the premier abbey may have been ready to shoulder other expenses, particularly those at the Curia, it is difficult

not to believe that a new attitude to the government of the
Order lay behind the change of wording.

   In the 1380s Cîteaux does not seem to have had the confidence to organise Collections on the scale of those undertaken by the Urbanist abbots. Contributions continued to
trickle in. Nothing at all came in the winter of 1380-81,
recorded the bursar,[181] but on 2 May 1381 10 *fr.* arrived
from the abbey of Mont-Sainte-Marie.[182] For the most part
the Mother House was kept afloat by the rents which individual abbots were persuaded to pay.[183] It is not always easy
to distinguish them from contributions in the bursar's
Accounts. No doubt, from the point of view of Cîteaux,
there was little difference. Nor needed the bursar be
scrupulous about place-names, since the record was for his
eyes alone. He would not have to explain to anyone from
which of the many abbeys called *Gardum, Benedictio Dei*
or *Bona Vallis* payments had come. It is fairly clear, however, that in the years immediately after the Great Schism
Cîteaux received financial support from a small number of
abbeys in France. Throughout the 1380s the repayments for
the loan of 1357 provided a small but steady source of
income.[184] There were also a few benefactions. Jean de Cros,
'the cardinal of Limoges',[185] made an annual gift of 200 *fr.*[186]
It was a striking reversal of the older financial relationship
between the Cistercians and the Sacred College.

   There was more vigorous financial activity from 1389. In
that year the Chapter General decreed a Collection to raise
9,000 *fl.* The preamble to the statute stated that the Order's
debts to individuals and institutions were insupportable.
Receptores were appointed and payments were to be in two
instalments, at Easter and the September Chapter General.[187]
After this Collections became, once again, an annual feature.
12,000 *fl.* were to be raised in 1390,[188] 6,000 *fl.* in 1391,[189]
12,000 *fl.* in 1392[190] and 1393,[191] 6,000 *fl.* in 1394,[192]
9,000 *fl.* in 1395,[193] 6,000 *fl.* from 1396-99,[194] 12,000 *fl.* in
1400.[195] There were also frequent enquiries to find out who

owed money to the Order.[196] The surviving statements for
Audits at this period never reveal how much money was
actually raised on these occasions, but always manage to give
the impression that the financial situation was desperate. At
the Audit of 1390 it was stated that the Order's debt to the
Mother House was 24,967 *fl.* 3 *gr.t.* In addition all the expenses for the year, including the cost of the Chapter
General, were unpaid. The total for these came to 521 *fl.*
Cîteaux had not received its annual 100 *fl.*[197] In 1391 the
Order's debt was estimated as 25,488 *fl.* 3 *gr.t.*[198] This sum
was copied into every statute dealing with finance until
1400.[199]

The size of the debt, and the urgency of the language used,
require some explanation. Although the Order's sources of
income were much reduced, the Chapter General at Cîteaux
was now attended by only a handful of abbots, and
the cost of feeding and housing them was very modest.[200]
According to the statutes the money was owed to the Proctor
General at the Curia, and the masters and bachelors at the
Studia had not received their bursaries.[201] One can only
guess that the heaviest demands came from Avignon, whose
popes, like those of the rival lines, expected support from
the Cistercians and other religious Orders of their obedience.

In these circumstances Cîteaux needed more help than it
could get from a few loyal abbeys in France. If money was to
come from the other side of the Pyrenees, however, a special
effort would be necessary. In 1397 three Spanish abbots
were appointed to carry out visitations of Cistercian abbeys
in Castile, León, Galicia, and Portugal. Their commission was
to last for three years. They were to visit every house and
restore discipline. As for contributions, they were to make
detailed enquiries about what was owed. They had full
powers to make terms and issue receipts, and every year,
whilst their commission lasted, they were to send whatever
they had gathered to the Chapter General.[202] It was still
possible, on occasions, to put on a show of severity. The

abbot of Royaumont's debts were exactly calculated in 1395-96, and he was made to pay, at least in part, to the cellarer of St Bernard's in Paris.[203] In 1399 the abbot of Bellebranche was excommunicated for non-payment over many years.[204]

No doubt these victims were carefully chosen. With its jurisdiction reduced, Cîteaux needed the good will of those abbeys which remained faithful to it. On the whole, a conciliatory tone was advisable. In 1395 the abbey of L'Estrée, which had paid no contributions for forty years, was excused, because of extreme poverty, all arrears except for a small sum, which it could pay over four years.[205] The arrears of Breuil were similarly reduced.[206] Because L'Arrivour was unable to go on paying its rent, it was allowed to give the Mother House a small estate to be quit.[207] In 1389 the abbeys of Igny and Longuay were excused contributions altogether, because of pestilence and storms.[208]

In the altered circumstances it was clearly politic to deal with the vexed question of assessments so that the arguments, which had been such a feature of the Cistercian financial system,[209] could be avoided. The statute which dealt with the matter in 1392 was not as sweeping as it appeared, at first sight, to be.[210] The apologetic language in which it was couched was, however, wholly without precedent.

> Chapter has listened with sympathy to the eloquent complaints, occasioned by the heavy burdens of many of the abbots and monasteries of our Order. They declare that from the very beginning and in all the time which has followed, the monasteries of our Order were too heavily burdened. Now they are oppressed by even greater damage and impoverished in many places, because of the almost complete destruction and ruin caused by crop failures, wars, floods, the dearth of labourers, and the catastrophic fall in their rents, income,

revenues, and resources. As for the taxes and charges placed upon them and their monasteries, even when they were far more prosperous than they are now in worldly goods and revenues, the quotas and contributions which were imposed upon them year after year for the Collections of the Chapter General (however justified these may have been), were in excess of reason and equity. Yet these quotas are still imposed by the Chapter General every year.

It looks as if frustration with the financial system, which had been seething for many years, boiled over in 1392. The language used in the preamble to the statute is clearly that of the opposition, not of the authorities. It was agreed that no abbey should ever have been assessed at a rate higher than 3 *l.t.* for every 1,000 *l.t.* which were to be raised from the whole Order. A higher rate was not valid, especially if it had been imposed without the agreement of the abbey concerned. Three for one thousand, whatever the currency used, was in future to be the maximum which could be taken from any abbey for a Collection. The concession was to be valid for five years from 1392. Arrears were to be collected at the same rate, for Chapter was pledging itself to right an ancient wrong. An abbey rated higher than this was to have its quota reduced to the defined level. Houses assessed at a lower rate were not affected, and were to pay their traditional quota. In 1397 the concession was renewed for another five years.[211] In 1402 it was made permanent.[212]

Between 1392 and 1400 the totals demanded from the Order at Collections were 6,000 *fl.,* 9,000 *fl.,* and 12,000 *fl.*[213] No house would therefore be liable to pay more than 18 *fl.,* 27 *fl.,* or 36 *fl.,* as the case might be. A study of the Modena Tax Book shows that, out of a total of over 650 houses, only around 80 would have qualified for these reductions. Of these, some 58 were in territories firmly within the Avignon obedience. The reductions did not, therefore, affect the majority of Cistercian abbeys, but they placated the richest, which were able to make the most trouble. For some of these the load was considerably lightened. Lannoy, for instance, had been liable to contributions of 69 *l.t. (Moderata),* or 92 *l.t. (Mediocris).*[214] The new arrangements meant, however, that the traditional monetary targets were unattainable.

The Cistercian financial records of the fourteenth century show the marks of firm direction, and of a clear if somewhat desperate financial policy. The five seniors were keenly aware of the Order's debts, and of the pressures from the Curia. They tried their utmost to spread the burdens evenly, and used the Accounts as well as the statutes to achieve this end. The problem hardly changed from 1290 to 1400, though a solution was even more elusive in the troubled times of the Great Schism.

NOTES TO CHAPTER FOUR

1. See above, pp. 7f.
1a. See above, p. 20.
2. *Fulgens,* 18; *Statuta,* iii, p. 421.
3. See below, p. 104.
4. See Buczek, 'Medieval Taxation', 42-106.
5. *Statuta* 1289, 15.
6. Sens MS. 129, ff. 164b-165a.
7. See Fournial, *Histoire monétaire,* 88; Favier, *Philippe le Bel,* 114-5; Cazelles, 'Quelques réflexions . . . ' , 274.
8. I am grateful to Dr. J.H. Munro for pointing out the complexities of the monetary mutations in 1290.
9. *Statuta* 1291, 30.
10. *Statuta* 1292, 6.
11. Sens MS 129, ff. 165a-b.
12. See below, pp. 136-7.
13. On the process in France see Strayer and Taylor, *Studies in early French Taxation,* 24-43. For the parallel story in England, Denton, *Robert Winchelsey and the Crown,* 60-135. The story as it affected the French Cistercians is told in some detail by Buczek, 72-91.
14. *Comptes du Trésor,* Nos. 551, 593.
15. Buczek, 95.
16. *Les journaux du Trésor de Philippe IV,* Nos. 417, 827. The words must also apply to the other Cistercian entries, *ibid.,* Nos. 993, 1281, 3328, 3460, 3501, 5842.
17. *Statuta* 1295, 15; 1296, 4; 1298, 8; 1300, 7; 1301, 8; 1305, 3; 1308, 4; 1310, 3; 1311, 3; 1314, 7; 1316, 1; 1318, 19; 1320, 13; 1322, 11, 17; 1327, 1; 1328, 13; 1331, 11.
18. *Statuta* 1322, 17; 1327, 1.
19. N. Valois, 'Un plaidoyer du XIV siècle en faveur des cistercians'.
20. See H.S. Lucas, 'The great European famine of 1315, 1316, and 1317'.
21. 'Un plaidoyer', 366.
22. *Ibid.,* 365-6.
23. *Ibid.,* 367.

24. *Ibid.*, 365.

25. Lecler, *Vienne*, 121-4.

26. *Inventaire d'anciens comptes royaux dressé par Robert Mignon,* No. 2517; *Les journaux du Trésor de Philippe IV le Bel,* Nos. 840, 895, 1239, 1289, 1807, 2162.

27. *Statuta* 1296, 4; 1305, 3; 1314, 7.

28. See H.S. Lucas, 'The great European famine'.

29. Mollat, *The Popes of Avignon,* 330. For the rate of exchange between the *l.t.* and the *florin* at this period, see Spufford and Wilkinson, 216-7.

30. *Statuta* 1316, 1.

31. *Statuta* 1300, 7.

32. *Statuta* 1316, 1.

33. *Statuta* 1314, 7; 1320, 13; 1328, 13; 1331, 11.

34. See below, pp. 100-101.

35. See above, p. 151.

36. *Statuta* 1322, 17; 1327, 1.

37. *Statuta* 1330, 3, 8.

38. *Statuta* 1331, 11.

39. *Statuta* 1333, 4.

40. Sens MS 129, f. 80b.

41. Sens MS 129, ff. 80b-81a.

42. J.M. Canivez, 'Cîteaux—abbaye', 857.

43. Longecourt-en-Plaine, an estate of the abbey of Cîteaux, see *Répertoire numérique des . . . archives ecclésiastiques . . . abbaye de Cîteaux,* 27-8.

44. See below, p. 188.

45. See above, p. 90.

46. See King, 'Cistercian financial organisation', 130-1.

47. *Statuta* 1336, 7.

48. Accts., ff. 1a, col. 1–2a, col. 2.

49. *Ibid.,* f. 2a, col. 2.

50. All the payments in the Accounts are consistent with a *contributio mediocris,* ff. 2b, col. 1–9a, col. 2. The statute for September 1337, however, orders a *contributio moderata, Statuta* 1337, 6.

51. Accts., f. 8a, col. 2.

52. *Ibid.,* f. 9a, col. 2.

53. *Ibid.*

54. See above, p. 98.

55. See below, p. 157.

56. *Statuta* 1338, 6.

57. Accts., f. 8b, col. 1.

58. *Ibid.,* f. 9a, col. 1.

59. *Statuta,* 1339, 4. The statute is not consistent with the other financial decision of 1339, and must date from the previous year. The Accounts of 1339 are headed, 'Recepta contributionum . . . facta pro arreragiis'. Accts., f. 9b, col. 1.

60. Accts., f. 11a, col. 1.

61. *Ibid.*

62. *Ibid.,* f. 11b, col. 2.

63. See below, p. 158.

64. See below, pp. 176f.

65. See below, p. 180.

66. Accts., f. 11b, col. 1.

67. *Statuta* 1339, 9.

68. *Ibid.*

69. Accts., ff. 12a, col. 1–17b, col. 2.

70. See above, pp. 74-5.

71. Accts., f. 17b, col. 1.

72. *Ibid.,* f. 17b, col. 2.

73. *Ibid.,* f. 17b, col. 2.

74. See below, p. 158.

75. *Ibid.,* f. 17b, col. 1.

76. *Statuta* 1340, 14.

77. On the change to *florins* see below, p. 163.

78. *Statuta* 1340, 14.

79. *Statuta* 1340, 14.

80. Accts., f. 20b, col. 2.

81. *Ibid.,* f. 21a, col. 1.

82. See below, p. 158.

83. See below, pp. 176f.

84. *Ibid.*

85. Accts., f. 21a, col. 1.

86. *Statuta* 1341, 14.

87. Accts., f. 21b, col. 2.

88. *Ibid.,* f. 22a, col. 2.

89. E.g. Gerkeskleaster, *ibid.,* f. 22a, col. 2.

90. *Ibid.,* f. 21a, col. 2; f. 21b, col. 1.

91. *Ibid.,* ff. 21a, col. 2; 21b, col. 1; 22a, col. 2.

92. *Ibid.,* f. 22b, col. 2.

93. *Ibid.,* f. 23a, cols. 1, 2.

94. *Ibid.,* f. 23a, col. 2.

95. *Ibid.,* f. 23a, col. 2.

96. *Ibid.,* f. 23a, col. 1.

97. See below, p. 166.
98. *Statuta* 1342, 6.
99. Accts., f. 25a, col. 2.
100. *Ibid.,* f. 25b, col. 1.
101. Accts., f. 25b, col. 1. Not mentioned in *Statuta.*
102. Accts., f. 27a, col. 1.
103. *Ibid.,* f. 27a, col. 2.
104. *Ibid.*
105. *Ibid.*
106. *Ibid.,* f. 27b, col. 1. 12,000 *fl.* according to *Statuta* 1344, 6.
107. Accts., f. 27b, col. 1. On the money of Poitou, see Spufford and Wilkinson, *Interim Listing,* 227.
108. Accts., f. 27b, col. 1.
109. *Ibid.*
110. See below, p. 176.
111. Accts., f. 27, col. 1.
112. *Ibid.,* f. 27b, col. 2. Not mentioned in *Statuta.*
113. Accts., f. 27b, col. 2.
114. *Ibid.,* f. 28a, col. 1.
115. *Ibid.*
116. *Ibid.,* f. 27b, col. 2.
117. Accts., f. 27b, col. 2.
118. *Ibid.,* 28a, col. 1. Not in *Statuta.*
119. Accts., f. 29b, col. 1.
120. *Ibid.*
121. *Ibid.*
122. See above, p. 103.
123. Accts., f. 29b, col. 1.
124. *Ibid.,* f. 29b, col. 2.
125. Samaran et Mollat, *La fiscalité pontificale en France au xive siècle,* 16; Henneman, *Royal Taxation in fourteenth century France 1322-56,* 179.
126. *Statuta* 1348, 5.
127. Sens MS 129, ff. 169a-b.
128. See above, p. 104.
129. See above, p. 103.
130. Griesser, 'Unbekannte Generalkapitelstatuten', 4-5; *Statuta* 1357, 2.
131. *Statuta* 1352, 2.
132. Griesser, 'Unbekannte Generalkapitelstatuten', 3.
133. *Statuta* 1352, 4; Griesser, *op. cit.,* 8-9.
134. Griesser, 8-9.
135. Griesser, 6.

136. Griesser, 8,
137. Griesser, 9-10.
138. *Statuta* 1356, 2.
139. See below, p. 175.
140. Sens MS 129, f. 169b.
141. *Ibid.,* ff. 170b-172a.
142. See above, p. 104.
143. See discussion by Griesser, 'Unbekannte Generalkapitelstatuten', 1-2.
144. See above p. 000.
145. See above p. 000.
146. Accts., f. 45b, col. 2.
147. *TB,* 2b, 19; *MTB,* f. 11a.
148. *TB,* 9b, 16; *MTB,* f. 15b.
149. See above, p. 38.
150. Accts., f. 45b, col. 2.
151. 'Nonnus'.
152. São Critovão de Lafões in Portugal (Beira Alta).
153. São Paulo de Almaziva, Portugal (Beira Litoral).
154. *Peregrinatio Hispanica,* ed. M. Cocheril, i, 86 (map). On Dom Edme at Valmagne and Villelongue, see *ibid.,* 132-5; 144-7.
155. *Ibid.,* 124-7.
156. *Ibid.,* 144-5.
157. *Ibid.,* 318-9; 512-5.
158. Accts., f. 46a, col. 1.
159. Accts., f. 50a, cols. 1, 2.
160. *Ibid.,* f. 46a, col. 1.
161. *Ibid.,* f. 50a, col. 2.
162. *Ibid.*
163. See below, p. 113.
164. On Conrad and the Schism, see E. Krausen, 'Generalkapitel ausserhalb Cîteaux während des Grossen Schismas', Nachtrag (by J. Marilier), 10-11.
165. Griesser, 'Statuten von Generalkapiteln ausserhalb Cîteaux', 65-66.
166. *Ibid.,* 66.
167. Griesser, 'Statuten von Generalkapiteln ausserhalb Cîteaux', 66.
168. *Ibid.,* 66-67.
169. *Ibid.*
170. *Ibid.,* 67.
171. *Ibid.,* 67-8; 72-9.
172. *Ibid.,* 79.

173. E. Krausen, 'Generalkapitel ausserhalb Cîteaux während des Grossen Schismas', 7.
174. *Ibid.,* 7-10.
175. Sens MS 129, f. 172a.
176. See above p. 107.
177. Sens MS 129, ff. 173a-b.
178. Accts., f. 29b, col. 2.
179. Sens MS 129, f. 169a.
180. See below, p. 175.
181. Accts., f. 78b, col. 1.
182. *Ibid.,* f. 84a, col. 2.
183. See above, p. 38.
184. See below, p. 175.
185. Eubel, *Hierarchia Catholica,* i, 21, 301.
186. Accts., f. 94b, col. 1.
187. *Statuta* 1389, 48.
188. *Statuta* 1390, 7.
189. *Statuta* 1391, 2.
190. *Statuta* 1392, 3.
191. *Statuta* 1393, 1.
192. *Statuta* 1394, 2.
193. *Statuta* 1395, 3.
194. *Statuta* 1396, 3; 1398, 7; 1399, 7.
195. *Statuta* 1400, 7.
196. *Statuta* 1390, 6, 19; 1393, 4; 1397, 54; 1399, 12.
197. Fifteenth century copy, *Archives de l'Aube,* 3 H 153; Sens MS 129, ff. 174a-177a.
198. *Statuta* 1391, 2.
199. E.g. *Statuta* 1400, 7.
200. See below, pp. 190f.
201. *Statuta* 1390, 6.
202. *Statuta* 1397, 54.
203. Accts., f. 201b, col. 2.
204. *Statuta* 1399, 12.
205. *Statuta* 1395, 16.
206. *Statuta* 1395, 27.
207. *Statuta* 1392, 6.
208. *Statuta* 1389, 17, 22.
209. See above, pp. 65f.
210. *Statuta* 1392, 23.
211. *Statuta* 1397, 13.
212. *Statuta* 1402, 10.

213. See above, p. 114.
214. *MTB,* f. 15a. See list in *TB,* p. 30, to which Chaalis should be added.

CHAPTER FIVE

The Statistics and Distribution
of the Collections, 1337–47.

THE AUTHORITIES of the Cistercian Order liked to give the impression that payment of contributions was a touchstone of loyalty. It is worth investigating the extent to which this view was held outside the charmed circle which directed the Chapter General. Enough records survive the period 1337-47 to make it possible to estimate the proportion of Cistercian abbeys which were prepared to shoulder the Order's financial burden. In order to do this, however, it is first necessary to establish more exactly the total number of Cistercian houses at this period.

Medieval Cistercians were proud of the way their Order had grown from modest beginnings. This feeling was eloquently expressed in the preamble to Clement IV's bull *Parvus Fons,* in the composition of which the Cistercian cardinal Guy de Paré was no doubt involved:[1]

> There was once a little spring which became a river, and when it emerged under the sun's light, grew into a mighty flood. Such is the famous Cistercian Order. At the beginning of its history it was small, obscure, meek, poorly endowed, and committed to humility. Because of the number of those who have made their profession to it, it may not inaptly be compared to a spring, which it resembles in every detail. This spring provides water to irrigate the gardens of other religious Orders, cleansing them all through its example. It is

a spring made lovely by the rich variety of its health-giving powers, outstanding for its charity and limpid purity, well known for its devotion to religious observances, and never failing to give examples of holy living. For all these reasons it was found worthy to grow from a fountain into a river . . . Like an aqueduct from Paradise it has an unending supply of water with which to irrigate with streams of grace its innumerable gardens, that is to say its vast quantity of religious houses.[2]

This Cistercian triumphalism, with its insistence on numbers and geographical spread, informed all the Order's records with a statistical element, from the *Tabulae* to seemingly prosaic financial records. Across the bottom of the fourteenth-century portion of the Modena Tax Book, where presumably the manuscript once ended, was written in large letters, 'Total number of all the abbeys of the Order of Cistercian monks—EIGHT HUNDRED AND SIXTY THREE'.[3] The *Coucher Book of Furness Abbey* had the following statistics to offer its readers:

In the generation of Cîteaux the number of monasteries is	96
In the generation of La Ferté the number of monasteries is	17
In the generation of Pontigny the number of abbeys is	46
In the generation of Clairvaux the number of abbeys is	425
In the generation of Morimond the number of abbeys is	214
Total	798[4]

In some respects these figures resemble those provided by modern authorities.[5] The figures for the generation of Clairvaux, however, to which Furness itself belonged, are notably exaggerated.

In fact, the Cistercian Order did not grow steadily. Throughout its history new houses were founded and old ones disappeared. For the fourteenth century the financial records can be used to form the basis of more accurate statistics, though complete accuracy is impossible. The chief authorities are the two Tax Books at Dijon and Modena, both of which date from the second half of the fourteenth century.

The Tax Books present a difficulty in that they listed separately every known place-name variant, and included every Cistercian abbey which had ever existed. The compilers thus gave a greatly inflated picture of the Order's size. Sometimes they may have been genuinely muddled. On the whole, however, it seems likely that they knew what they were doing. Fourteenth-century monks were well aware, for instance, that abbeys in Palestine and Syria had long ceased to exist. The compiler of the Modena Tax Book, indeed, wrote, 'Salvacium in Outremer was destroyed'.[6] Yet he still put it on his list. Without it, and other abbeys like it, he could not have come to the grand total of 863 abbeys of which, at the end of his manuscript, he was so proud. Foreign abbots could have given accurate information about the names of the houses whose contributions they brought to the Chapter General. The multiplication of place names, however, shows every sign of having been intentional. It reflected the Cistercians' pride in the growth and extent of their Order.

Although the Dijon Tax Book gives a very complete impression of the Cistercian financial system, a large number of abbeys are missing from it. Some of the omissions are surely the result of careless copying in the fifteenth century. It is difficult to believe, for instance, that the Norman abbey of La Trappe, which faithfully paid its contributions for the years 1337-47, would not have appeared in the fourteenth century original. Most of the omissions in the Dijon Tax

Book can be corrected from the one at Modena. There are, however, a number of abbeys missing from both compilations. The abbey of St Mary Graces in London was founded by king Edward III of England in 1350, during the Hundred Years' War.[7] It can never have paid contributions to the Chapter General, and its absence from all the Order's financial records is easily explicable. There is, however, no logical explanation for the absence from both Tax Books of such abbeys as Himmelstädt in Brandenburg. It seems that the information available to the compilers of the Tax Books was not always complete and that, as a result, some houses slipped through the net.

It is possible to compile a list of Cistercian abbeys by conflating the information in both Tax Books, using one place-name instead of the many variations, and adding houses which occur only in the Accounts. Since it is impossible to eradicate all place-name muddles, and some houses never appear in any of the financial records, the result will not give a definitive figure of all Cistercian abbeys for men in the fourteenth century. It will show the number of houses which, according to the surviving records, were expected to contribute to the Collections.[8] This definition applies to all the 'totals' in the statistics which follow.

Total Number of Cistercian Abbeys for Men in the Financial Records:

Seniors	5
Generation of Cîteaux	99
Generation of La Ferté	15
Generation of Pontigny	44
Generation of Clairvaux	356
Generation of Morimond	197
Total	716

To obtain realistic figures for the period 1337-47, however, some adjustments have to be made. The five seniors did not contribute to the Collections. The college of St Bernard in Paris appears in the Dijon Tax Book with an assessment.[9] At some time in the fourteenth century there must have been a decision that it need not pay contributions, since none appear in the Accounts. Alcántara and Calatrava, the two military houses in Spain dependent upon Morimond, appear in both Tax Books, though the spaces are left blank.[10] No attempt to obtain payments from them seems to have succeeded.

The abbey of S. Trinità della Magione in Palermo, which appears in both Tax Books[11] although it was suppressed in 1197,[12] must be omitted, as must all the houses in Outremer, and those in the short-lived Latin Empire of Constantinople, except for Daphni, which was still in existence. It is also necessary to leave out houses founded after 1347 and which can be found in the Modena Tax Book: the priory at Strasbourg,[13] and the new abbey in Valencia.[14] After the deductions have been made, the figures are as follows:

Generation of Cîteaux	98
Generation of La Ferté	13
Generation of Pontigny	44
Generation of Clairvaux	351
Generation of Morimond	190
Total	696

The figures which follow, culled from the Order's Accounts, are introduced with diffidence. The Accounts are not more free than other records from place-name muddles. All figures must, therefore, be approximate, but even a crude attempt to count the abbeys which contributed to Collections yields results which are of some significance.

The Collections of 1337 were for backpayments. If the surviving Accounts are complete, a comparatively small number of houses was involved:

Generation of Cîteaux	2
Generation of La Ferté	1
Generation of Pontigny	2
Generation of Clairvaux	14
Generation of Morimond	14
Total	33[15]

In 1338 a Collection for a *contributio mediocris* was taken from the whole Order, and money began to come in as early as January.[16] Between then and the September Chapter General, the number of abbeys which had contributed was as follows:

Generation of Cîteaux	63[17]
Generation of La Ferté	8[18]
Generation of Pontigny	38[19]
Generation of Clairvaux	161[20]
Generation of Morimond	110[21]
Total	380

The Collections of 1339 were, once more, for arrears. One of the *receptores* could not remember the names of all the foreign abbots in the generation of Morimond who had given him money.[22] Somewhat more abbeys were involved, therefore, than were listed:

Generation of Cîteaux	3
Generation of La Ferté	2
Generation of Pontigny	4
Generation of Clairvaux	35
Generation of Morimond	17+
Total	61+[23]

Payments for the *contributio excessiva* of 1340 were as follows:

Generation of Cîteaux	61[24]
Generation of La Ferté	13[25]
Generation of Pontigny	35[26]
Generation of Clairvaux	170[27]
Generation of Morimond	122[28]
Total	401

The response to the *contributio duplex* of 1341 was

Generation of Cîteaux	62[29]
Generation of La Ferté	9[30]
Generation of Pontigny	34[31]
Generation of Clairvaux	166[32]
Generation of Morimond	139[33]
Total	410

In 1342 a lump sum was sent by 'some abbots of Denmark and Sweden'.[34] For the rest, participation in the *contributio mediocris* was as follows:

Generation of Cîteaux	51[35]
Generation of La Ferté	7[36]
Generation of Pontigny	30[37]
Generation of Clairvaux	167[38]
Generation of Morimond	114[39]
Total	369+

The Collections of 1343 were for a *contributio duplex:*

Generation of Cîteaux	60[40]
Generation of La Ferté	6[41]
Generation of Pontigny	32[42]
Generation of Clairvaux	153[43]
Generation of Morimond	115[44]
Total	366

In 1344 some payments came from 'the abbots of Frisia',[45] and 'from many abbots in Italy'.[46] Other abbeys contributed to the *contributio mediocris* as follows:

Generation of Cîteaux	53[47]
Generation of La Ferté	7[48]
Generation of Pontigny	35[49]
Generation of Clairvaux	143[50]
Generation of Morimond	116[51]
Total	354+

Contributing abbeys were not listed in the meagre Accounts for 1345 and 1346.[52] In 1347 the Order collected a *contributio moderata*. The arrangement of the Accounts for the year is very peculiar. In the generation of Cîteaux, La Ferté, and Pontigny, there are lists of houses and the sums they paid, followed by further lists, in which the names are closely crowded together and there are no sums against them.[53] In the list below the first figure gives the number of houses which are recorded with their payments, the second the total number listed:

Generation of Cîteaux	45[54]	69[55]
Generation of La Ferté	5[56]	17[57]
Generation of Pontigny	15[58]	45[59]
Generation of Clairvaux	136[60]	
Generation of Morimond	84[61]	

In the ten years 1337-47 the number of abbeys which contributed to Collections can be counted for six. The totals are as follows:

1338	380
1340	401
1341	410
1342	369+
1343	366
1344	354+

Throughout this period, therefore, more than half of the abbeys in the Order contributed whenever there was a Collection. In the years 1338-41 the number of abbeys which responded to the Collections was increasing. From 1342 there was some decline. Nevertheless, the Chapter General could count on significant financial support during these years.

An analysis of contributions by generations show that a high proportion of abbeys in that of Morimond contributed to the Collections:

Total number of abbeys in generation of Morimond		190
	1338	110
	1340	122
	1341	139
	1342	114
	1343	115
	1344	116
	1347	84

The decline in 1347 may have begun earlier. Up to 1344 more than half the abbeys in this generation contributed. The abbot of Morimond was sometimes personally involved as a *receptor* of Collections.[62] He seems to have kept a watchful eye on payments from abbeys of his generation and was prepared to use sanctions against the recalcitrant.[63]

Abbeys in the generation of Cîteaux also had a good record. The abbot of Cîteaux was responsible for the Order's financial policy at many levels and the abbeys of his line may have felt some loyalty to him:

Total number of abbeys in generation of Cîteaux		98
	1338	63
	1340	61

1341	62
1342	51
1343	60
1344	53

The small generation of Pontigny also presented a satisfactory picture:

Total number of abbeys in generation of	
Pontigny	44
1338	38
1340	35
1341	34
1342	30
1343	32
1344	35

The generation of Clairvaux was the largest in the Order. Nearly half the abbeys belonged to it. The proportion of abbeys in this line which contributed to the Collections was rather low. Undoubtedly the almost complete absence of abbeys in the British Isles, most of which belonged to the generation of Clairvaux, affected the figures:

The number of abbeys in generation of	
Clairvaux	351
1338	161
1340	170
1341	166
1342	167
1343	153
1344	143
1347	136

The smallest generation in the Order was that of La Ferté. The figures here are satisfactory enough. The number of

abbeys involved was so small, however, that these contributions can have made little difference to the total amount of
cash collected:

The number of abbeys in generation of La Ferté	13
1338	8
1340	13
1341	9
1342	7
1343	6
1344	7

A regional survey of contributions shows that the Cistercian abbeys of France[64] provided the greater part of the
Order's financial support:

Total[65] number of abbeys in France	224
1338	207[66]
1340	208[67]
1341	205[68]
1342	186[69]
1343	193[70]
1344	188[71]

The lowest number contributed in 1342, but even in that
year the majority of abbeys in the kingdom paid. During the
period studied, the overwhelming number of houses in
France supported the Collections. There was no French
abbey which did not send something in these years, and
most contributed to every subsidy demanded by the Chapter General. The record is the more impressive in that the
abbeys of France were hard pressed by the monarchy at this
time. From 1337 the popes regularly granted clerical tenths
to the king of France.[72] It is just possible that in 1345-7 the

French Cistercians were helped to pay their share by a contribution from the Collections.[73] In any case French financial support for the Chapter General was clearly of great significance, and may have reflected a French majority at its meetings.

Contributions from abbeys in the Empire (except Bohemia) show a pattern somewhat similar to that of France. The proportion of abbeys which made regular payments was somewhat smaller. In 1338 it was less than half the total:

Total number of abbeys in the Empire (except Bohemia)	103[74]
1338	45[75]
1340	71
1341	79
1342	68
1343	74
1344	67+

A collective contribution came in 1344 from 'the abbots of Frisia'.[76] Except in 1338 the proportion of contributing abbeys was always more than half. The Order could count on substantial financial aid from the Empire.

In Bohemia, too, contributions reached their peak in 1341. 1340 and 1343 were bad years, but on the whole the majority of abbeys in this distant but rich kingdom contributed to the Collections:

Total number of abbeys in the kingdom of Bohemia	13
1338	8
1340	6
1341	10
1342	7
1343	3
1344	8

Contributions from the Italian peninsula were much less reliable:

Total number of abbeys in the Italian peninsula	82[77]
1338	40
1340	40
1341	34
1342	30
1343	15
1344	27+

In 1344 a number of unnamed abbots forwarded money through the abbot of San Galgano.[78]

The Italian pattern is different from those so far listed. The abbeys of the peninsula played no part in the effort that was being made elsewhere in 1341. From that area there was, on the contrary, a decline in contributions which began in that year. The lowest point was reached in 1343. After that there was an improvement, perhaps because the abbot of San Galgano, who by 1350 had become one of the Order's *receptores*,[79] took matters in hand. It is not easy to generalise, however, about this area. Some houses were meticulous in their payments. Such was the abbey of San Tommaso di Torcello near Venice, which annually paid all its contributions in full.[80] Not far away, the abbey of S. Maria dell' Ospedale del Piave paid much less often, and never as much as was owed.[81]

A somewhat different pattern is discernible in the payments from abbeys in Castile, Aragon and Navarre:

Total number of abbeys in the Spanish kingdoms	51
1338	31
1340	17
1341	27

1342	24
1343	22
1344	28

These abbeys were clearly reluctant to pay the *contributio excessiva* in 1340, or the *duplex* in 1343. They made an effort in 1341, but the peak years were 1338 and 1344. On the whole, about half the abbeys in these regions supported the Collections.

Further west were the Cistercian abbeys in the kingdom of Portugal:

Total number of abbeys in the kingdom of Portugal	13
1338	9
1340	10
1341	3
1342	7
1343	6
1344	5

In 1340 'a number of Portuguese abbots at the Chapter General' paid a very large sum—279 *l.t.*—in advance of future demands.[82] It was an unusual arrangement, and it probably explains the drop in contributions in 1341. When this is taken into account it can be seen that the Portuguese abbeys contributed generously to the Collections until 1342. After that a slow decline began.

There were nineteen Cistercian abbeys in Scandinavia. One Scandinavian payment was recorded in 1342, and ten in 1343. In 1339 a monk of Esrom brought money from three Danish abbeys (including his own), some of it in silver of doubtful value.[83] A lump sum arrived from abbots in Denmark in 1340.[84] In 1342 arrears were paid by 'abbots in Denmark and Sweden' of the generation of Cîteaux.[85] There were only three abbeys of this line in Scandinavia—Holm

and Løgum in Denmark, and Herrevad in Scania. The latter
province, formerly in Denmark, had been seized by king
Magnus Eriksson of Sweden in 1332. Altogether this area was
too far from Cîteaux for contributions to come with any
regularity. Nevertheless it is clear that some kind of financial
relationship with the Order was maintained.

Place-name muddles are not lacking in the Accounts of
1337-47. On the whole, abbeys from France, Italy, and the
Iberian peninsula stand out clearly from the page. The dis-
tortion of German place-names is sometimes grotesque, but it
may have been intentional.[86] These houses remain identifi-
able. Names from eastern Europe, however, clearly presented
the scribes at the Mother House with considerable difficulties.
Since identification is uncertain, statistics cannot be presented with any great confidence. Among the payments in
1338 there appear to be three from Poland.[87] At least nine
Polish abbeys contributed to the Collections in 1340,[88]
eight in 1341,[89] and ten in 1342.[90] Four Polish abbeys can
be identified among those who paid their quotas in 1343,[91]
and one in 1344.[92] Hungarian abbeys are the most difficult
to identify. It would appear that nine Hungarian abbeys
were among the number which sent contributions in 1338,[93]
six in 1340,[94] five in 1341,[95] two in 1343,[96] and four
in 1344.[97]

Money occasionally came from much further afield. The
Livonian abbeys appear in the Accounts from time to time.
Falkenau sent arrears in 1337,[98] a large sum in backpayments in 1342,[99] and more arrears in 1347.[100] Padis sent
arrears in 1339,[101] and contributions to the Collections of
1341 and 1342.[102] Daphni, the only surviving Cistercian
abbey in the former Latin Empire of Constantinople, sent a
contribution in 1340.[103] A large sum in backpayments
arrived in 1344 from Beaulieu in Cyprus.[104] It is hardly
likely that collectors went to these outlying parts. It is more
probable that when distant abbots made their rare personal
appearances at Chapters General, they brought money with

them in order to satisfy, as far as possible, the financial demands of the Order.

The most conspicuous absentees from the Accounts of 1337-47 are the abbeys of the British Isles. In 1307 Edward I of England's Statute of Carlisle had forbidden any payments from English abbeys to foreign superiors.[105] The evidence from the Tax Books suggests that the statute did not immediately prevent all payments from England to the Cistercian Chapter General. It is at least clear that negotiations about quotas continued for a long time.[106] Both the Dijon and the Modena Tax Books contain evidence of much unfinished business. In the fourteenth century, English Cistercian abbots on visitation were still enquiring about arrears owed to the Chapter General from Collections.[107] After the outbreak of the Hundred Years' War the ban on the export of money out of the kingdom was strengthened.[108] Even this did not prevent all payments from English abbeys to Cîteaux. In 1343 visitors from the Chapter General were in England, and apparently brought up the question of contributions. The king's officials got wind of what happened and most of the money which had been collected was confiscated.[109] Some of it, however, got through to Cîteaux, as the Accounts of 1343 show:

From Rievaulx for the year '35	40 *écus*	
From the same, for '37	20 *écus*	
From Revesby for the year '37	37 *écus*	worth 212 *fl.*
From Kirkstall for the same year	30 *écus*	55 *s.*
From Woburn for arrears	34 *écus*	
From Stanley for the year '37	24 *écus*	

a little further down:

From Dublin for arrears	81 *l.t.*[110]

The sums were not large and may have been all the visitors were able to smuggle past the watchful customs officials. It seems that the English abbots had been asked for arrears, rather than the *contributio duplex* which was being collected in 1343. It is noteworthy that the contribution from Dublin was in a different currency, and is not recorded with the other abbeys. It was probably transmitted independently.

These payments led to the prosecution of a number of English Cistercian abbots. The abbot of Meaux was obliged to appear before the barons of the Exchequer, and questioned about the contributions which he had made since the beginning of the War. He replied that he was not bound to pay money to a superior beyond the sea. Neither he nor his predecessors had paid anything since the king's prohibition in 1337. He was told that he would have to appear before a jury. At a meeting at Beverley in September 1344 the abbot was able to persuade those present, by repeating his earlier denial on oath. A year later he swore before a jury at York that the abbey of Meaux had paid nothing to a foreign superior since 1337, or indeed, within living memory.[111] Thus the abbot had, like St Peter, denied his Lord three times. His assertions may, for all that, have been true. Some abbeys never contributed to the Collections. The name of his abbey does not appear on the list of those who sent money from England in 1343. Nevertheless Meaux was one of the abbeys which seem to have been negotiating with the Chapter General about their quota.[112]

In 1347, under arrears from the generation of Clairvaux, there were some payments from Irish abbeys:

From Mellifont for the year '45	8 *fl.*
From the same, for the year '46	12 *fl.*
From Corcomroe[113]	6½ *fl.*
From Monasteranenagh	6½ *fl.*[114]

The order was collecting a *contributio mediocris* in 1345, and a *contributio duplex* in 1346. The payments from Mellifont correspond exactly to the assessments in the Tax Books.[115]

For much of the period 1337-47 Scotland was in confusion. The attempt of Edward Balliol and a party of exiled Scots to reestablish themselves in the kingdom soon led to the intervention of Edward III of England, who mounted an invasion in 1333. By 1337 much of southern Scotland had been laid waste.[116] Churches were burned with those who had taken refuge inside them, abbeys laid under contribution to pay for the invader's castles.[117] A brief national recovery, whilst king Edward went off to ravage France, ended with the defeat of the Scots at Neville's Cross in 1346, and the capture of king David. After this, much of southern Scotland was under English occupation for more than a century.[118]

In these circumstances it was impossible for Scottish abbeys to make any contribution to the Collections. The houses of this kingdom are the only ones which never figure in any of the Order's financial records of the period. In February 1344, at a time when the Scots appeared to have recovered, a representative of the abbot of Cîteaux was at Melrose.[119] He discussed the pension owed by the abbey of Coupar Angus to the Mother House,[120] and other financial matters may have been on the agenda. In May 1348, when conditions in Scotland had much worsened, Lambert, a monk of Coupar Angus, met the abbot of Cîteaux at the Norman abbey of La Trappe. He gave news of the fighting, and described the plight of his own abbey. Coupar Angus had suffered so severely that it was deserted, and its monks, scattered about in various places, were living in great poverty. The abbot promised, for the time being, not to send representatives to Scotland to raise money for the Order.[121]

It remains to consider the part played in the Collections by the Cistercian nuns. A nunnery which had been incorporated into the Order and shared its privileges could logically be expected to help with its financial burdens. It is not easy to tell how consistently this inference was drawn. The whole question of incorporation was unclear,[122] and the attitudes of the Chapter General and of local Cistercian abbots were often contradictory.[123] The Cistercian Order had, at times, been reluctant to undertake responsibility for nuns.[124] It must therefore have been difficult to persuade communities that they were so involved in the Order that they must contribute to Collections.

For a very long time statutes of the Chapter General which referred to Collections used the masculine gender of those liable to pay. For most of the thirteenth century these enactments referred to 'abbots'.[125] The first statutes about finance which expressly mentioned women were issued in the very last years of the century. In 1297 the Chapter General, legislating about annual rents, spoke of 'abbots and abbesses'.[126] In 1298 there were regulations about 'abbots and abbesses and other persons in the Order who are under obligation to the Chapter General, the Mother House at Cîteaux, or their father abbots by reason of any contribution, subvention, rent, or debt'.[127] If the statutes can be used as evidence, therefore, it would seem that the Order tried to involve the nuns in its financial system at the end of the thirteenth century. It follows that around that time nuns were at last recognized as an equal and integral part of the Order.

Statutes about finance which mentioned nuns were, however, still the exception. The detailed regulations about assessments made in 1326, for instance,[128] spoke of 'abbots' and used the masculine gender about those involved.[129] Attempts to make the nuns contribute to Collections were intermittent, and short-lived. A statute of 1336 shows the Chapter General in a resolute mood:

> Since decrees are the more valuable if they advance the good of all rather than of a few, the Chapter General, after deliberation, approves and confirms those already made, namely that the nuns of our Order shall be obliged to pay contributions according to the wealth of their houses, that they shall be threatened if they are disobedient, and duly

punished if they do not pay. Since these decrees are ignored in many parts of the world, Chapter orders all father abbots, visitors, and commissioners to observe them with the utmost care, and manfully[130] to collect whatever they discover is owed by the nuns subject to them, as the past decisions of Chapter require. Let them compel payments, if necessary, by deposing abbesses, excommunicating obedientiaries, or putting convents under interdict, if protracted opposition makes this necessary. If father abbots and others are neglectful in this matter, they shall be suspended from the altar until they take action. From now on father abbots and visitors who take payments due from nuns for contributions, or who have taken any as far back as 1326, must bring the money to the next meeting of the Chapter General, and continue to do so annually, paying it to the *receptores* appointed for the year. If they fail to do this they will be excommunicated. The same punishment is incurred by abbesses, prioresses, cellaresses, and bursars who refuse to reveal the income of their convents to father abbots or visitors when they come on visitation.[131]

Chapter is here seen extending to the women the organisation for collecting money which had already been established in the Order. Each monastery of nuns was under the direct care of an abbey for men, whose abbot was the 'father abbot' of the women.[132] The father abbot, or a visitor appointed by Chapter, was to be responsible for assessing the quota due from a nunnery, according to its wealth. The same abbot or commissioner also had responsibility for collecting the actual contribution. There were powers to depose or suspend the recalcitrant. It must be presumed that the authorities knew what they meant by 'nuns of our Order'.

The statute of 1336 was issued by the Chapter which ordered a collection of arrears throughout the Order.[133] Thirty nunneries made payments in 1336-7: nine in the generation of Cîteaux, eleven in that of La Ferté, one from the line of Pontigny, nine from that of Clairvaux.[134] The abbot of Clairvaux also received a small lump sum 'from a number of nuns'.[135] The drive to bring in arrears from the women probably made abbots aware of the difficulties. A much more conciliatory tone was used by the Chapter General in September 1337. The assembled abbots now expressed sympathy with the poverty of the nuns and a readiness to be generous. All money owed for past Collections, and all penalties for non-payment were remitted. The contributions of 1335 were also excused. Father abbots, who must bear some of the responsibility for past failures, were forgiven. Nuns were, however, to play their full part in all the Collections to come, and in future the statute of 1336 was to be applied in all its rigour.[136]

In 1338, therefore, nuns were, in theory, equally liable with the men for the *contributio mediocris*. Contributions, as has been seen, came in from 380 abbeys of monks, over half the total. Comparable figures for nuns were:

Generation of Cîteaux	34
Generation of Clairvaux	44
Generation of Morimond	2
Total	80[137]

No complete list of Cistercian houses for women was ever drawn up in the Middle Ages.[138] Since the status of many nunneries which claimed to belong to the Order was doubtful, it was probably impossible to compile one, nor would it have served any useful purpose. A modern conspectus of all such houses, explaining in each case why it should be called 'Cistercian',[139] is urgently needed. Without it, it is not easy to put the figures from the Accounts into context. It may be noted that in the opinion of one modern authority there were more houses for women than for men in the Middle Ages.[140] If that is the case, only a minority of nunneries contributed to the Collections in 1338, and the criticisms of father abbots, voiced in 1336 and 1337[141] were justified. In 1339 there was a drive to bring in arrears throughout the Order. Altogether over 61 monasteries sent backpayments. Results among the women were as follows:

Generation of Cîteaux	2
Generation of Clairvaux	3
Generation of Morimond	1
Total	6[142]

A study of contributions from women in the years 1337-9 shows that payments came mostly from houses directly subject to the five major abbots.[143] In some cases these abbots may themselves have set out to collect the money. A list of forty-four nunneries which paid contributions in 1338 is headed, 'From certain daughters of Clairvaux, paid to the abbot and forwarded by him.'[144] There may have been an agreement between the abbots of Cîteaux and Clairvaux to bring in payments from the nunneries of either filiation as convenience dictated. In 1339, for instance, five nunneries paid 'through the abbot of Clairvaux' and were listed in his generation: Nonnenmünster, Chumbd, Val-des-Roses, Katarinental, and La Ramée.[145] The last two were actually in the Generation of Cîteaux.[146]

It is noticeable that most of the houses involved can be found in well-defined areas. The three German houses mentioned above are in the district of the Upper Rhine. Many of the nunneries which paid contributions in 1338 can be grouped geographically. It is possible to reconstruct a tour for Collections among houses for women in this year. Épinlieu, Saulchoir, and Marquette could easily be reached from the city of Tournai.[147] The nunneries of Audenarde, Biloque, Doorzelle, ter Hagen, Nouveau Bois, and Oostekloo were grouped around Ghent.[148] Someone based in Bruges could have collected the contributions from Nouvelle Jerusalem and Val-du-Ciel,[149] and perhaps have gone on to Val-des-Roses near Malines.[150] An abbot had worked his way through the area of northern France in the present departments of Pas-de-Calais, Nord, and Somme, to visit the nunneries of Beaupré, Blandecque, Espagne, Flines, Fontenelle, Ravensberg, Willencour, and Woestine.[151] Biache, Bouhan, Braille-lez-Annay, Monstreuil, L'Olive, and Le Sauvoir[152] were in Picardy. There was also activity in the Isle de France, reaching the convents of Abbaye-aux-Bois, Eau-le-Chartres, Fervaques, Lys, Maubuisson, Mouchy-le-Pereux, Panthemont, Pont-aux-Dames and Parc-aux-Dames.[153] In Champagne contributions came from Amour-Dieu, Argensolles, Belleau, Clairmarais, Cour-Notre-Dame, Jardin-lez-Pleurs, Notre-Dame-de-Consolation, Piété-Dieu, and St Jacques de Vitry.[154] It was natural that there should also be contributions from the bishopric of Liège, which had seen a flowering of the religious life among women during the thirteenth century. Payments were collected from Diest, Florival, Herkenrode, Marche-les-Dames, Paix-Dieu, Parc-aux-Dames,[155] La Ramée, Rothem, Solières, Val-Notre-Dame, and Wevelghem.[156] The areas in which these houses were to be found were contiguous to one another. It is impossible not to conclude that there was an organised campaign to collect money from nunneries in this region, under the aegis of the abbots of Cîteaux and Clairvaux, and in parts conducted by them personally.[157]

In 1337 some very obscure nunneries of the generation of La Ferté paid arrears. These houses, as far as they can be identified, seem to have been in northern Italy.[158] In the same year money came from a group of convents in the main cities of central Italy: Florence, Siena, Pisa, Perugia, and Rieti.[159] Contributions from these houses could well have been collected by an abbot on his way to the Chapter General, acting on behalf of the major abbots.

In 1337 and 1339 the Order was collecting arrears. Only the Accounts of 1338 show what nuns contributed at a regular Collection. In that year the Chapter General decreed a *contributio mediocris*. Many of the payments from the women were for 1 *l.t.* or less. The contribution from Béton in Savoy came to 2 *s.t.*[160] None of the men paid as little as this. In 1338 the lowest payments from abbeys of men came from Jubin (near Genoa) and Rosières. These two houses paid 2 *l.t.* each.[161] It would be a mistake, however, to think of all nunneries as small and obscure. In these very years the abbey of Biloque was erecting the magnificent building which remains one of the showpieces of the city of Ghent. It could surely have afforded more than a paltry 4 *l.* 6 *s.t.*[162] Some of the highest payments from the women came from houses in northern France—8 *l.* 15 *s.t.* from Marquette, 9 *l.* 14 *s.* 2 *d.t.* from Maubuisson, 10 *l.t.* from Amour-Dieu.[163] Houses of men which paid at this level were Belle-branche and Pontrond, which paid 9 *l.* 10 *s.t.*,[164] and Zinna, which paid 10 *l.t.*[165] These contributions rank rather low among those which came from abbeys of monks in that year. The only substantial sum from a nunnery was 31 *l.t.* from Woestine, another house in northern France.[166] This was higher than most of the payments from abbeys of men; it compares with the 30 *l.t.* from Quincy and Fontaine-jean,[167] though there were even higher payments in 1338; Preuilly and Royaumont each contributed 58 *l.* 6 *s.* 8 *d.t.*[168]

Very little evidence exists about the assessment of the nunneries. The statute of 1336 makes it clear that it was the duty of the father abbot to impose the quota. It is possible to read into the wording the suggestion that the task had not yet been completed. There is some information about the assessment of Boos, in Baden-Würtemberg, now in the German Federal Republic. An entry about this abbey slipped into the Dijon Tax Book even though it was compiled long after the nuns had been exempted from all contributions. It was probably included because of an oversight by a scribe who was copying from an older list. Three out of the four columns are blank. Under *mediocris* the house is assessed at 14 *l.t.*[169] Judging by the eight other abbeys which have this assessment for their *contributio mediocris,* Boos' *contributio moderata* would have been between 10 *l.* 10 *s.t.* and 11 *l.* 10 *s.t.*[170] In fact Boos did not contribute to the 1338 Collection. Its only known payment is 5 *s.t.* in arrears for 1336, paid the following year.[171]

The money collected from the nuns was always very little compared to payments from the rest of the Order. In 1337, 4,751 *l.* 5 *s.t.* were collected,[172] of which 96 *l.* 2 *s.* 4 *d.t.* came from women.[173] In 1338 they contributed 181 *l.* 7 *s.* 7 *d.t.*[174] to a total of 8,964 *l.* 10 *s.* 8 *d.t.*[175] The drive for arrears in 1339 brought in a total of 2,371 *l.* 3 *s.* 8 *d.t.*[176] of which 12 *l.* 15 *s.t.* came from the nuns.[177] In 1336 the Chapter General had tried threats, in 1337 blandishments. Neither had worked. The abbots of Cîteaux and Clairvaux had acquired personal experience of the difficulties in collecting money from this source and no doubt took a more lenient view of the failures of other father abbots. In 1339 Chapter decided that the nuns should be exempted from the Collections. The statute enacting this has been preserved only in an abbreviated form: 'The Chapter General, viewing with sympathy the pitiable poverty of our nuns, excuses them from the payment of contributions, whenever they are raised in the Order, until the Chapter General shall decide otherwise'.[178] After 1339 the only houses of women which had financial relations with the Order were those which were paying annual rents.[179]

It seems that a serious attempt to involve the nuns in the Order's Collections was only made at the end of the thirteenth century. Some convents were poor, however, and the affiliation of many more with the Order was doubtful. In fact contributions came mostly from houses directly under the five major abbots, and Collections from nuns were successful in very restricted areas. Attempts to extend them more generally among houses of women failed. The amount of money which could be brought in was small, and the cost and effort involved probably never justified the small return.

A far more serious blow to the Cistercian financial system came, however, from the withdrawal of the houses in the British Isles, many of which were rich and famous. Edward III's prohibitions were the latest in a long series of attempts by English kings to stop monasteries, sending money to foreign superiors. The effect of these policies was to make it impossible for the Order to attain the monetary targets of the Collections. The Chapter General made strenuous efforts to make up for this loss. The idea of a *contributio excessiva,* most probably new in 1340, may have been part of a plan for economic recovery. There is evidence that in the years 1340-44 many abbeys, particularly in France and the Empire, responded well. The exceptional effort involved, however, could not be maintained for many years.

NOTES TO CHAPTER FIVE

1. On *Parvus Fons* see Lekai, *The Cistercians*, 70-2.
2. *Parvus Fons* 1, *Statuta*, iii, p. 22.
3. *MTB*, f. 27a.
4. *CB*, iii, 638.
5. F. Hervay, 'Kritische Bemerkungen', 137.
6. *MTB*, f. 27a.
7. Hadcock and Knowles, *Medieval Religious Houses of England and Wales*, 113, 121.
8. See appendix.
9. *TB*, 13b, 25.
10. *TB*, 23b, 2; 27b, 24; *MTB*, ff. 23b, 24a.
11. *TB*, 18b, 16; *MTB*, f. 21b.
12. See above, p. 14.
13. *MTB*, f. 12a.
14. *MTB*, f. 20b.
15. Accts., ff. 1a, col. 1—1b, col. 2.
16. *Ibid.*, f. 2b, col. 1.
17. *Ibid.*, ff. 2b, col. 1—3a, col. 2; 7b, col. 1.
18. *Ibid.*, ff. 3a, col. 2—3b, col. 1.
19. *Ibid.*, ff. 3a, col. 1—3b, col. 2; 7b, col. 1.
20. *Ibid.*, ff. 4a, col. 1—5b, col. 1; 7b, col. 2.
21. *Ibid.*, ff. 6a, col. 2—7a, col. 2; 8a, cols. 1, 2.
22. See above, p. 74.
23. *Ibid.*, ff. 9b, col. 1—10b, col. 2.
24. Accts., ff. 12a, cols. 1, 2; 13a, col. 1; 15b, col. 1; 16a, col. 2—16b, col. 1.
25. *Ibid.*, ff. 13a, col. 1; 15b, col. 2; 16b, col. 1.
26. *Ibid.*, ff. 13a, col. 2; 15b, col. 2; 16b, col. 2.
27. *Ibid.*, ff. 13b, col. 1—14b, col. 2; 16a, col. 1; 16b, col. 2—17a, col. 2.
28. *Ibid.*, ff. 14b, col. 2—15b, col. 1; 16a, col. 2; 17a, col. 2—17b, col. 2.
29. *Ibid.*, f. 18a, cols. 1, 2.
30. *Ibid.*, f. 18b, col. 1.

31. *Ibid.*, f. 18b, col. 1, 2.
32. *Ibid.*, ff. 18b, col. 2–19b, col. 2.
33. *Ibid.*, ff. 19b, col. 2–20b, col. 1.
34. *Ibid.*, f. 21a, col. 2.
35. *Ibid.*, ff. 18b, col. 2–19b, col. 2.
36. *Ibid.*, f. 21b, col. 1.
37. *Ibid.*
38. *Ibid.*, ff. 21b, col. 2–22a, col. 2.
39. *Ibid.*, f. 21b, cols. 1, 2.
40. *Ibid.*, f. 23b, col. 1.
41. *Ibid.*, f. 23b, col. 2.
42. *Ibid.*
43. *Ibid.*, ff. 24a, col. 1–24b, col. 1.
44. *Ibid.*, ff. 24b, col. 2–25a, col. 1.
45. *Ibid.*, f. 26a, col. 1.
46. *Ibid.*, f. 26b, col. 1.
47. *Ibid.*, f. 25b, cols. 1, 2.
48. *Ibid.*, f. 25b, col. 2.
49. *Ibid.*, f. 25b, col. 2–26a, col. 1.
50. *Ibid.*, ff. 26a, col. 1–26b, col. 2.
51. *Ibid.*, ff. 26b, col. 2–27a, col. 1.
52. See above, p. 21.
53. *Ibid.*
54. Accts., f. 28a, col. 1.
55. *Ibid.*, f. 28a, cols. 1, 2.
56. *Ibid.*, f. 28a, col. 2.
57. *Ibid.*, incl. some houses belonging to a different generation.
58. *Ibid.*
59. *Ibid.*
60. *Ibid.*, ff. 28b, col. 2–29a, col. 1.
61. *Ibid.*, ff. 29a, col. 2–29b, col. 1.
62. See above p. 76.
63. Accts., f. 8a, cols. 1-2.
64. Including territories briefly claimed by the emperor Charles IV.
65. As defined above, p. 129.
66. Accts., ff. 2b, col. 1–8a, col. 1.
67. *Ibid.*, ff. 12a, col. 1–17b, col. 1.
68. *Ibid.*, ff. 18a, col. 1–20b, col. 1.
69. *Ibid.*, ff. 21a, col. 2–22b, col. 2.
70. *Ibid.*, ff. 23b, col. 1–25a, col. 1.
71. *Ibid.*, 25b, col. 1–27a, col. 1.
72. Samaran et Mollat, *La fiscalité pontificale*, 16; Henneman,

Royal Taxation . . . 1322-56, 113-14; 129; 179.

73. See above, pp. 104-5.

74. The list of abbeys 'im deutschen Sprach- und Kulturraum' in Schneider, *Die Cistercienser*, 555-610, includes abbeys from Bohemia, Hungary and Poland. When these are omitted the total comes to 106.

75. For references see above, p. 136, nn. 66-71.

76. Accts., f. 26a, col. 1.

77. 88 in Bedini, *Breve Prospetto*.

78. Accts., f. 26b, col. 1. See above p. 133.

79. See above p. 105.

80. Accts., ff. 6a, col. 2; 8a, col. 1; 14b, col. 2; 17a, col. 2; 19b, col. 2; 20a, col. 2; 24b, col. 2; 26b, col. 2; 29a, col. 2.

81. *Ibid.*, ff. 16a, col. 1; 17a, col. 1; 22a, col. 2.

82. Accts., f. 17b, col. 1.

83. See below, p. 162.

84. Accts., f. 17a, col. 2.

85. *Ibid.*, f. 21a, col. 2.

86. See above, p. 19.

87. Including Silesia, Accts., f. 7a, cols. 1, 2.

88. *Ibid.*, ff. 15b, col. 1; 17a, col. 1; 17b, cols. 1, 2.

89. *Ibid.*, ff. 20a, col. 2; 20b, col. 1.

90. *Ibid.*, ff. 21b, col. 2; 22b, col. 1.

91. *Ibid.*, ff. 24a, col. 1; 24b, col. 2; 25a, col. 1.

92. *Ibid.*, f. 27a, col. 1.

93. *Ibid.*, ff. 3b, col. 2; 5b, col. 1; 7a, cols. 1, 2; 7b, col. 2; 8a, col. 1.

94. *Ibid.*, ff. 16b, col. 2; 17a, cols. 1, 2; 17b, col. 1.

95. *Ibid.*, ff. 19a, cols. 1, 2; 19b, cols. 1, 2.

96. *Ibid.*, ff. 24a, col. 1; 25a, col. 1.

97. *Ibid.*, ff. 25b, col. 2; 26a, col. 2; 26b, col. 2.

98. *Ibid.*, f. 1b, col. 1.

99. *Ibid.*, f. 22b, col. 2.

100. *Ibid.*, f. 29a, col. 1.

101. *Ibid.*, f. 10b, col. 2.

102. *Ibid.*, ff. 20a, col. 2; 22b, col. 1.

103. *Ibid.*, f. 17b, col. 1.

104. *Ibid.*, f. 27a, col. 1.

105. *Rotuli Parliamentorum*, i, 217. See L.A. Desmond, 'The Statute of Carlisle and the Cistercians', *Studies in Medieval Cistercian History presented to Jeremiah O'Sullivan*, 138-62.

106. See above, p. 65.

107. Harper Bill, 'Cistercian Visitation in the late Middle Ages', 105.

108. Desmond, 156.
109. *CCR* 1343-1346, pp. 74-75; Desmond, *op. cit.,* 156-7.
110. Accts., f. 24b, col. 1.
111. *Chronica de Melsa,* iii, 29-30. See Desmond, *op. cit.,* 157.
112. See above, p. 66.
113. ? *(De Collameboria)*
114. Accts., f. 29a, col. 1.
115. *TB,* 21b, 26; *MTB,* f. 18b.
116. Nicholson, *Scotland, the later Middle Ages,* 124-135.
117. *Chron. Fordun,* 361.
118. Nicholson, 146-8.
119. King, 'Coupar Angus and Cîteaux', p. 60, doct. No. 10.
120. See above, p. 35.
121. King, p. 61, doct. No. 11.
122. Lekai, *The Cistercians,* 349.
123. See examples in A. Wienand, 'Die Cistercienserinnen' in A. Schneider, ed., *Die Cistercienser,* 350.
124. Lekai, *The Cistercians,* 347-51.
125. See e.g. Statuta 1262, 1; 1274, 14.
126. Statuta 1297, 2.
127. Statuta 1298, 3.
128. See above p. 62.
129. Statuta 1326, 4.
130. *Viriliter.* Did Chapter use this word on purpose?
131. Statuta 1336, 8.
132. Lekai, *The Cistercians,* 351.
133. See above p. 99.
134. Accts., ff. 1a, col. 1—1b, col. 1.
135. *Ibid.,* f. 1b, col. 1.
136. Statuta 1337, 9.
137. Accts., ff. 3a, cols. 1, 2; 5b, col. 2—6a, col. 1; 7b, col. 1.
138. Canivez, for his list of nunneries in 'Cîteaux (Abbaye)', 860-62 used an edition by Winter of a copy of a 17th century catalogue, which is limited in scope.
139. A task shirked, for the most part, even by *Monasticon Belge.*
140. M. Kuhn-Rehfus, 'Zisterzienserinnen in Deutschland', 125.
141. See above, p. 144.
142. Accts., f. 10b, cols. 1, 2.
143. For partial lists see Canivez, 'Cîteaux (Abbaye)', 860-2; 'Clairvaux', 1052-3.
144. Accts., f. 5b, col. 2.
145. *Ibid.,* f. 10b, col. 1.

146. Canivez, 'Cîteaux (Abbaye)', 860-61.
147. Accts., ff. 3a, col. 1; 5b, col. 2.
148. *Ibid.,* ff. 3a, col. 2; 5b, col. 2.
149. *Ibid.*
150. *Ibid.,* f. 3a, col. 2.
151. *Ibid.,* ff. 5b, col. 2; 6a, col. 1.
152. *Ibid.,* ff. 3a, cols. 1, 2; 5b, col. 2; 6a, col. 1.
153. *Ibid.*
154. *Ibid.*
155. Not to be confused with the other nunnery of his name in the Isle de France.
156. Accts., ff. 3a, col. 2; 5b, col. 2; 6a, col. 1.
157. Apart from the articles by Canivez above, the following are a help in identifying Cistercian nunneries: Cocheril, *Dictionnaire,* Schneider, *Cistercienser,* 611-29; *Monasticon Belge.*
158. Accts., f. 1a, col. 2.
159. *Ibid.,* f. 1b, col. 1.
160. Accts., f. 3a, col. 2.
161. *Ibid.,* ff. 5a, col. 2; 6a, col. 2.
162. *Ibid.,* f. 5b, col. 2.
163. *Ibid.,* ff. 3a, col. 1; 5b, col. 2; 6a, col. 1.
164. *Ibid.,* ff. 2b, col. 2; 4a, col. 2.
165. *Ibid.,* f. 6a, col. 2.
166. *Ibid.,* f. 6a, col. 1.
167. *Ibid.,* f. 3b, col. 1.
168. *Ibid.,* f. 2b, col. 1.
169. *TB,* 7b, 6.
170. Cf. *TB,* 7b, 7; 10b, 7; 12b, 4; 14b, 23; 25b, 2; 25b, 9; 27b, 29; 28b, 26.
171. Accts., f. 1a, col. 2.
172. See above, p. 99.
173. Accts., ff. 1a, col. 1, 2; 1b, col. 1.
174. *Ibid.,* f. 3a, cols. 1, 2; 5a, col. 2; 6a, col. 1.
175. See above, p. 99.
176. See above, p. 100.
177. Accts., f. 10b, cols. 1, 2.
178. *Statuta* 1339, 12.
179. See above, p. 39.

CHAPTER SIX

Monetary Problems

LIKE MOST MEDIEVAL INSTITUTIONS the Cistercian Order received credit from bankers and relied upon their expertise. The seniors liked to paint a gloomy picture of financial affairs on Audit Day, and relations with the bankers were depicted in lurid colours. 'Our Order is subject to heavy debts, with interest, at the Roman Curia' ran the official statement in September 1339.[1] In fact the debt of 1339 was paid off in two years.[2] The figures revealed at the Audit simply afford glimpses of the Order's account with certain merchants.

Until 1341 the Chapter General dealt with 'Lapo and his companions'.[3] This individual was almost certainly Lapo di Ruspo, head of a Florentine banking firm closely connected with the Avignon popes from John XXII to Gregory XI.[4] Transactions took place at the Curia,[5] where the Order was represented by its proctor.[6] Lapo may, however, have sent an agent to the September Audit at Dijon. After the account with his firm was closed, there were no dealings with bankers for some years. Nicholas Francisci of Savoy to whom the Cistercians turned in 1346, and with whom they were still doing business in 1350,[7] is not known from other sources.

Transactions with Lapo are recorded in the *Expensa* sections of the Accounts for the years 1338-41. In 1338 2,000 *fl.* were sent to the proctor at Avignon so that he could settle two outstanding debts to the firm. The bursar of Cîteaux sent Lapo a further 5,800 *fl.* The total of 7,800 *fl.*

sent to the Bank in that year was equivalent, at the current rate of exchange, to 5,850 *l.t.*[8] It was only possible to make these payments by borrowing money at the Fairs of Champagne.[9] In November 1338 the Order borrowed 6,268 *fl.* from Lapo at 20%; the sum had grown to 7,544 *fl.* a year later.[10] The purpose of these rather circular transactions was, no doubt, to keep the interest on the loan from Lapo down to a manageable level.

Thanks to the vigorous financial campaigns of 1340 and 1341, the new loan was cleared. By September 1340 it had been reduced to 6,654 *fl.*[11] Although it had risen, through interest and other charges, to 7,369 *fl.* by the following year, the seniors could announce at the Audit on St Lambert's day, that it had been paid off in full.[12] The abbeys which had contributed, for two years running, to Collections raised at unprecedented rates, deserved most thanks.[13] Individual abbots had helped by lending money. The abbot of Cîteaux had lent 200 *l.t.* at 20%,[14] the abbot of La Charité lent 600 *l.t.*[15] (his rates are not recorded), the proctor of the Order lent 500 *l.t.* at 12%.[16] No further dealings with Lapo and his company are recorded after this, though it should be noted that the Order's Accounts were less detailed after 1345.[17] In 1346 250 *l.t.* were paid to 'merchants of Savoy'.[18] In September 1347 the Order owed 1,500 *fl.* to 'Nicholas Francisci of Savoy'.[19] By 1350 the debt had risen to 2,000 *fl.*[20]

In the middle years of the fourteenth century, the policies of those who directed the affairs of the Order required ample funds. The Order's ability to raise money from its constituent abbeys was impressive. In spite of the jeremiads at the annual Audit, loans from Italians did not create insoluble problems in the 1340s. A generation later the popes of the Schism still thought it worth while to seek financial support from the Cistercians.[21]

The instability of French money in the period covered by the Accounts, however, sometimes made it difficult to calculate profit and loss accurately. Since abbots came to the Chapter General from different areas of Christendom, they were likely to bring their contributions in different currencies. In the Accounts of 1337-47, therefore, rates of exchange between the *livre tournois* and the Florentine *florin,* and the French *écu* as well, are prominently recorded, written across the top of every two facing pages. Such rates were extremely sensitive to market conditions and foreign news, and could vary, in bills of exchange, from one day and place to another. The rates quoted in the Accounts were no doubt decided by bankers at Avignon, and were valid at the time of the September Chapter General and Audit:

Year	Value of *fl.* in *s.t.*	Value of *écu* in *s.t.*
1337	15 *s.t.*[22]	
1338	15 *s.t.*[23]	
1339	15 *s.t.*[24]	
1340	30 *s.t.*[25]	
1341	30 *s.t.*	40 *s.t.*[26]
	50 *s.t.*	62 *s.* 6 *d.t.*[27]
1342	50 *s.t.*	62 *s.* 6 *d.t.*[28]
1343	48 *s.t.*	60 *s.t.*[29]
	57 *s.* 6 *d.t.*[30]	
1344	12 *s.* 6 *d.t.*[31]	
1345-6	12 *s.* 6 *d.t.*[32]	
	25 *s.t.*[33]	
1347	25 *s.t.*[34]	
1347-8	25 *s.t.*[35]	

The listing graphically illustrates the successive devaluations of French money, as a result of reverses in the war with the English. They were often followed by attempts to return to 'good money', but it seldom proved possible to maintain the initiative.[36] Some of the rates quoted in the Accounts can be corroborated from other sources. The rate available to the Cistercians for the *florin* in 1337-39 was also used in

France and the Curia in those years.[37] The dramatic improvement in the value of French money noticeable at the Chapter General in 1344 was brought about by a reform of the currency in the previous year.[38] Too many of the old coins remained in circulation, however, for this improvement to be completely effective. As early as January 1344 merchants at Avignon had to distinguish between 'bad' and 'good' money of France,[39] and a general downward slide is reflected in the Cistercian list from 1346.

The rates recorded across the tops of the pages of the Accounts were not, however, always used. In 1340 the abbot of La Colombe was given a rate of 25 *s.t.* to the *florin*,[40] Staffarda had 27 *s. 6 d.t.*,[41] and the abbey of S. Pantaleo 35 *s.t.*[42] It must be remembered that not all abbeys paid during the September Chapter General.

Two rates are quoted in the Accounts for the years 1341, 1343, and 1345-46. On most of the pages of the Accounts for 1341 the value of a *florin* is given as 30 *s.t.* and there are 40 *s.t.* for the *écu*. Over one page the rate is 50 *s.t.* for the *florin* and 62 *s. 6 d.t.* for the *écu*. A study of the actual payments made in that year shows that the lower rate was normally used. The abbey of Bithaine, however, appears to have paid its arrears of rent at the higher rate.[43]

For 1343 the rates are given as 48 *s.t.* for the *florin* and 60 *s.t.* for the *écu*. Halfway through the Accounts for that year a new rate for the *florin* of 57 *s. 6 s.t.* appears at the top of the pages. The latter appears to have been the rate actually used, though a few houses got 55 *s.t.* for the *florin*.[44] It is likely that when money was not actually paid at the Chapter General, the transactions took place at Avignon, where the proctor of the Order had access to the latest financial information.

There are also two rates for 1345-6; 12 *s. 6 d.t.,* or 25 *s.t.* to the *florin*. For some reason the effect of the last currency reforms was felt longer at Cîteaux than elsewhere, but confidence seems to have ebbed in the end. The Accounts for 1345-46 are too sparse to allow an analysis of individual payments.

When money was paid in different currencies, it was necessary to find one in terms of which all payments could be recorded in the Order's Accounts. Until 1341 the Cistercians used as their 'money of account' the French silver *petit denier tournois,* in which assessments of individual quotas had always been made,[45] even for houses in England.[46] In the thirteenth century the *denier tournois* had been a convenient currency to use at the Fairs of Champagne, at which the money from the Collections was usually gathered in and counted.[47] It is expressly mentioned in the Accounts of 1290[48] and 1294.[49] As late as 1339 the Chapter General insisted that all payments must be made in this currency.[50] No doubt compliance would have made the task of the Order's financial officers easier, but by this time such a demand was quite impractical. In fact payments came in a variety of currencies. In 1340, for instance, the abbot of La Colombe brought 14 gold *florins* valued at 25 *s.t.* each, one French gold piece worth 30 *s.t.,* and 20 *s.t.*'s worth of 'black money'. The whole was equivalent to 20 *l.t.* leaving him, as a marginal note recorded, with 13 *s.* 4 *d.t.* to pay.[51] In 1337 the abbot of Buillon made a payment in the silver of Paris.[52] In 1339 the Portuguese abbey of Seiça paid the equivalent of 24 *l.t.* in the recently minted pavillons of France,[53] and the queen of France used them to pay her 100 *l.t.* of annual alms.[54] Italian abbeys like Chiaravalle della Colomba, Ferrara, and Fontevivo, found it more convenient to pay in Florentine *florins.*[55]

Naturally there could be arguments about the value of the money brought. In 1338 the abbess of Groeninghe near Courtrai, whose house owed a rent of 15 *l.t.* a year,[56] made a payment of 12 French *écus.* This, stated the Order's accountants, would have been worth 15 *l.* in the money of Flanders, but was worth only 12 in that of Tours.[57] The abbess of Verguines in Flanders, who owed an annual rent of 25 *l.* paid that amount in Flemish silver, and found that it was worth only 21 *l.t.*[58] It has already been noted that the original charters had specified that payments from these houses should be in Flemish silver.[59] Clearly the Order was using the rate of exchange as a means of raising the rents owed by these abbesses.

In 1339 Andrew, a monk of Esrom in Denmark, arrived with gold coins from various Danish abbeys. Sixteen *fl.* from the abbey of Ryd were of good quality and were accepted without difficulty at the current rate as 12 *l.t.* Fifteen *fl.* from his own abbey of Esrom, however, and 5 *fl.* from Tvis were judged to be of inferior quality and were accepted at the official rate only after demur.[60] Brother Andrew had possibly come to the Chapter General with some of the newly minted gold *écus* of the emperor Lewis the Bavarian. They were freely available in the Low Countries, and were struck on the basis of Lewis's alliance with Edward III of England. Four of them were worth five *florins* of Florence,[61] and they may well have been unacceptable at Cîteaux for political as well as economic reasons.

The troubles of Brother Andrew illustrate the shortage of gold specie in the first half of the fourteenth century. On his way from Denmark he had, no doubt, looked for a safe currency for which to exchange his Baltic silver, and had hunted in the Netherlands for gold coins. The Cistercians had similar difficulties in 1340 when they had some large payments to make at Avignon. They had to satisfy Cardinal Guillaume Court, to whom they had been ordered, in 1338, to pay a pension of 3,000 *fl.* a year.[62] He had seen very little of it so far. Chapter did not really have the money, but its agents also found it difficult to obtain sufficient gold for a large payment. Towards the sum he was owed in arrears the cardinal was paid 600 *fl.* The equivalent of another 400 *fl.* was paid in 'white' money. In order to pay part of the current pension in gold, the abbot of Clairvaux borrowed 540 *pavillons* and 578 *lions d'or.* The latter were no longer legal currency in France and must have been obtained, at a price, on the

money market. The abbot kept a little back for his own purposes, and paid the cardinal the equivalent of 1,400 *fl.* in
French gold coins.[63]

At the Curia only a few tips and minor payments could be
made in silver.[64] Whenever it used a silver currency, the
Order had to cope with the consequences of monetary
fluctuations. The expenses of the Chapter General of 1338,
for instance, were left unpaid for some years. When they
were incurred the *florin* had been worth 15 *s.t.* and the
amount owed to the Mother House was 219 *l.t.* In 1340 the
florin was worth 30 *s.t.* The debt was still unpaid, and
Cîteaux reckoned that it should now receive 438 *l.t.*[65]

Altogether there were good reasons, in the 1340s, for
abandoning the shaky *livre tournois* as money of account,
and going over to the Florentine *florin,* one of the most stable international currencies of the time. At the Chapter
General of September 1340 the Order was asked to raise
12,000 *fl.* for the next year.[66] The seniors clearly aimed to
pay off the debt to Lapo by September, and this may partly
have prompted the departure from Cistercian monetary
traditions. There is no reason to believe, however, that all
the abbeys actually paid in gold. Cambron, for instance, paid
in silver *gros,* probably of Tours.[67] It was also considered
too complicated to calculate arrears from past years in a different currency. These, as well as rents and the traditional
alms were paid, or at least reckoned up, in *livres tournois.*[68]

In 1340 and 1341 the *florin* had been valued at 30 *s.t.* at
the Chapter General.[69] A demand for 12,000 *fl.* was therefore
equivalent to a *contributio duplex* of 18,000 *l.t.* The assessments on the old lists could be used without difficulty. It was
even possible to recalculate the contribution to the advantage
of one's own abbey. The abbey of Grandselve, for instance, is
one of those whose assessment in the 1340s was almost
certainly unchanged when it was recorded in the Dijon Tax
Book. Its *contributio duplex* was 75 *l.* 11 *s.* 6 *d.t.,* and,
since it chose to pay in two instalments, would have owed,

on each occasion 37 *l.* 15 *s.* 9 *d.t.*[70] How was the small silver to be expressed in a different currency? Grandselve solved the problem by making two payments of 25 *fl.* each, which was the equivalent of 75 *l.t.*[71] The loss to the Order of 11 *s.* 6 *d.t.* may not have been great, but other abbeys took the opportunity of 'rounding off' their assessments in this way, and the cumulative effect may have been worrying. Examples from the Accounts for 1341 are shown over:[72]

[SEE PAGE 165]

The Order's *receptores* were accustomed to note even the smallest part of a quota which was left unpaid.[74] In 1341 they must have felt powerless. In 1342 the value of French silver fell from 30 *s.t.* to 50 *s.t.* to the *florin*. There was some compensation for the Chapter General therefore, when abbeys paid arrears from the previous year:

CALERS
> *Duplex* assessment: 16 *l.* 10 *s.t.*[75]
> First instalment 1341—5½ *fl.*[76]; value at 30 *s.t.* to the *fl.*: 8 *l.* 5 *s.t.*
> Arrears 1342—5½ *fl.*[77]; value at 50 *s.t.* to the *fl.*: 13 *l.* 15 *s.t.*

CERRETO
> *Duplex* assessment: 24 *l.* 15 *s.t.*[78]
> First instalment 1341—8 *fl.*[79]; value at 30 *s.t.* to the *fl.*: 12 *l.t.*
> Arrears 1342—8 *fl.*[80]; value at 50 *s.t.* to the *fl.*: 20 *l.t.*

FONTEVIVO
> *Duplex* assessment: 31 *l.t.*[81]
> First instalment 1341—9 *fl.*[82]; value at 30 *s.t.* to the *fl.*: 13 *l.* 10 *s.t.*

Abbey	Contributions in *fl.*	Value in *l.t.*	Assessment (TB)
Bellebranche	4½ *fl.* 6 *s.* 4½ *fl.* 6 *s.* }	14 *l.* 2 *s.t.*	14 *l.* 5 *s.t.*
Cambron	33 *fl.* 4 *s.* 4 *d.t.* 33 *fl.* (in *gros t.*) }	99 *l.* 4 *s.* 4 *d.t.*	100 *l.t.*
Capolago	7 *fl.* 7 *fl.* }	21 *l.t.*	22 *l.* 10 *s.t.*
Carnoët	2½ *fl.* 2½ *fl.* }	7 *l.* 14 *s.* 6 *d.t.*	7 *l.* 19 *s.t.*
Chambons	9 *fl.* 3 *gr.* 2 *s.* 6 *d.t.* 9 *fl.* 12 *s.t.* }	28 *l.* 2 *s.t.*[73]	29 *l.* 5 *s.t.*
Chezery	6½ *fl.* 6½ *fl.* 9 *s.* 6 *d.t.* }	19 *l.* 19 *s.* 6 *d.t.*	20 *l.t.*
Clairmarais	53 *fl.* 6 *s.* 8 *d.t.*	79 *l.* 8 *s.* 6 *d.t.*	81 *l.t.*
Cour Dieu	11½ *fl.* 3 *s.* 4 *d.t.* }	34 *l.* 16 *s.* 8 *d.t.*	34 *l.* 18 *s.t.*
Grandselve	11½ *fl.* 3 *s.* 4 *d.t.* 25 *fl.* 25 *fl.* }	75 *l.t.*	75 *l.* 11 *s.* 6 *d.t.*
Duinen, Ter	66 *fl.*	99 *l.t.*	100 *l.t.*
Orval	11½ *fl.* 12½ *fl.* }	36 *l.t.*	37 *l.* 10 *s.t.*
Valbenoîte	1½ *fl.* 1½ *fl.* 1½ *fl.* }	4 *l.* 10 *s.t.*	5 *l.* 3 *s.* 9 *d.t.*

Arrears 1342–9 *fl.*[83]; value at 50 *s.t.* to the *fl.*:
22 *l.* 10 *s.t.*

VALSERENA
Duplex assessment: 35 *l.t.*[84]
First instalment 1341–11½ *fl.*[85]; value at 30 *s.t.*
to the *fl.*: 17 *l.* 5 *s.t.*
Arrears 1342–11½ *fl.*[86]; value at 50 *s.t.* to the *fl.*:
28 *l.* 15 *s.t.*

_____

It is not easy to tell how much actual profit or loss there
was as a result of these fluctuations. In 1342 Chapter recorded
a small loss from bad silver of 6 *l.* 6 *d.t.*[87] It is more likely
that the difficulties in book-keeping were found disturbing.
In 1342 the Order returned to *livres tournois* as its money of
account, and asked for a contribution of 12,000 *l.t.*[88]
Arrears were reckoned, as has been seen, in *florins,* and some
payments were made in *écus.*[89] The arithmetic presented
unusual difficulties. The authorities may not have been too
dissatisfied with the financial situation, but the Audit of
St Lambert's day was an accounting disaster.[90]

For 1343 the Chapter General expressed its financial
needs once more in *florins,* and continued to use this
currency for the Collections for the rest of the Middle Ages.
The sum demanded for 1343 was 18,000 *fl.*[91] The *livre
tournois* was continuing to lose value,[92] and the ancient
assessments could no longer be used as they stood. The Order
hit upon the simple expedient of substituting *florins* for
livres. The Collection for 18,000 *fl.* was a *contributio duplex*
in gold. Thus the abbey of Longvillers which, if the Dijon
Tax Book is any guide, owed a *contributio duplex* of
58 *l.* 10 *s.t.*,[93] paid 58½ *fl.*[94] Cherlieu, assessed in the Dijon
Tax Book at 22 *l.* 10 *s.t.*,[95] paid 22½ *fl.*[96] In this way the
old lists could continue to be used. Each page in the Dijon
Tax Book is headed, 'florenos vel libras'.[97] In the Tax Book
at Modena only *florins* are used for the assessments.

The adoption of *florins* as money of account may have simplified book-keeping, but actual payments continued to be in a variety of currencies. When the money was being counted for the Audit of 1345, a little *poitevin* was found in the heap. There is no record of how it got there. Too small to be expressed in terms of any other currency, it had to be separately recorded in all the different stages of reckoning up the final totals.[98] The amount of money payable to the Order in rents and expected in alms had been fixed in *livres tournois* many years ago. These payments continued unchanged,[99] even though this could involve losses. In 1345 the annual alms from the queen of France were partly paid in adulterated silver worth 26 *s.t.* less than its nominal value.[100] At St Bernard's College in Paris, the senior members received their bursaries in gold, and the rest in silver.[101] The *florin* was not the only gold currency used. The English payments in 1343 were made in *écus*.[102] The total of 185 *écus* from this source was valued at 212 *fl.* 55 *s.t.*[103] Not all the gold currencies of the period maintained the same quality as the the Florentine *florin*.[104] The Order's losses from inferior gold coins amounted to 77 *fl.* in 1344,[105] and 67½ *fl.* in 1347.[106]

In 1360 the French royal government began to mint gold *francs*. The *franc à cheval* came first; the somewhat lighter *franc à pied* was issued in 1365.[107] From this time the bursar of Cîteaux usually kept his account in *francs* and *florins*. On 14 May 1378, for instance, he received a number of payments in *florins* which he also recorded in *francs*:[108]

Abbey	Payment in *florins*	Value in *francs*
Vaux de Cernay	25 *fl.*	20 *fr.* 10 *g.t.*
Igny	20 *fl.*	16 *fr.* 8 *g.t.*
Fontainejean	33 *fl.*	22½ *fr.*
St. Andrew[109]	16 *fl.*	13 *fr.* 4 *g.t.*

Le Valasse	8½ *fl.*	7 *fr.* 1 *g.t.*
Our Lady[110]	16½ *fl.*	13 *fr.* 9 *g.t.*
Preuilly	29 *fl.* 3 *s.* 4 *d.t;*	24 *fr.* 3½ *g.t.*
Jouy	14 *fl.* 4 *g.t.*	12 *fr.*
Echarlis	30 *fl.*	25 *fr.*

Of the 55 abbots who brought money to the Chapter General in 1378, 24 paid in *francs* and 31 in *florins*. Most of the money which the abbot of Cîteaux had been collecting had been paid in the latter currency.[111] Although the *franc* was important to the bursar of Cîteaux, who was concerned with the economic affairs of his abbey, the *florin* continued to be the official currency of the Order. It was used as the money of account during the Audits of 1380 and 1390.[112] Both halves of the Order expressed their financial requirements in this currency when holding Collections during the period of the Schism.[113]

Throughout the fourteenth century the authorities of the Order clung to the view that they could decide what money should be used when individual payments were made. At the Chapter General of 1392 the opposition to the Cistercian financial system won many concessions.[114] It was agreed, however, that payments should always be 'in the money used by the Chapter General'.[115] No doubt the seniors felt that, since they had been ready to meet their critics halfway, they had a right to expect monetary discipline in return.

NOTES TO CHAPTER SIX

1. *Statuta* 1339, 4.
2. See below p. 101.
3. Accts., ff. 8b, col. 1; 11b, col. 2; 17b, col. 2.
4. See Renouard, *Les relations des papes d'Avignon et des compagnies commerciales,* passim.
5. 'In curia', Accts., f. 11b, col. 2, 'eidem Lapo de pecunia missa Avinionensi', *ibid.,* f. 8b, col. 1.
6. See below p. 180.
7. See below p. 105.
8. Accts., f. 8b, col. 1.
9. See above p. 100.
10. Accts., f. 11b, col. 2.
11. *Ibid.,* f. 17b, col. 2.
12. *Ibid.,* f. 20b, col. 2.
13. See above pp. 100-101.
14. Accts., f. 11b, col. 2.
15. *Ibid.,* f. 17b, col. 1.
16. *Ibid.,* f. 11b, col. 1.
17. See above p. 21.
18. Accts., f. 27b, col. 2.
19. *Ibid.,* f. 29b, col. 1.
20. Sens MS 129, f. 169b. See above p. 105.
21. See above p. 112.
22. Accts., ff. 1a-2a.
23. *Ibid.,* ff. 2b-9a.
24. *Ibid.,* ff. 9b-11b.
25. *Ibid.,* ff. 12b-17a.
26. *Ibid.,* ff. 17b-21a.
27. *Ibid.,* f. 21a.
28. *Ibid.,* ff. 21b-23a.
29. *Ibid.,* ff. 23b-24a.
30. *Ibid.,* ff. 24a-25b.
31. *Ibid.,* ff. 25b-27a.
32. *Ibid.,* f. 27b.

33. *Ibid.*, f. 28a.

34. *Ibid.*, ff. 28b-29a.

35. *Ibid.*, ff. 29b-30a. List first published in King, 'Cistercian Financial Organisation 1335-92', *Journal of Ecclesiastical History*, 24 (1973) 138.

36. Fournial, *Histoire monétaire*, 98-101.

37. Spufford and Wilkinson, *Interim Listing*, 218.

38. Fournial, *Histoire monétaire*, 98-101.

39. Spufford and Wilkinson, *Interim Listing*, 219.

40. Accts., f. 12a, col. 1.

41. 13 *fl.* = 17 *l.* 17 *s.* 6 *d.t.*, *ibid.*, f. 15b, col. 2.

42. 16 *fl.* = 20 *l.t.*, *ibid.*

43. *Ibid.*

44. Staffarda, Pontaut, Ardorel, Accts., f. 23b, col. 2.

45. See *TB*, passim.

46. See above p. 65.

47. See above p. 91.

48. Sens MS 129, f. 164b.

49. *Ibid.*, f. 165b.

50. *Statuta* 1339, 9.

51. Accts., f. 12a, col. 1.

52. *Ibid.*, f. 4b, col. 2.

53. *Ibid.*, f. 10a, col. 2. On *pavillons,* see Fournial, *Histoire monétaire*, 102.

54. Accts., f. 11a, col. 1.

55. *Ibid.*, ff. 5a, col. 2; 10a, col. 2.

56. *TB*, 30a, 24.

57. Accts., f. 8a, col. 2. On the various currencies in use in Flanders see Spufford and Wilkinson, *Interim Listing,* 262.

58. Accts., f. 8a, col. 2.

59. See above pp. 41f.

60. Accts., f. 10a, col. 1.

61. Suhle, *Deutsche Münz- und Geldgeschichte,* 160-1.

62. See below p. 176.

63. Accts., f. 17b, col. 2. On *Lion d'or* see Fournial, *Histoire monétaire*, 102.

64. See below p. 180.

65. Accts., f. 17b, col. 2.

66. *Statuta* 1340, 14.

67. Accts., f. 19a, col. 2.

68. *Ibid.*, ff. 19b, col. 2; 20b, col. 2.

69. See above p. 159.

70. *TB*, 9b, 9.
71. Accts., f. 19a, col. 1.
72. *Ibid.*, ff. 18a, col. 1–19b, col. 1.
73. For the value of *gros tournois* at this period see Spufford and Wilkinson, *Interim Listing*, 231.
74. See e.g. Accts., ff. 10a, col. 1; 12a, col. 1.
75. *TB*, 20b, 15.
76. Accts., f. 19a, col. 1.
77. *Ibid.*, f. 22a, col. 1.
78. *TB*, 17b, 21.
79. Accts., f. 19a, col. 1.
80. *Ibid.*, f. 22a, col. 2.
81. *TB*, 19b, 9.
82. Accts., f. 19a, col. 1.
83. *Ibid.*, f. 22a, col. 2.
84. *TB*, 21b, 7.
85. Accts., f. 19a, col. 1.
86. *Ibid.*, f. 22a, col. 2.
87. *Ibid.*, f. 25a, col. 2.
88. *Statuta* 1341, 8.
89. Accts., f. 23a, col. 1.
90. See above p. 102.
91. *Statuta* 1342, 6.
92. Spufford and Wilkinson, *Interim Listing*, 219.
93. *TB*, 10b, 27.
94. Accts., f. 24a, col. 2.
95. *TB*, 7b, 15.
96. Accts., f. 24a, col. 2.
97. *TB*, passim.
98. Accts., f. 27b, cols. 1, 2.
99. See e.g. *ibid.*, f. 27a, col. 2.
100. *Ibid.*, f. 27b, col. 1.
101. *Ibid.*, f. 25a, col. 2.
102. For the use of this currency by the English see Prestwich, 'Early fourteenth century exchange rates', 477.
103. See above p. 141.
104. See Fournial, *Histoire monétaire*, 103-7.
105. Accts., f. 27a, col. 2.
106. *Ibid.*, f. 29b, col. 2.
107. Fournial, *Histoire monétaire*, 119; Spufford and Wilkinson, *Interim Listing*, 242, 4.
108. Accts., f. 46a, col. 1.

109. S. Andrea di Sesto, or St. André de Gouffern.
110. Perhaps Le Val.
111. Accts., ff. 50a, col. 1–50b, col. 1.
112. See above pp. 113, 115.
113. See above pp. 112, 113.
114. See above p. 116.
115. 'Monetae ipsius Capituli generalis', *Statuta* 1392, 23.

CHAPTER SEVEN

The Expenses of the Chapter General

A T THE END of the Accounts for every year there is a section headed *Expensa* which lists expenditure since the last Chapter General. It is never easy to devise a logical arrangement for miscellaneous items. Nevertheless the *receptores* had been successful in ordering the material for these columns fairly systematically. The heaviest items of expenditure came first, the smallest and most domestic last. For the rest, like was grouped with like. The *Expensa* columns for 1344, for instance, began with the heavy payments to the cardinal protector and to the Order's proctor at Avignon. Next came pensions and student fees. Last came the cost of the Chapter General and the money spent at Cîteaux whilst it was meeting. Miscellaneous items difficult to categorise had to find a place where they could.[1] Sometimes there was a separate list of payments made on the Order's behalf by the proctor at the Curia.[2] After *Expensa*, and closely connected with it, came *Expendenda*,[3] sometimes needed *Erat Ordo obligatus.*[4] This was a list of the Order's debts, and largely dictated the financial policy for the next year. In 1342, when many of the expenses at the Curia were unpaid, this list was particularly long.[5]

It is clear that the financial demands of the popes and cardinals constituted the heaviest burdens upon the Order. Already in the thirteenth century papal tax collectors had been bought off with the promise of lump sums from the Order.[6] The demands of the Avignon popes were as heavy as those of their predecessors. The increasing centralisation of

173

the Church was expensive. Clement VI needed money to buy Avignon from queen Joan of Naples; Innocent VI wished to finance his wars in Italy. It was for financial reasons that the popes extended to monasteries the system of provision, thus depriving monks of their ancient right to elect their superiors. Whether abbots had been directly appointed by the popes or elected by their monks, they had to pay common services or annates.[7] The indebtedness of individual Cistercian houses to the Curia is not irrelevant to a discussion of the finances of the whole Order, for abbeys thus impoverished would be less able to contribute to Collections.

Although as a Cistercian pope Benedict XII was counted a friend of his old Order, he did not hesitate to take considerable sums from it. In 1338 the Chapter General sent him 800 *fl.*[8] In 1340 he received 3,411 *l.t.* and 825 *fl.*[9] In September 1342 an unspecified sum in *florins* went to the new pope, Clement VI, and it was stated that a further 6,000 *fl.* were owed.[10] It seems likely that these debts had been contracted in the time of Benedict XII. Pope Clement, in spite of his famed prodigality, asked much less from the Cistercians. Only one payment to him is recorded: 800 *fl.* in 1345.[11]

The heaviest demands upon the Order came from pope Innocent VI. The reconquest of the papal lands in Italy, which he had undertaken, required vast sums.[12] In September 1355 the pope wrote to individual abbeys which were reputed to be rich and asked for voluntary contributions. Most of the houses thus approached were Benedictine, but there were twenty-five Cistercian abbeys on the list: Hautecombe, Fontfroide, Cambron, St Bernard-sur-l'Escaut, Poblet, Boulbonne, Vaucelles, Franquevaux, Valbonne, Santes Creus, Benifaçar, Escarp, Grandselve, Eaunes, Belleperche, Feuillants, Villelongue, Gimont, Valmagne, Piedra, Leire, Oliva, Cîteaux, Clairvaux, La Ferté.[13] The list shows clearly the geographical area from which Innocent could still hope for some financial support. English abbeys were inaccessible.

Those in Italy were probably too poor. As for the Empire, a papal subsidy was being raised there,[14] but the pope probably did not think it politic to approach individual abbeys, many of which stood under the protection of Charles IV.

This left abbeys in France and the Iberian peninsula. In France, the clergy had been subject, since 1351, to a particularly onerous papal thirtieth, which took years to collect and caused conflict and bitterness for the rest of Innocent's pontificate.[15] In September 1355, no doubt in order to obtain a collective Cistercian contribution, the pope sent cardinal Guillaume Court, protector of the Order, to the Chapter General, to ask for a subsidy.[16] When Chapter pleaded poverty, Innocent appointed two legates to visit all the houses of the Order and demand procurations in cash. The visitation began and had reached England, the papal agents taking as much money as possible everywhere, when cardinal Guillaume Court interceded for his fellow-Cistercians. It was agreed to call off the visitation on condition that the Order paid the pope 8,000 *fl.* The matter had been settled in principle by July 1356.[17] It took most of 1357 to raise the money. The abbey of Cîteaux lent the Order 2,000 *fl.,*[18] Clairvaux lent 4,000 *fl.,*[19] and La Ferté lent another 2,000 *fl.*[20] Repayment was to come out of Collections at the rate of 100 *fl.* a year each to Cîteaux and La Ferté,[21] and 200 *fl.* a year to Clairvaux.[22] These repayments were being made throughout most of the fourteenth century, as can be seen from occasional references in the Order's financial records. In 1383 the Chapter General paid Cîteaux 200 *fl.* for two years running.[23] In 1389 the rights of Clairvaux and La Ferté to their respective shares out of the Collections were expressly guaranteed.[24] At the 1390 Audit the Mother House complained that the payment for the current year had not been made.[25]

In 1343 the Cistercian Order had been able to raise over 10,000 *fl.* from the Collections.[26] In 1341 it had finally paid its debt of over 7,000 *fl.* to the Italian bankers. In the

context of these figures the papal demand for 8,000 *fl.* may
not seem excessive. It must be remembered, however, that it
had taken two years to pay off the Italians. Lapo had been
content to wait (charging interest the while).[27] Some of the
Order's difficulties in 1355-57 may have arisen from the fact
that pope Innocent wanted his money at once. It is also
clear that the Order's income from Collections was declining,
as was the number of abbeys ready to contribute. In 1351
the Chapter General had ordered a Collection of 6,000 *fl.*
every year until further notice.[28] This may have been
regarded as a realistic estimate of annual income. Out of this,
as will be seen,[29] an annual pension of 3,000 *fl.* had to be
paid to cardinal Guillaume Court. Since already in the 1340s
Collections had not reached their target, it may be doubted
whether the Cistercians were able to raise even one half of
the sum demanded by the pope.

The Order was also very heavily burdened by obligations
to the cardinals. Its cardinal protector[30] usually enjoyed a
substantial pension from the Chapter General. In the early
fourteenth century beneficiaries had been cardinals Arnaud
Nouvel,[31] and later Jacques Fournier, the future Benedict XII himself.[32] A study of the Accounts of 1337-47
bears out the Order's complaint that expenses at the Curia
and especially the pensions of cardinals Guillaume Court and
Napoleon Orsini were among its heaviest burdens.[33]

Guillaume Court was a Cistercian, and had become abbot
of Boulbonne, where pope Benedict XII had once been a
monk. In 1337 he became in quick succession bishop of
Nîmes and then of Albi, and in December 1338 he was made
a cardinal.[34] A month later the pope ordered the Cistercians
to pay him an annual pension of 3,000 *fl.*[35] As a Cistercian
and the protector of the Order Guillaume was sometimes
referred to as 'our cardinal',[36] but his good will was dearly
bought. In 1339, at the first Chapter General after he had
been granted his pension, it proved impossible to pay him
anything.[37] In 1340 he was given the equivalent of 1,000 *fl.*,

nearly half of it in silver, towards the payment owed in the previous year. For what was owed in 1340, the equivalent of 1,400 *fl.* was found, paid in French gold which had been borrowed for the purpose by the abbot of Clairvaux. A debt of 1,600 *fl.* was acknowledged, and the rest of the money owed for 1339 was not mentioned.[38] In 1341, with a payment of 1,000 *fl.* the debt was reduced to 6,000 *fl.*, but the whole pension for the current year was unpaid.[39] Nothing was available for the cardinal in the next year.[40] In 1343 he had to accept two scarlet gowns and a camel hair coat valued at 100 *fl.*[41]

In 1344 a gigantic effort was made. The bursar of Cîteaux paid the cardinal 3,314 *fl.*, the *receptores* handed over 1,000 *fl.* and the Order's proctor at Avignon 649 *fl.* Two hundred *fl.* were made available to him for buying wine, making a total of 5,163 *fl.*[42] This still did not cover all that was owed. The year 1345 proved to be another difficult one—the Cistercians could only give him 279 *fl.* 4 *s.* 8 *d.t.*[43] In the next year he received 1,500 *fl.*, exactly half the current pension owed.[44] In 1347 the Chapter General was able to pay him 7,923 *fl.* 7 *s.* 5 *d.t.*[45] This sum covered the pension for that year, what was owed from 1346, and a little towards what had been unpaid since 1339. One of the last entries in the Accounts of 1347 records a debt to him of 1,700 *fl.*[46] By 1350 it had gone up to 6,082 *fl.*—the pension for the current year and for 1349.[47]

In later years Guillaume Court was remembered for his gifts to the Cistercian College in Paris. He restored the church and decorated it with jewels and ornaments, he gave books to the library, improved the revenues, and left an endowment for the permanent upkeep of the buildings. The Chapter General decreed in 1395 that there should be a solemn requiem for him every year on the anniversary of his death.[48] By this time no one could remember that his benefactions to the Order had been paid for by the Order itself.

The Chapter General's other pensioner in the Sacred

College was Napoleon Orsini, who had been a cardinal since 1288. He belonged to an ancient Roman family, many members of which had become popes. In normal times he could have expected to rise to the same heights, and he had played a vital part in the conclave of Perugia in 1305. Acting as agent of Philip IV of France he had secured the election of Bertrand de Got as Clement V. The papacy's move to the south of France and the flooding of the college of cardinals with Gascons and southern Frenchmen had dashed his hopes and left him isolated and embittered. At Avignon he became a focus of opposition, sometimes clashing openly with the pope at consistory, more often attempting to thwart papal policy through intrigues.[49]

During the period covered by the Cistercian Accounts Napoleon was at the end of a very long life. It is not known how he had obtained his pension from the Cistercians. It may have been during the thirteenth century. It is unlikely that any of the Avignon popes would have approached the Chapter General on his behalf. For him the pension was probably a useful help towards maintaining his independence. It is difficult to see what the Cistercians could hope to gain from his labyrinthine policies. The pension was worth 400 *fl.* a year and he was paid in full in 1338 and 1339.[50] In 1340 the Order had to face the implications of paying the much higher pension of cardinal Guillaume Court. Napoleon was therefore left unpaid.[51] In 1341 he received 200 *fl.* towards what was owed him.[52] The pension of the current year, however, could not be paid. The Order could only acknowledge the debt, and add that 200 *fl.* must also be found for the previous year.[53] One hundred *fl.* went towards the debt in September 1342.[54] By this time cardinal Napoleon was dead,[55] and the money must have been paid to his heirs. Whether any other settlement was made is not known. There is no further reference to this pension in the Accounts.

After direct payments to the popes and pensions to cardinals, the heaviest expenses at Avignon came from lawsuits.

The autonomy of the Cistercian Order, as conceived in the bull *Parvus Fons,* was greatly undermined in the fourteenth century. It proved to be impossible for the Chapter General to be the supreme and unchallenged governing body of an Order of nearly seven hundred abbeys. The Cistercian exemptions were under attack from bishops.[56] The Curia dealt with matters which should have gone before the Chapter General. Individual abbots and monasteries, for instance, appealed to the pope against sentences of father abbots, visitors, or the Chapter General itself, and Chapter was obliged to meet the costs of the ensuing lawsuits.[57] Even the Order's new *Libellus Diffinitionum* projected in 1338[58] could not be compiled without outside interference. Since the old book was out of date, the task of revision had been entrusted to the abbots of Hautecombe and Chassagne.[59] They had completed their work by September 1339, and the Chapter General gave the new book its approval and ordered it to be observed throughout the Order.[60] Cardinal Guillaume Court, however, was extremely critical. 'The reverend father and Lord, the Cistercian cardinal has, as it seems, informed the Chapter General that in the *Libellus Diffinitionum* which was recently approved, certain matters are very obscure and require clearer definition', was the Chapter General's report in 1340. The new book had to be withdrawn.[61] The cardinal's reservations may have been shared by Benedict XII, who took a keen if stifling interest in his old Order, but neither of these two men had any standing in the Chapter General, and their scrutiny of a purely internal matter was without precedent. The abbot of Hautecombe's visits to Avignon in 1339 and 1340, the expenses of which appear in the Order's Accounts, were almost certainly in connection with this affair.[62] In 1340, 50 *l.t.* were spent 'on the corrections of the *Libellus Diffinitionum*'[63] but a definitive version was not ready before 1350.[64]

To watch over its interests at the Curia the Order had a proctor who was paid an annual fee. In the thirteenth century

two secular clerks had represented the Order at the papal
court. In the fourteenth century the work was done by a
senior Cistercian, possibly of abbatial status.[65] In the period
of 1337-47 his name was Bernard.[66] He handled the Order's
money affairs at Avignon, collecting the contributions of
those who preferred to pay them there,[67] making payments
on behalf of the Chapter General,[68] and arranging loans.[69]
When lawyers or agents were required in the papal city it is
likely that he made the contacts and negotiated the fees. He
was paid an annual pension of 250 *fl.*, for which, like the
cardinals, he sometimes had to wait. Everything was a year
behind in 1338-40.[70] In 1340 the Chapter General was only
able to make a payment in silver of 132 *l.* 4 *s.t.,* some of it
sent through a special courier called Raymond.[71] The rest of
the debt was expressed as 162 *fl.* and may have included
some of the money owed in the past.[72] In 1341 Bernard
received 500 *fl.* for the current year and the previous
one.[73] The next payment, in 1343, was again for two years
running.[74] Possibly the proctor's dissatisfaction with this
state of affairs explains a present to his nephew worth
10 *fl.*[75] In the three years which followed Bernard received
his pension regularly.[76] The extra 66 *fl.* he was paid in 1346
may have been in settlement of past accounts.[77] He resigned
in 1347, and was given a final payment of 213 *fl.* 10 *gr. t.*[78]
The new proctor was immediately paid his fee of 250 *fl.* and
an initial extra sum of 11 *fl.* 17 *s.* 1 *d.t.*[79]

The Accounts of 1337-47 also give information about some
of the lesser expenses at the papal court. In a structured
society it is difficult to distinguish gifts from bribes. One did
not go empty-handed to the court of any prince, and one
remembered his servants. It is not easy to define the payments in the Accounts described as 'gifts'. They involve every
grade of the hierarchy at Avignon. In 1338 and 1339 gifts to
the cardinals and bishops at the papal palace cost 20 *fl.*[80] In
1338 a robe worth 4 *l.* 10 *s.t.* was given to John of Viterbo.[81]
John must have been, at that time, a lowly member of

the pope's guard. About ten years later he appears regularly in the papal Accounts as one of the pope's men-at-arms.[82] Another guard, at one of the palace gates, was given presents to the value of 15 *s.t.* in 1338.[83] In 1339 20 *fl.* were distributed among the master ushers, gatekeepers, servants, couriers, 'and others' at Avignon.[84]

The settlement of the popes at Avignon brought a large court within reach of the vineyards of Burgundy, many of which were owned by the Cistercians. The frugal Benedict XII made small use of his opportunities. He encouraged cultivation of the somewhat inferior local wines, and drank Burgundy only when it came as a present from Cistercian abbots.[85] The gifts of wine to this pope recorded in the Cistercian Accounts are fairly small. It is clear that transport costs were prohibitive. On the roads the wagons rattled and much of the wine was spilled; on the rivers the casks had constantly to be unpacked and repacked, and tolls payable at many points added to the expense.[86] In 1338, for instance, the Cistercians spent 20 *l.t.* on wine for the papal court. The pay of the barges, of the navvies who loaded and unloaded the casks and carried them from one craft to another, and the various fines and taxes on the way, cost another 32 *l.* 6 *d.t.*[87] For all that the Cistercians must have thought the exercise worthwhile, for in 1339 wine for the papal court was provided by the abbot of Mazières and transported to Avignon at a total cost of 202 *l.t.*[88] At the Audit of that year the Chapter General decided to set aside 160 *l.t.* which were to be spent on eight casks of wine for the pope.[89] In 1340 and 1341 the Order spent altogether 82 *fl.* on wine for the Curia,[90] and the abbot of Echarlis demanded repayment for the products of his vineyard which had gone to the pope in those years.[91]

Clement VI, that great prince, was determined to improve the quality of the wine consumed at the papal palace. He was prepared to pay, and purchasers were regularly sent to the wine-growing areas to make an informed choice.[92] No doubt the change of policy was to the profit of the Cistercian abbeys of Burgundy, but there was less scope for gifts. The ten cases of wine sent to the Curia in September 1342 were no doubt a courteous present from the Cistercian Chapter General to the recently elected pope. They cost the Order 25 *fl.* and 115 *l.,* 4 *s.t.*[93] The abbot of La Ferté sent a large consignment of wine, valued at 300 *fl.* to the papal court on behalf of the Order in 1347.[94]

Thus the complexity of the relations between the Order and the papacy made it necessary to have a dignitary—the proctor—whose task it was to take special, though not exclusive, charge of them. The Chapter General could also appoint individual abbots to undertake business, at Avignon or elsewhere, on its behalf. For this it often turned to the abbot of Clairvaux, whose abbey remained one of the richest in the Order throughout the Middle Ages.[95] In 1357, as we have seen, he was prepared to advance half the money demanded by pope Innocent VI.[96] In 1340 he borrowed, on the Order's behalf, the gold currency needed to pay cardinal Guillaume Court.[97] In 1342 the Chapter General stated that it owed the abbot 4,000 *fl.,*[98] in 1343 it paid him 7,300 *fl.*[99] This may have been a settlement of the debt contracted in 1340. Altogether it is clear that the Chapter General often turned to the abbot of Clairvaux for help in financial matters.

In return he expected favours and ready cash. In 1340, he borrowed 150 *l.t.* from the Order and promised to repay out of the profits of the sale of his wool—'so he says,' added the scribe, exhibiting a certain scepticism about this particular deal.[100] In 1342 a number of other payments to him were recorded:[101]

[TABLE ON NEXT PAGE]

The list gives an idea of the miscellaneous business the abbot undertook for the Order during the year. The duchess may have been Jeanne, the wife of Eudes IV, duke of Burgundy.

For the lord abbot of Clairvaux	300 *fl.*
For him also	237 *l.* 16 *s.t.*
For him again	63 *l.t.*
A payment to him for various services	500 *fl.*
For him also, for visiting the duchess	5 *fl.* 2 *gr. t.*
For him also, for the cost of transporting *florins* to the Curia	20 *fl.*
For him also, for the death of his sumter horse	30 *fl.*
For him again, for the expenses of the abbot of Pontigny and his own	685 *l.* 2 *s.* 2 *d.t.*

She was a daughter of king Philip V of France.[102] The last item refers to the visitation of the Cistercian College in Paris, which the Order had entrusted to the abbots of Clairvaux and Pontigny at the Chapter General of 1341.[103] Bernard, who succeeded as abbot of Clairvaux in 1345,[104] was paid 213 *fl.* in the following year for the expenses of a journey to Paris.[105] This may also have been in connection with the affairs of the College.

The abbey of La Ferté seems also to have been in a fairly healthy financial state during the fourteenth century. It came to the Order's aid in 1357.[106] In 1347 its abbot sent a considerable amount of wine to the pope on the Chapter General's behalf.[107] None of the other seniors were considered rich at this period. Indeed the abbot of Pontigny obtained a loan of 800 *fl.* from the Chapter General in 1345.[108] Other Cistercian abbots occasionally occur in the Accounts. In 1339 the abbot of Mazières sent wine to the pope;[109] in 1339 and 1340 the abbot of Hautecombe was journeying to Avignon on the Order's behalf, no doubt in connection with the affair of the *Libellus Diffinitionum*.[110] In 1337 the abbot of Mazan, staying in Dijon for the Chapter General, found that his lodgings needed repair and charged the Order 20 *s.t.* for the work.[111] In 1346 the abbot of

Esrom in Denmark was paid 4 *fl.* 10 *s.t.* for his expenses on behalf of the Order.[112]

The College of St Bernard in Paris figures frequently in the Accounts of 1337-47. In 1335 pope Benedict had established the size of the bursaries to be paid to students. Those following the Arts courses were to be entirely supported by their own abbeys, and were to receive an annual 12 *l.t.* The *Biblicus* or bachelor who had begun to lecture upon the Bible, was to get 20 *l.t.* a year from his abbey and an additional 10 *l.t.* from the Chapter General. A bachelor lecturing upon the *Sentences* was to receive 25 *l.t.* from his own abbey and the same sum from the Chapter General. After obtaining his Theology degree the master who stayed at the College to teach would also be paid an annual 25 *l.t.* from home, and 80 *l.t.* by the Chapter.[113] The principle was established that the Order would bear more of the burden of supporting the senior members of the College.

It had long been possible for Cistercian abbots to obtain papal permission to leave their abbeys for a time in order to study in Paris. Pope Benedict himself, when abbot of Font-froide, had done this.[114] In 1342 seven abbots were living at the College. They were the abbot of Cîteaux himself, who was taking his master's degree, the abbot of Mortemer, who was about to become a regent master, and the abbots of Chaalis, Isle-de-Ré, Prières, Valmagne, and Villers.[115] The number of abbots in the *Studium* seems to have been thought excessive. In 1343 the Chapter General decreed that no abbot could stay at the University for longer than one year after taking his degree in Theology. A special exception was made for the abbot of Mortemer, who was acting as regent master. He was allowed to stay until the chancellor of the University appointed another.[116] In fact the abbot of Mortemer is not found on the lists in the Accounts after 1343.[117] The abbot of Cîteaux's stay may have been cut short by the complaints at the Chapter General. He was not on the 1343 list; neither were the abbots of Valmagne or Chaalis. The

abbot of Isle-de-Ré was still there in 1343,[118] but had gone
by the next year. The abbot of Villers stayed until 1344,[119]
and the abbot of Prières until 1345.[122] Chapter had
managed, however, to prevent St Bernard's from becoming a
net which caught up every abbot who went there to do his
studies.

Pope Benedict wished to curb the festivities which marked
a student's progress through the University. Banquets were
not allowed for those who became bachelors. As for masters,
at their inception friends and relatives were to spend no
more than 1,000 *l.t.*[123] The enactment did not involve the
Chapter General at all. This body seems, however, to have
been ready to make occasional extra grants. At the inception
of the abbot of Cîteaux in 1342, for instance, Chapter contributed 626 *l.t.*[124] None of the other grants were quite
as generous. 'Master V.', perhaps the abbot of Villers, was
allowed 50 *l.t.* for his inception in 1338.[125] In 1340 Chapter
gave 110 *l.t.* for the inception of a master.[126] Later payments
were in *florins:* 240 *fl.* for the inception of three masters in
1344,[127] and 71 *fl.* 6 *s.t.* for the inception of master Michael
in 1346.[128]

Benedict XII had clearly not foreseen that abbots might
wish to stay on in Paris after their studies or spell of teaching
were over. It looks as if this particular abuse was checked in
1343. The effect of inflation on some of the bursaries was
more troublesome. The system outlined in the bull *Fulgens*
had to be revised, but some new arrangements made by the
Chapter General were considered inadequate at St Bernard's,
and led to a vehement protest by the united academic body
some time in 1340 or 1341.[129] Although Chapter expressed
itself shocked by this demonstration and some of the intem-
perate things which had been said, it realised that bursaries
must be raised. It chose to do this by placing the burden on
individual abbots. In 1342 and 1343 it asked them to pay
their student monks increased bursaries in the silver of Paris.
The concessions were to be for one year only.[130] The

currency of Paris was slightly heavier than that of Tours,[131] but it had not escaped notice that Chapter did not raise its own support for the students. It was not surprising that the abbots refused to pay.[132] Some of the students likely suffered hardship. Until 1344, for instance, the *Biblicus* received 10 *l.t.* from the Order, as pope Benedict had decreed.[133] In 1345, perhaps as a result of complaints, he was given two *ex gratia* payments of 10 *fl.* and 16 *fl.*[134] In 1347 his bursary was 8 *fl.*[135] For the bachelor lecturing upon the *Sentences* pope Benedict's tariff of 25 *l.t.* was paid unchanged until 1343.[136] In 1344 it was raised to 40 *fl.* and in 1347 he was paid 20 *fl.*[137] One may reflect that the students in St Bernard's received little encouragement from the Chapter General in these years, and it is not altogether surprising that this was a period of indiscipline in the College.[138]

It appears from the Accounts of 1337-47 that a number of persons were receiving pensions from the Order. A certain Marcellus occurs every year until 1346. He is sometimes called *magister* and sometimes *nunnus*. The latter word survives in most modern European languages only in its feminine form as 'nonne' or 'nun'. The masculine means 'old monk' and was sometimes used, in Cistercian records, for retired abbots.[139] This may have been Marcellus's status, in which case he was receiving a pension from his own abbey as well as the small annual sum which, for some reason, the Chapter General paid him. Until 1343 it was 3 *l.t.* a year.[140] In 1344 he received 5 *fl.*,[141] roughly the equivalent of the previous payment according to the current rate of exchange. In 1345 and 1346 he was paid 3 *fl.*[142] Richard of Scotland was another individual who received a small sum: 3 *l.t.* described as 'alms' in 1338 and 1342.[143] An old monk called Nicholas was paid 3 *l.t.* in 1342.[144]

There were also some more substantial pensions. Master Jacques de Fausselettre received 50 *l.t.* a year from 1338-43.[145] During that time his pension was losing value steadily. In 1344 he was paid only 4 *fl.*[146] He obtained his usual

50 *l.t.* in 1345,[147] and a payment to him in the following
year of 71 *fl.* 6 *s.t.* looks like an attempt to settle a debt.[148]
He may also have received compensation for what was owed
in goods and services. His payment in 1347 was 40 *fl.*[149]
Master Jean de Montbéliard, who appeared as a new pensioner in 1345, was paid in gold from the first. His pension
was 40 *fl.* and he received it regularly until 1347.[150]

Couriers and messengers figure regularly in the Accounts.
Bringing money was dangerous and could be highly rewarded.
A man who brought money to Cîteaux in 1341 was paid
40 *l.* 10 *s.t.*, though it is possible that this exceptionally high
sum was for several journeys.[151] It was right that the messenger of the queen of France who brought her annual alms to
the Order should be well rewarded. In 1339 he got 100 *s.t.*
(5 *l.t.*),[152] in 1340 6 *l.t.*[153] The queen's alms were duly paid
in 1341,[154] but since her messenger is not mentioned, she
must have sent the money in another way. She sent nothing
in 1342,[155] but her messenger appeared again with her alms
in 1343 and was paid 10 *l.t.*[156] In 1344 he received 2 *fl.*,[157]
his first payment in gold. He received 6 *fl.* in the next
year.[158]

Other payments to couriers appear more like tips. The
two men who took money to Avignon in 1340 shared
15 *s.t.* between them.[159] Fifty five *s.t.* were distributed
among 'various runners' in 1341,[160] 19 *fl.* 2 *s.* 6 *d.t.* was
spent on 'various messengers and runners' in 1344,[161] 16 *fl.*
was paid to couriers in 1345.[162] Here it seems that an estimate was made, at the time of the Audit, of the total amount
spent in this way during the previous year.

The Accounts record occasional payments to the abbot of
Cîteaux. One hundred *l.t.* in 1338,[163] and 143 *fl.* in 1346,[164]
were described as *'de gratia'*. In 1343 the Order paid him
250 *fl.*[165] None of these sums are as large as those paid to
the abbot of Clairvaux.[166] No details are given, nor is much
enlightenment to be gained from the statement that 32 *l.* 5*s.*
6 *d.t.*, paid to him and some other abbots, were 'for various

expenses'.[167] The abbot of Cîteaux was paid 53 *l.t.* in 1340 for visiting the abbey of Reigny.[168] The abbot of La Ferté had gone there the previous year.[169] These two journeys may have been undertaken in order to quell some disorder. In 1340 the abbot of Cîteaux received 100 *l.t.* for travelling to the Curia.[170] There is nothing very remarkable about these entries.

Since the Chapter General met at Cîteaux, certain customary payments were made every year to the community and its obedientiares. The list for 1341 may be taken as typical:[171]

For the community of Cîteaux	20 *l.t.*
For the gatekeeper	2 *l.t.*
For the cellarer	10 *l.t.*
For the bursar	10 *l.t.*
For the precentor	2 *l.* 10 *s.t.*

There were also payments to be made to the notaries and proctors directly appointed by the abbot of Cîteaux whilst the Chapter General was meeting. The proctor of the *Audientia*—that part of the Chapter which was not in the *Diffinitorium*[172]—was an important official who received an annual fee of 25 *fl.*,[173] which was sometimes in arrears.[174] His salary, paid in gold, was exactly one-tenth of that of the proctor in Avignon,[175] which implies perhaps some kind of relationship with him. The abbot of Cîteaux also had his own notary at the Chapter General, who was known as the notary '*ad pedes*'.[176] This functionary was paid 5 *l.t.* from 1340 to 1344,[177] 24 *l.t.* in 1345,[178] 7 *fl.* 2 *s.t.* in 1346,[179] and 4 *fl.* in 1347.[180] There is a quite extraordinary rise in 1345, explicable perhaps by his undertaking some extra duties in that year.

The Cistercian financial system began with the need to help the Mother House meet the cost of hospitality during the Chapter General. Some figures appear for this every year in the Accounts. It is difficult to compare these entries one with another, however, because the *receptores* seem to have hit upon a uniform way of making them. There was also some inconsistency in the way sums, carried over from one year to the other, were recorded.

1337
For the Chapter   1,000 *l.t.*[181]
For St Lambert's Day   100 *l.t.*[182]
The sum of 111 *l.t.* was not paid off until 1338.[183]

1338
For the Chapter   982 *l.* 18 *s.* 2 *d.t.*[184]
For St Lambert's Day   111 *l.t.*[185]
The sum of 219 *l.t.* remained unpaid in 1339. Add interest—
    40 *l.t.*[186]
The debt was paid in 1340, by which time, owing to infla-
    tion, it was calculated as 438 *l.t.*[187]

1339
For the Chapter   1,140 *l.t.*[188]
For the Chapter   1,410—according to the Ac-
                                      counts of 1340.[189]
For St Lambert's Day   100 *l.t.*[190]

1340
For the Chapter   1,500[191]

1341
For the Chapter   1,600 *l.t.*
The Order was unable to pay the bill.[192]

1342
For the Chapter   3,300 *l.t.*[193]

1343
For the Chapter   4,300 *l.t.*[194]

1344
For the Chapter   1,500 *l.t.* = 2,400 *fl.*[195]

1345
For the Chapter   2,000 *fl.*[196]

1346
For the Chapter   1,308 *fl.* 8 *s.t.*[197]

1347
For the Chapter   1,500 *fl.*[198]

1350
For the Chapter   1,500 *fl.*
For St Lambert's Day   50 *fl.*[199]

It would appear that the bill for 1341 was never paid. In the years 1342-4 the figures follow the fluctuations of the *livre tournois,* as they affected the Cistercians at the time of the Chapter General.[200]

Probably only the figures for 1338 and 1346 represent, with anything like meticulous accuracy, what was actually spent. At other times the Mother House preferred round numbers, which probably made possible a small profit. The Accounts of 1337-47 fail to make clear exactly what was being included in the bill. In later decades the formula used on St Lambert's day was, 'The purchase and provision of bread, wine, and other necessities at past Chapters General of our Cistercian Order by the abbot and obedientiaries of the said abbey of Cîteaux'.[201] A number of late fourteenth-century lists of purchases by the bursar show what was involved when the Chapter General met.[202] They do not give a complete picture of all that was consumed on these occasions. Cîteaux had its own produce, and the bursar went shopping only for what he did not have, or for extra quantities.[203] This explains the variety of these lists, the absence from them of such necessities as bread and wine, and the rare mention of fruit. No conclusions can be drawn from the quantities bought.

The list of 1384[204] will serve as an example. For local expenditure the bursar used, as has been seen,[205] the *franc* for payments in gold, and for silver the *gros tournois*.

For the Chapter General.

For 208 glasses	2 *fr.*	6 *gr.t.*	
For 200 earthenware jars	1 *fr.*	8 *gr.t.*	
For 25 large earthenware jars and 8 other jars	1 *fr.*	15 *d.t.*	
For 100 tallow dips	4 *fr.*	5 *gr.t.*	
For 6 lb. gingerbread and pepper	2 *fr.*		
For ½ lb. saffron	1 *fr.*	6 *gr.t.*	
For ½ lb. cloves		8 *gr.t.*	
For ½ lb. cinnamon		8 *gr.t.*	
For ½ lb. grain of Paradise		4 *gr.t.*	
For ½ lb. sugar		4 *gr.t.*	
For 12 lb. almonds		9 *gr.t.*	
For 6 lb. wax	1 *fr.*	3 *gr.t.*	
For 1 pint of ink		2 *gr.t.*	
For 8 reams of paper		8 *gr.t.*	
For 12 skins of parchment		9 *gr.t.*	
For 2 lb. sweets		10 *gr.t.*	
For 22 kids	4 *fr.*	8 *gr.*	5 *d.t.*
For coal bought in Dijon		1 *gr.*	
For a bucket		3 *gr.*	12 *d.t.*
For one crate of fish		5 *gr.t.*	
For 4 ells of cloth		4 *gr.t.*	
For 2,000 eggs	3 *fr.*		
For 3 calves	1 *fr.*	9 *gr.t.*	
For 2 lecterns		6 *gr.t.*	
For 5 locks and 10 keys		1 *s.t.*	

For 18 sacks of coal	4 *gr.t.*	
For the man who brought the glasses	1 *gr.t.*	
For a servant from another household	2 *gr.t.*	
For the man called La Mofle	4 *gr.t.*	
For shoeing the lord Abbot's horses at Bligny	3 *gr.*	10 *d.t.*
For the men who served 2 *fr.*	7 *gr.*	9 *d.t.*
the abbots of Bligny during the time of the Chapter General in the kitchen, and in the Chamber		

The imminence of the Chapter General was often the pretext for repairs to the buildings. In 1367 there was a special reason for this. Cîteaux had been burned by the 'free companies' and the community was living in the abbot's town house in Dijon.[206] It was necessary and entirely reasonable to build a bakehouse between the kitchen and the garden, to acquire new altar-cloths for the chapel, and to charge all this to the Chapter General. Even after Cîteaux had been reoccupied, the house at Dijon could be regarded as a responsibility of the whole Order, since by tradition, the St Lambert's Day Audit took place there. In 1387 and 1388 the Chapter General was charged for repairs in the cook's quarters and the bath house. At Cîteaux itself there were extensive repairs in the stables in 1388. It is clear from the words used in the list for 1384 that some of the meetings of the Chapter General in that year took place in Cîteaux's country house at Bligny-sur-Ouche. This seems to have been the case also in 1386, when various improvements in the cook's quarters there were required. Clearly it was in the interests of the Mother House to charge the Chapter General for repairs at Cîteaux and its properties, but the work detailed in the lists is mostly of a minor character.

Cîteaux's workforce was also paid by the Chapter General

for the extra work which its assembly involved. In the 1380s the rate appears to have been 12 *d.t.* to 15 *d.t.* a day for each man. The work included looking after the abbey furnace, which occupied four men for twelve days in September 1386, bringing in extra bedding and making the beds, which provided work for two other men during the same period, and working in the stables. There were men who waited on the abbots at Bligny. These were possibly men of the district who had charge of the buildings. The man called La Mofle, who occurs in 1384 and 1386, may have acted as a kind of foreman. Men could also be sent on errands, like Thierry Brichet, who made purchases for the Chapter General on several occasions.

During the fourteenth century the consumption of meat became common for all classes.[207] As a consequence, Cistercians found abstention from it difficult, especially when they were travelling and being provided with hospitality by strangers. Already during the thirteenth century many Cistercians regarded the dietary regulations of the Order, which forbade them to eat meat or anything cooked in fat, as antiquated and irksome.[208] The rule continued to be, however, that meat could only be eaten in the infirmary by the sick. This applied even to guests in a Cistercian house. In 1244 St Louis, who was attending the Chapter General at Cîteaux, was given special permission to eat meat in a house near the abbey.[209] The frequent embarrassments, particularly when abbots were travelling, persuaded even the austere pope Benedict XII to make some concessions. The ancient rule that meat could be eaten regularly only in the infirmary, and there only by the sick, was reaffirmed. With the permission of the reigning abbot, a very old retired abbot could join the sick and eat meat with them. Abbots and very senior members of the Order who were visiting another abbey could, with the permission of the reigning abbot, eat meat, either in the infirmary, or in the abbot's room.[210]

The items relating to food and particularly meat in the bursar's lists may be understood in the light of these regulations. In 1367 the bursar purchased a quantity of fish, 4,900 eggs and 700 cheeses, and slaughtered two geese which belonged to Cîteaux. In 1384 he bought, as has been seen, three calves, 22 kids, a crate of fish, 2,000 eggs, and two pounds of sweets. The 1387 list has three dozen hens, six kids, and the usual large quantity of eggs and fish. Purchases in 1388 were particularly imaginative. Huntsmen on a neighbouring estate were paid to organise a hunt and bring in game. Eighteen partridges were bought in Dijon. Thierry Brichet was sent to town to buy hens, and 3,000 eggs were obtained from various places. A Dijon pastrycook was paid to make cakes.

The crates of fish surely only supplemented the catch from the abbey's own fishponds. It was never necessary to buy wine or bread, of which the Mother House must have had enough for its own guests. The abbeys orchards too will have supplied most of the fruit required and purchases for the Chapter General were very rare. Cîteaux must also have had plenty of hens, but eggs were used for cooking and there can never have been enough. Cheese appears to have been regarded as something of a luxury in the fourteenth century.[211] It does not appear as a regular item on the bursar's lists. Seven hundred cheeses were bought in 1384 and an unspecified quantity in 1388. Sweets were purchased in 1384 and 1388, probably to serve as dessert after the main courses.

An early statute of the Order had forbidden the use of pepper, cinnamon, and other spices in Cistercian houses. Monks were to be content with the herbs produced in their own gardens.[212] By the fourteenth century this enactment had been forgotten. For the upper classes spices and condiments were important ingredients of every meal. They form a distinct section of each of the bursar's lists. Gingerbreads and pepper, always mentioned together, were among the most expensive items. Five to six pounds were bought each year for the Chapter General, at a cost of two *francs*. Saffron was even more expensive; in 1384 half a pound cost 1 *fr.* 6 *gr.t.;* in 1388 a quarter pound cost 2 *fr.* 5 *gr.t.* These spices had to be bought with gold. The rest, usually bought half a pound at a time, and costing three to six *gr.t.,* included cloves, cinnamon, mustard, and grain of Paradise. The latter was a kind of pepper, like Hungarian paprika.[213] A large quantity of almonds was also required every year.

The bursar bought a considerable amount of table ware and cutlery for every Chapter General. Twelve wooden spoons were bought in 1387, and eleven more in the following year. Two hundred medium-sized earthenware jars holding one pint, and 25 to hold three pints, were an almost annual feature of his lists. In addition eight 'French jars' were bought in 1386. In the next year there was a great variety of size. The list included 100 one-pint jars, and 35 four-pint jars. The apparently short life of these earthenware vessels is noteworthy, and they were certainly very cheap. In 1387 all the purchases in earthenware cost together 20 *gr.t.* In the next year there seems to have been an inclination for better quality. Thierry Brichet was sent to a fair and came back with 55 jars—50 had cost 55 *d.t.* each, and five had cost 2½ *gr.t.* each. Since no further lists are preserved there is no means of knowing how well these vessels lasted. The bursar was also, by modern standards, very prodigal about glassware. A new set of glasses seems to have been thought necessary for every Chapter General. Four hundred were bought in 1367, 208 in 1384, 250 in 1386, 250 in 1387, 212 in 1388. Carriers were paid to bring them from Dijon, no doubt specially packed to prevent breakages.[214]

For the business of the Chapter General the bursar bought each year six pounds of sealing wax, a pint of ink, eight reams of paper, and up to eighteen skins of parchment. More ink was made in the kitchen using gall-nuts,[215] which were bought in most years for this purpose. In 1384 it was necessary to acquire two lecterns. The five locks and ten keys purchased that year may have served to secure the money collected in contributions. It appears that the kitchen at Cîteaux did not produce enough tallow and fat for all the extra candles required during the Chapter General. About 100 tallow dips were bought every year. Finally, steps had to be taken to keep the visitors warm. In 1384 coal was bought in Dijon, and a bucket to carry it. A new bucket was needed in 1386 for the furnace which was kept going that year, as we have seen, for twelve days.

A study of these lists shows that the accommodation of the Chapter General was well organised in the last decades of the fourteenth century. The bursar was clearly concerned about the comfort of his guests and showed considerable resourcefulness. He knew how to exploit the opportunities of the local market, and was able to put something new on the menu every year. It would be easy to draw the wrong conclusions. During this period the kings of England were regaled with swan, peacock, mallard, teal, woodcock, snipe, lark, and a large variety of other river and singing birds, as well as pork, capon, and veal.[216] A generation later Dijon was to be the location of the gargantuan banquets of the dukes of Burgundy. Within this context it will be seen that the fare at Cîteaux during the Chapters General satisfied the standards of generous hospitality, but did not depart from the modesty and sobriety which could be expected from religious.

NOTES TO CHAPTER SEVEN

1. Accts., f. 27a, col. 2.
2. *Ibid.*, ff. 8b, col. 1; 11b, col. 1.
3. *Ibid.*, f. 11b, col. 1.
4. *Ibid.*, ff. 17b, col. 2; 21a, col. 1; 23a, col. 1.
5. *Ibid.*, f. 23a, cols. 1, 2.
6. See above p. 50.
7. Mollat, *The Popes at Avignon*, 319-23.
8. Accts., f. 9a, col. 1.
9. *Ibid.*, f. 17b, col. 2.
10. *Ibid.*, f. 23a, cols. 1, 2.
11. Accts., f. 27b, col. 1.
12. Baluze, *Vitae Paparum Avenionensium*, i, 328, 331.
13. Innocent VI, *Lettres secrètes et curiales*, iii, Nos. 1718, 1720.
14. Baluze, *Vitae Paparum Avenionensium*, i, 331, 336-37.
15. Samaren et Mollat, *La fiscalité pontificale*, 17-18.
16. Innocent VI, *Lettres secrètes et curiales*, iii, No. 1674.
17. *Ibid.*, iv, No. 2289; *Chron. de Melsa*, iii, 153.
18. Archives de l'Aube 3 H 154.
19. Archives de l'Aube 3 H 153.
20. Manrique, *Annales cistercienses*, i, 494.
21. Archives de l'Aube 3 H 154; *Statuta* 1389, 48.
22. Archives de l'Aube 3 H 153.
23. Accts., f. 94b, col. 1.
24. *Statuta* 1389, 48.
25. See above p. 115.
26. See above p. 103.
27. See above p. 158.
28. Griesser, 'Unbekannte Generalkapitelstatuten', 6; see above, p. 106.
29. See below.
30. On the cardinal protector see Lekai, *The Cistercians*, 34.
31. *Statuta* 1316, 1.
32. *Statuta* 1328, 13.
33. *Statuta* 1340, 14.

34. On the career of cardinal Guillaume Court see Baluze, *Vitae Paparum Avenionensium,* ii, 320-24.

35. Benoît XII, *Lettres closes . . . se rapportant à la France.* Nos. 561; 564; *Lettres communes,* No. 7489.

36. Accts., f. 11b, col. 2.

37. *Ibid.*

38. *Ibid.,* f. 17b, col. 2. On the French gold see above p. 162.

39. *Ibid.,* ff. 20b, col. 2—21a, col. 1.

40. *Ibid.,* f. 23a, col. 1.

41. *Ibid.,* f. 25a, col. 1.

42. Wrongly added as 5,463 in Accts., f. 27a, col. 2.

43. *Ibid.,* f. 27b, col. 1.

44. *Ibid.,* f. 27b, col. 2.

45. Accts., f. 29b, col. 2.

46. *Ibid.*

47. Sens MS 129, ff. 169a—b.

48. *Statuta* 1395, 8.

49. For a study of the character and career of Napoleon Orsini see Guillemain, *Le Cour pontificale d'Avignon,* 241-4.

50. Accts., ff. 8b, col. 2; 11b, col. 1.

51. Accts., f. 17b, col. 2.

52. *Ibid.,* f. 20b, col. 2.

53. *Ibid.,* f. 21a, col. 1.

54. *Ibid.,* f. 23a, col. 2.

55. Died 23 March 1342, Eubel, *Hierarchia Catholica,* i, 11.

56. Lecler, *Vienne,* 120-5.

57. *Statuta* 1352, 2.

58. *Statuta* 1338, 11.

59. *Ibid.*

60. *Statuta* 1339, 5.

61. *Statuta* 1340, 3.

62. Accts., ff. 11a, col. 2; 17b, col. 2.

63. *Ibid.,* ff. 11b, col. 2; 17b, col. 2.

64. On the affair of the *Libellus Diffinitionum,* see Lekai, *The Cistercians,* 76.

65. Lekai, 74.

66. Accts., ff. 27b, col. 1; 29b, col. 2.

67. *Ibid.,* ff. 2b, col. 2—3a, col. 1; 9b, cols. 1, 2; 15b, col. 1—16a, col. 2.

68. *Ibid.,* ff. 8b, col. 1; 11b, col. 1.

69. *Ibid.,* f. 11b, col. 1.

70. *Ibid.,* ff. 11b, cols. 1, 2; 17b, col. 2.

71. *Ibid.,* f. 17b, col. 2.
72. *Ibid.*
73. *Ibid.,* f. 20b, col. 2.
74. *Ibid.,* f. 25a, col. 2.
75. *Ibid.*
76. *Ibid.,* ff. 27a, col. 2; 27b, cols. 1, 2.
77. *Ibid.,* f. 27b, col. 2.
78. *Ibid.,* f. 29b, col. 2.
79. *Ibid.*
80. Accts., ff. 8b, col. 2; 11b, col. 1.
81. *Ibid.,* f. 8b, col. 2.
82. Schäfer, *Die Ausgaben der Apostolischen Kammer unter Benedikt XII, Klemens VI und Innozenz VI,* 361, 419, 461, 487, 537, 597, 615, 654, 685.
83. Accts., f. 8b, col. 2. On the keepers of the gates at Avignon see Guillemain, *La cour pontificale,* 418-19.
84. Accts., f. 11b, col. 1.
85. See Renouard, 'La consommation des grands vins de Bourgogne et du Bourbonnais à la cour pontificale d'Avignon', 223-4.
86. See Renouard, 'Le grand commerce des vins de Gascogne', 265-6; 'La capacité du tonneau bordelais', 402.
87. Accts., f. 8b, col. 2.
88. *Ibid.,* f. 11b, col. 1.
89. *Ibid.,* f. 11b, col. 2.
90. *Ibid.,* f. 20b, col. 2.
91. *Ibid.,* f. 21a, col. 1.
92. Renouard, 'La consommation des grands vins . . . ' , 224-6.
93. Accts., f. 23a, col. 2.
94. *Ibid.,* f. 29b, col. 2.
95. See Dautrey, 'Croissance et adaptation chez les cisterciens au 13ᵉ siècle', 148.
96. See above p. 175.
97. See above p. 162.
98. Accts., f. 23a, col. 1.
99. *Ibid.,* f. 25a, col. 2.
100. *Ibid.,* f. 17b, col. 2.
101. *Ibid.,* f. 23a, col. 2.
102. See Anselme, *Histoire Genealogique,* i, 94.
103. *Statuta* 1341, 3.
104. A. King, *Cîteaux and Her Eldest Daughters,* 282-83.
105. Accts., f. 27b, col. 2.
106. See above p. 175.

107. See above p. 182.

108. Accts., f. 27b, col. 1.

109. See above p. 181.

110. See above p. 179.

111. Accts., f. 8b, col. 1.

112. *Ibid.,* f. 27b, col. 2.

113. *Fulgens,* 34, *Statuta,* iii, pp. 430-1; see table in Mahn, *Le pape Benoît XII et les cisterciens,* 57.

114. Mahn, 63-4.

115. Accts., f. 23a, col. 2.

116. *Statuta* 1343, 2.

117. Accts., f. 25a, col. 1.

118. *Ibid.,* f. 25a, col. 2.

119. *Ibid.,* f. 27a, col. 2.

120. *Ibid.,* f. 27b, col. 1.

121. *Ibid.,* f. 25b, col. 1.

122. *Ibid.,* f. 27b, col. 1.

123. *Fulgens,* 40; *Statuta,* iii, pp. 434-5.

124. Accts., f. 23a, col. 2.

125. *Ibid.,* f. 8b, col. 1.

126. *Ibid.,* f. 17b, col. 2.

127. *Ibid.,* f. 27a, col. 2.

128. *Ibid.,* f. 27b, col. 2.

129. *Statuta* 1341, 3.

130. *Statuta* 1342, 5; 1343, 1.

131. On the relationship between the two currencies, see Spufford and Wilkinson, *Interim Listing,* 211, 234.

132. *Statuta* 1344, 1.

133. Accts., ff. 8b, col. 1; 11a, col. 2; 17b, col. 1; 20b, col. 2; 27b, col. 2.

134. *Ibid.,* f. 27b, col. 1.

135. *Ibid.,* f. 29b, col. 2.

136. *Ibid.,* ff. 8b, col. 1; 11a, col. 2; 17b, col. 2; 20b, col. 2; 25b, col. 1.

137. *Ibid.,* ff. 27a, col. 2; 29b, col. 2.

138. See Mahn, 61-2.

139. See e.g. *Statuta* 1344, 11, 12.

140. Accts., ff. 11b, col. 1; 17b, col. 2; 21a, col. 1; 25b, col. 1.

141. *Ibid.,* f. 27a, col. 2.

142. *Ibid.,* ff. 27b, col. 2; 28a, col. 1.

143. *Ibid.,* ff. 8b, col. 1; 23a, col. 2.

144. *Ibid.,* f. 23a, col. 2. Not to be confused with master Nicholas,

resident in St Bernard's College, who occurs in the same column.
145. Accts., ff. 9a, col. 1; 11a, col. 2; 17b, col. 2; 23a, col. 2; 25a, col. 2.
146. *Ibid.*, f. 27a, col. 2.
147. *Ibid.*, f. 27b, col. 1.
148. *Ibid.*, f. 27b, col. 2.
149. *Ibid.*, f. 29b, col. 2.
150. *Ibid.*, ff. 27b, cols. 1, 2; 29b, col. 2.
151. *Ibid.*, f. 23a, col. 2.
152. *Ibid.*, f. 11b, col. 1.
153. *Ibid.*, f. 17b, col. 2.
154. *Ibid.*, f. 20b, col. 2.
155. See above p. 48.
156. Accts., f. 25a, col. 2.
157. *Ibid.*, f. 27a, col. 2.
158. *Ibid.*, f. 27b, col. 1.
159. *Ibid.*, f. 17b, col. 2.
160. *Ibid.*, f. 20b, col. 2.
161. *Ibid.*, f. 27a, col. 2.
162. *Ibid.*, f. 27b, col. 1.
163. *Ibid.*, f. 9a, col. 1.
164. *Ibid.*, f. 27b, col. 2.
165. *Ibid.*, f. 25a, col. 2.
166. See above p. 183.
167. Accts., f. 11a, col. 2.
168. *Ibid.*, f. 17b, col. 2.
169. *Ibid.*, f. 11a, col. 2.
170. *Ibid.*, f. 17b, col. 2.
171. *Ibid.*, ff. 20b, col. 2–21a, col. 1.
172. Müller, 'Studien über das Generalkapitel' (1902), 310.
173. Accts., ff. 11b, cols. 1, 2; 20b, col. 2; 25a, col. 2; 27a, col. 2; 27b, col. 1; 29b, col. 2.
174. *Ibid.*, ff. 21a, col. 1; 23a, cols. 1, 2.
175. See above p. 180.
176. Müller, 123.
177. Accts., ff. 17b, col. 2; 20b, col. 2; 25a, col. 2; 27a, col. 2.
178. *Ibid.*, f. 27b, cols. 1, 2.
179. *Ibid.*, f. 27b, col. 2.
180. *Ibid.*, f. 29b, col. 2.
181. Accts., f. 2a, col. 1.
182. *Ibid.*
183. *Ibid.*, f. 9a, col. 1.

184. *Ibid.,* f. 11a, col. 2.

185. *Ibid.,* f. 9a, col. 1.

186. *Ibid.,* f. 11b, col. 2.

187. *Ibid.,* f. 17b, col. 2. What happened to the interest?

188. *Ibid.,* f. 11b, col. 2.

189. *Ibid.,* f. 17b, col. 2.

190. *Ibid.,* f. 11b, col. 2.

191. Accts., f. 17b, col. 2.

192. *Ibid.,* f. 21a, col. 1.

193. *Ibid.,* f. 23a, col. 2.

194. *Ibid.,* f. 25a, col. 2.

195. *Ibid.,* f. 27a, col. 2.

196. *Ibid.,* f. 27b, col. 1.

197. *Ibid.,* f. 27b, col. 2.

198. *Ibid.,* f. 29b, col. 2.

199. Sens MS 129, f. 169b.

200. See above p. 159.

201. Sens MS 129, ff. 171a; 173b; 175a.

202. Accts., ff. 44b, col. 2 (1367); 123a, cols. 1, 2 (1384); 138b, col. 2–139a, col. 1 (1386); 146a, cols. 1, 2 (1387); 162b, col. 2 (1388).

203. See comments on this kind of material in Stouff, *Ravitaillement,* 225.

204. There is no entry for 1384 in *Statuta.*

205. See above p. 167.

206. Lekai, *The Cistercians,* 97.

207. See Stouff, 222-5.

208. See Müller, 'Der Fleischgenuss im Orden', 26.

209. *Ibid.,* 59-60.

210. *Fulgens,* 22; *Statuta,* iii, p. 425; Müller, *op. cit.,* 184-5.

211. See Stouff, 244.

212. *Instituta Capituli Generalis,* LXIII, *Statuta,* i, p. 27.

213. Grieve, *A Modern Herbal,* 628.

214. Cf. Purchases in earthenware and glassware for the coronation of Clement VI at Avignon in 1342; Stouff, 268-9.

215. For a contemporary recipe for making ink, see Schrader, *Die Rechenbücher der hamburgischen Gesandten,* 17.

216. W.E. Meade, *The English Medieval Feast,* 37-8.

CHAPTER EIGHT

Conclusions

IN SPITE OF THE FACT that late medieval rulers were increasingly able to tax both their regular and secular clergy, the Cistercian Order was able to create machinery for acquiring funds of its own which would guarantee it a certain independence. From the late twelfth century the Chapter General had its own endowments. In the middle of the thirteenth century a system of Collections was devised, through which every Cistercian house contributed, according to its wealth and the Order's needs, to a central fund. The Chapter General was never able to gather quite as much as it had planned. Nevertheless the Collections became increasingly efficient, and reached their peak during the first half of the fourteenth century. In 1340-44 the authorities of the Order were able to make quite heavy demands, and the response was sufficient to pay off many debts. After this there was a decline. Many of the abbeys in France, from which much of the financial support for the Chapter General had come, were ruined by the Hundred Years' War. The Black Death was no doubt also responsible for the disintegration of the Order's financial organisation. In addition to this, the demands of the Papacy became excessive. By the end of the fourteenth century the profits from Collections had dwindled, and the papal Schism of 1378, which divided the Order into two obediences, was a further blow.

The aim of this study has been to describe the Cistercian financial system during the fourteenth century. The historian of the Order's activities in this field is faced with a number of questions. Was the whole elaborate exercises a departure from the Cistercian spirit? How did these exertions affect the Order's life and spiritual health? What was their ultimate purpose?

The answers to these questions would require further reflection from historians of the Order as a whole. Only a few tentative suggestions can be made here. It has been noted that the Collections were specifically sanctioned by the 'papal statutes' which governed the lives of Cistercians in the late Middle Ages.[1] It is not at all evident that the statutes, in this respect, departed from the spirit of the *Carta Caritatis.* It is true that in that document abbot Stephen and his community had promised not to exact a tax from the other abbeys.[2] The abbot, however, was careful to explain his motives: 'Lest while seeking to enrich ourselves from their poverty, we ourselves should fail to avoid the evil of avarice which, according to the Apostle, is the service of idols'.[3] The founders of Cîteaux were critical of the abbots of Cluny, who took tribute from dependent priories and used the proceeds for the benefit of their own abbey, which they adorned with magnificent buildings and treasures. When it became necessary for the Cistercians to organise their Collections on the other hand, only a small part of the money went to Cîteaux and this was to pay the expenses of the Chapter General. Most of what was raised went to pay taxes to popes or cardinals, or was spent on lawsuits at Avignon. One may legitimately criticise an ecclesiastical system of which these expenses were a part, but there was never any question of the Mother House enriching itself from the Order.

The effect of the Collections on morale in the Order is more difficult to gauge. Every Cistercian abbot who came to the Chapter General in the fourteenth century knew that he would be asked how much money he had brought. The prospect can hardly have encouraged attendance, and it is possible that the experience discouraged a second visit, especially from those who had a long journey. An institution which is constantly appealing for money becomes unpopular, however justified the requests. Collections may therefore have been partly responsible for sparse attendance at the Chapter General. There is plenty of evidence, moreover, of haggling and argument about contributions. The energy and ingenuity of those involved could surely have been put to better use.

The Cistercian Chapter General was, of course, powerless to resist the financial pressures which made the Collections necessary, and there was little room for manoeuvre. Occasionally, when circumstances were favourable, the authorities in the Order were able to introduce a note of realism into financial affairs. They gave up trying to raise money from nuns; they yielded, albeit at the very end of the fourteenth century, on the question of assessments. Such concessions to the world around them, however, were rare. In the Late Middle Ages the Order suffered greatly from the fact that leading Cistercians lived in the past. Although attendance at the Chapter General had dwindled, and many abbeys were ruined and deserted, the senior abbots still used language as grandiloquent as if they commanded the obedience of hundreds of populous and fervent religious houses. Theirs was 'the sacred Cistercian Order', 'bright as the morning star amidst lowering clouds'.[4] It seemed obvious to them that the Order must be defended. There could be no question but that all must bestir themselves and find the funds required. Such anachronistic and hopelessly romantic views could only be a handicap to religious who tried to grapple with the changed realities of life during the fourteenth century.

NOTES TO CHAPTER EIGHT

1. See above p. 52.
2. *Carta Caritatis prior*, I, *Les plus anciens textes de Cîteaux*, 91.
3. Translation from *Carta Caritatis posterior*, in Lekai, *The Cistercians*, 462. Identical words in *Carta Caritatis prior*, *Les plus anciens textes de Cîteaux*, 91.
4. 'Fulgens sicut stella matutina in medio nebulae', *Fulgens* 1, *Statuta*, iii, p. 410.

APPENDIX

Cistercian Statistics for the Fourteenth Century

The following abbeys for men (listed under their modern names) occur in the Cistercian financial records of the fourteenth century. Citations from the Tax Books are to the first reference, or to the first reference under the correct generation. Abbeys not identified by the editors of TB are included when they occur under that name in both Tax Books, or in the Accounts of 1337-47. Abbeys marked with an asterisk were either not in existence in the period 1337-47, or not liable to contribute to the Collections.

ABBREVIATIONS

(for details of printed books, see the bibliographies)

Accts.	Dijon, *Archives de la Côte d'Or* 11 H 1160
CB	The Coucher Book of Furness Abbey
MTB	Modena MS Latino 142
TB	The Tax Book of the Cistercian Order

Generation of Cîteaux
Reference

Aumône, L'	*TB*, 1b, 4	*MTB*, f. 11a
Barbeau	*TB*, 1b, 25	*MTB*, f. 11a
Barzelle	*TB*, 2b, 26	*MTB*, f. 11a
Beaugerais	*TB*, 3b, 20	*MTB*, f. 11a
Beaulieu (Hants.)	*TB*, 1b, 14	*MTB*, f. 11a
Bégard	*TB*, 2b, 23	*MTB*, f. 11a
Bellaigue	*TB*, 2b, 20	*MTB*, f. 11a
Bellebrache	*TB*, 3b, 19	*MTB*, f. 11a
Biddlesden	*TB*, 3b, 2	*MTB*, f. 11a
Bindon	*TB*, 3b, 7	*MTB*, f. 11a
Bonaigue	*TB*, 3b, 26	*MTB*, f. 11a
Bonneval	*TB*, 2b, 18	*MTB*, f. 11a

Bonnevaux (Isère)	*TB*, 1b, 3	*MTB*, f. 11a
Bonport	*TB*, 2b, 6	*MTB*, f. 11a
Bonrepos	*TB*, 3b, 14	*MTB*, f. 11a
Boquen	*TB*, 3b, 12	*MTB*, f. 11a
Bordesley	*TB*, 3b, 1	*MTB*, f. 11a
Bruern	*TB*, 3b, 3	*MTB*, f. 11a
Bussière, La	*TB*, 1b, 7	*MTB*, f. 11a
Carnoët	*TB*, 3b, 17	*MTB*, f. 12a
Carracedo	*TB*, 1b, 6	*MTB*, f. 11a
Cercanceaux	*TB*, 2b, 3	*MTB*, f. 12a
Chambons	*TB*, 2b, 19	*MTB*, f. 11a
Clarté Dieu	*TB*, 1b, 21	*MTB*, f. 11a
Coëtmaloën	*TB*, 3b, 9	*MTB*, f. 12a
Colombe, La	*TB*, 1b, 24	*MTB*, f. 11a
Combe	*TB*, 2b, 30	*MTB*, f. 11a
Cour-Dieu, La	*TB*, 1b, 2	*MTB*, f. 11a
Dieulacres	*TB*, 11b, 17	*MTB*, f. 11a
Dunkeswell	*TB*, 3b, 8	*MTB*, f. 11a
Élan	*TB*, 2b, 5	*MTB*, f. 11a
Épau	*TB*, 1b, 19	*MTB*, f. 12a
Escarp	*TB*, 1b, 15	*MTB*, f. 12a
Flaxley	*TB*, 3b, 6	*MTB*, f. 11b
Ford	*TB*, 2b, 28	*MTB*, f. 11a
Frenade, La	*TB*, 3b, 28	*MTB*, f. 11b
Garde-Dieu, La		*MTB*, f. 11b
Garendon	*TB*, 2b, 27	*MTB*, f. 11b
Gourdon	*TB*, 3b, 30	*MTB*, f. 11b
Grace Dieu (Monmouth)	*TB*, 3b, 27	*CB*, iii, 641
Grosbos	*TB*, 3b, 29	*MTB*, f. 11b
Hailes	*TB*, 4b, 4	*MTB*, f. 11b
Herrevad	*TB*, 1b, 12	*MTB*, f. 11b
Holm	*TB*, 4b, 2	*MTB*, f. 11b
Iranzu	*TB*, 2b, 4	*MTB*, f. 12b
Junhas		*MTB*, f. 11b
Kingswood	*TB*, 3b, 15	*MTB*, f. 11b
Landais, Le	*TB*, 2b, 12	*MTB*, f. 11b
Langonnet	*TB*, 2b, 25	*MTB*, f. 11b
Lanvaux	*TB*, 3b, 13	*MTB*, f. 11b
Léoncel	*TB*, 2b, 10	*MTB*, f. 11b
Løgum	*TB*, 4b, 3	*MTB*, f. 11b
Loroux	*TB*, 1b, 5	*MTB*, f. 12a
Loroy	*TB*, 1b, 26	*MTB*, f. 11b

Mazan	*TB*, 2b, 7	*MTB*, f. 11b
Melleray	*TB*, 3b, 21	*MTB*, f. 11b
Merevale	*TB*, 3b, 4	*MTB*, f. 11b
Miroir, Le	*TB*, 1b, 8	*MTB*, f. 11b
Montpeyroux	*TB*, 2b, 8	*MTB*, f. 11b
Netley	*TB*, 4b, 5	*MTB*, f. 11b
Newenham	*TB*, 4b, 6	*MTB*, f. 11b
Obazine	*TB*, 1b, 11	*MTB*, f. 11b
Olivet	*TB*, 2b, 2	*MTB*, f. 11b
Peñamayor	*TB*, 3b, 24	*MTB*, f. 12a
Perseigne	*TB*, 1b, 13	*MTB*, f. 12a
Pontrond	*TB*, 3b, 18	*MTB*, f. 12a
Preuilly	*TB*, 1b, 1	*MTB*, f. 12a
Real Valle	*TB*, 4b, 7	*MTB*, f. 12a
Relec, Le	*TB*, 3b, 11	*MTB*, f. 12a
Rewley	*TB*, 1b, 27	*MTB*, f. 12a
Royaumont	*TB*, 1b, 16	*MTB*, f. 12a
S. Andrea di Sestri	*TB*, 1b, 9	*MTB*, f. 12a
Saint-Aubin-des-Bois	*TB*, 3b, 10	*MTB*, f. 12a
S. Maria della Vittoria	*TB*, 3b, 22	*MTB*, f. 12b
S. Salvatore de Monte Amiata	*TB*, 1b, 17	*MTB*, f. 11b
S. Salvatore di Monte Acuto	*TB*, 1b, 20	*MTB*, f. 11b
St William, Strasbourg[1] *		*MTB*, f. 12a
Sauveréal	*TB*, 2b, 12	*MTB*, f. 21b
Sénanque	*TB*, 2b, 17	*MTB*, f. 12a
Silvanès	*TB*, 2b, 15	*MTB*, f. 12a
Sotosalbos	*TB*, 1b, 18	*MTB*, f. 12a
Stoneleigh	*TB*, 3b, 5	*MTB*, f. 12a
Tamié	*TB*, 2b, 9	*MTB*, f. 12a
Thame	*TB*, 2b, 29	*MTB*, f. 12a
Thoronet, Le	*TB*, 2b, 16	*MTB*, f. 11a
Tihan	*TB*, 1b, 22	*MTB*, f. 12a
Tintern (Monmouth)	*TB*, 2b, 24	*MTB*, f. 12a
Tintern (Wexford)	*TB*, 3b, 16	*MTB*, f. 12b
Tvis	*TB*, 4b, 1	*MTB*, f. 12a
Val, Le	*TB*, 2b, 1	*MTB*, f. 12a
Valbenoîte	*TB*, 2b, 13	*MTB*, f. 12b
Valcroissant	*TB*, 2b, 14	*MTB*, f. 12b

Valette, La	TB, 3b, 25	MTB, f. 12b
Valloires	TB, 1b, 10	MTB, f. 12a
Valmagne (Ulmet)[2]	TB, 2b, 11	MTB, f. 12b
Varennes	TB, 1b, 28	MTB, f. 12b
Vauluisant	TB, 1b, 23	MTB, f. 12a
Villanueva de Osco	TB, 3b, 23	MTB, f. 12b
Waverly	TB, 2b, 22	MTB, f. 12b

Generation of La Ferté

Acqualunga	TB, 5b, 2	MTB, f. 12b
Barona[3]*	TB, 5b, 8	MTB, f. 12b
Casanova	TB, 4b, 13	MTB, f. 12b
Castagnola	TB, 4b, 14	MTB, f. 12b
Jubin[4]	TB, 5b, 1	MTB, f. 12b
Locedio	TB, 4b, 9	MTB, f. 12b
Mazières	TB, 4b, 10	MTB, f. 12b
Preallo	TB, 5b, 3	MTB, f. 12b
Rivalta Scrivia	TB, 4b, 15	MTB, f. 12b
Rivalta di Torino	TB, 5b, 7	MTB, f. 13a
St Sergius*	TB, 4b, 11	MTB, f. 13a
S. Severo	TB, 5b, 5	MTB, f. 12b
Staffarda	TB, 4b, 12	MTB, f. 13a
Sturzelbronne	TB, 5b, 4	MTB, f. 13a
Tiglieto	TB, 4b, 8	MTB, f. 13a

Generation of Pontigny

Ardorel	TB, 6b, 15	MTB, f. 13a
Aubignac	TB, 6b, 23	MTB, f. 13a
Beuil	TB, 6b, 20	MTB, f. 13a
Bonlieu (Creuse)	TB, 6b, 21	MTB, f. 13a
Bonlieu (Gironde)	TB, 6b, 29	MTB, f. 13a
Bonnevaux (Vienne)	TB, 6b, 17	MTB, f. 13a
Bouras	TB, 5b, 9	MTB, f. 13a
Bugedo	Accts., f. 18b, col. 1	
Cadouin	TB, 5b, 10	MTB, f. 13a
Cercamp	TB, 6b, 3	MTB, f. 13a
Chaalis	TB, 5b, 16	MTB, f. 13b
Chalivoy	TB, 6b, 11	MTB, f. 13a
Chassagne	TB, 7b, 3	MTB, f. 13a
Dalon	TB, 5b, 11	MTB, f. 13a

Egres	*TB*, 6b, 10	*MTB*, f. 25a
Estrée, L'	*TB*, 6b, 5	*MTB*, f. 14a
Étoile, L'	*TB*, 6b, 6	*MTB*, f. 14a
Faise	*TB*, 6b, 19	*MTB*, f. 13a
Faleri	*TB*, 7b, 2	*MTB*, f. 13b
Fontainejean	*TB*, 5b, 12	*MTB*, f. 13b
Fontguillem	*TB*, 6b, 14	*MTB*, f. 13b
Gondon	*TB*, 6b, 13	*MTB*, f. 13b
Isle-de-Ré	*TB*, 6b, 9	*MTB*, f. 13b
Jau, Du	*TB*, 6b, 16	*MTB*, f. 13a
Jouy	*TB*, 5b, 13	*MTB*, f. 13b
Kerc	*TB*, 6b, 12	*MTB*, f. 13a
Loc-Dieu	*TB*, 6b, 22	*MTB*, f. 13b
Merci-Dieu, La	*TB*, 6b, 1	
Noë, La	*TB*, 6b, 27	*MTB*, f. 13b
Palais-Notre-Dame	*TB*, 6b, 25	*MTB*, f. 13b
Pin, Le	*TB*, 6b, 4	*MTB*, f. 13b
Pontaut	*TB*, 6b, 28	*MTB*, f. 13b
Pré-Benoît	*TB*, 6b, 24	*MTB*, f. 13b
Quincy	*TB*, 5b, 14	*MTB*, f. 13b
Rivet	*TB*, 7b, 1	*MTB*, f. 13b
Roches	*TB*, 6b, 2	*MTB*, f. 13b
Szentkerest	*TB*, 7b, 5	*MTB*, f. 13b
St Léonard-des-Chaumes	*TB*, 6b, 26	*MTB*, f. 13b
St Marcel	*TB*, 6b, 18	*MTB*, f. 13b
S. Martino al Cimino	*TB*, 6b, 8	*MTB*, f. 13b
S. Sebastiano ad Catacumbas	*TB*, 7b, 4	*MTB*, f. 13b
St Sulpice-en-Bugey	*TB*, 5b, 15	*MTB*, f. 13b
Sellières	*TB*, 6b, 30	*MTB*, f. 14a
Trisay	*TB*, 6b, 7	*MTB*, f. 14a

Generation of Clairvaux

Abbey Cwmhir	*TB*, 19b, 14	*CB*, iii, 641
Abbeydorney	*TB*, 19b, 1	*MTB*, f. 18a
Abbeyknockmoy	*TB*, 10b, 8	*MTB*, f. 16a
Abbeylara	*TB*, 11b, 24	*MTB*, f. 17b
Abbeyleix	*TB*, 19b, 8	*MTB*, f. 18a
Abbeymahon	*TB*, 18b, 2	*MTB*, f. 17a
Abbeyshrule	*TB*, 18b, 26	*MTB*, f. 17a
Abbeystrowry	*TB*, 15b, 7	*MTB*, f. 20a

Abington	*TB*, 13b, 9	*MTB*, f. 23a
Ábrahám	*TB*, 21b, 21	*MTB*, f. 14a
'Acconnale'	*TB*, 14b, 16	*MTB*, f. 14a
Acey	*TB*, 12b, 24	*MTB*, f. 14a
Acquaformosa	*TB*, 18b, 14	*MTB*, f. 14b
Adwert	*TB*, 21b, 14	*MTB*, f. 20b
Aguiar	*TB*, 6b, 14	*MTB*, f. 12a
Aguias	*TB*, 16b, 16	*MTB*, f. 21a
Alcobaça	*TB*, 9b, 7	*MTB*, f. 14a
Almaziva	*TB*, 20b, 13	*MTB*, f. 12a
Altofonte		*MTB*, f. 14a
Alvastra	*TB*, 9b, 3	*MTB*, f. 14a
Arabona	*TB*, 19b, 24	*MTB*, f. 14a
Armenteira	*TB*, 9b, 29	*MTB*, f. 14b
Arnsburg	*TB*, 17b, 30	*MTB*, f. 14b
Arrivour, L'	*TB*, 8b, 23	*MTB*, f. 20a
Ås	*TB*, 14b, 2	*MTB*, f. 14b
Assaroe	*TB*, 14b, 1	*MTB*, f. 20b
Aubepierres	*TB*, 9b, 20	*MTB*, f. 14a
Auberive	*TB*, 8b, 16	*MTB*, f. 14a
Aulnay	*TB*, 10b, 23	*MTB*, f. 14a
Aulne	*TB*, 9b, 15	*MTB*, f. 14a
Aulps	*TB*, 8b, 14	*MTB*, f. 14a
Balerne	*TB*, 8b, 13	*MTB*, f. 14b
'Baliazes'	*TB*, 12b, 29	*MTB*, f. 14b
Balmerino	*TB*, 16b, 4	*MTB*, f. 14b
Baltinglass	*TB*, 18b, 22	*MTB*, f. 22b
Barbery	*TB*, 11b, 4	*MTB*, f. 14b
Basingwerk	*TB*, 11b, 20	*MTB*, f. 14b
Baudeloo	*TB*, 20b, 29	*MTB*, f. 15a
Beaubec	*TB*, 10b, 2	*MTB*, f. 14b
Beaulieu (Haute Marne)	*TB*, 10b, 15	*MTB*, f. 14b
Beaulieu (Tarne-et-Garonne)	*TB*, 8b, 21	*MTB*, f. 14b
Beaupré	*TB*, 12b, 20	
Bebenhausen	*TB*, 18b, 1	*MTB*, f. 14b
Bective	*TB*, 10b, 7	*MTB*, f. 14b
Bélakut	*TB*, 12b, 9	*MTB*, f. 26b
Bél-Harom-Kúti	*TB*, 15b, 24	*MTB*, f. 22a
Belleperche	*TB*, 9b, 5	*MTB*, f. 14b
'Belle Locus Hungariae'	*TB*, 15b, 21	*MTB*, f. 14b
	(also):	Accts., 7 entries

Belmonte	*TB*, 15b, 2	*MTB*, f. 18a
Benavides	*TB*, 19b, 30	*MTB*, f. 15a
Benifaçar	*TB*, 19b, 3	*MTB*, f. 15a
Bénissons-Dieu, La (Loire)	*TB*, 8b, 20	*MTB*, f. 15a
Bloemkamp	*TB*, 21b, 13	*MTB*, f. 17a
Bohéries	*TB*, 12b, 14	*MTB*, f. 15a
Bois-Groland	*TB*, 21b, 11	*MTB*, f. 15a
Boissière, La	*TB*, 10b, 22	*MTB*, f. 15b
Bonmont	*TB*, 7b, 16	*MTB*, f. 15a
Bonnecombe	*TB*, 20b, 23	*MTB*, f. 15a
Bonnefontaine	*TB*, 12b, 17	*MTB*, f. 15a
Boschaud	*TB*, 12b, 19	*MTB*, f. 15a
Boulancourt	*TB*, 9b, 22	*MTB*, f. 15b
Bouro	*TB*, 20b, 9	*MTB*, f. 15b
Boxley	*TB*, 9b, 11	*MTB*, f. 15a
Boyle	*TB*, 9b, 17	*MTB*, f. 15b
Breuil-Benoît	*TB*, 11b, 7	*MTB*, f. 15a
Brondolo	*TB*, 18b, 4	*MTB*, f. 15a
Buckfast	*TB*, 10b, 29	*MTB*, f. 15a
Buckland	*TB*, 14b, 17	*MTB*, f. 15a
Buildwas	*TB*, 10b, 30	*MTB*, f. 15a
Buillon	*TB*, 9b, 16	*MTB*, f. 15b
Buonsolazzo	*TB*, 13b, 28	*MTB*, f. 15a
Buzay	*TB*, 8b, 10	*MTB*, f. 15b
Byland	*TB*, 11b, 2	*MTB*, f. 14b
Cabuabbas	*TB*, 13b, 12	*MTB*, f. 15b
Calder		*MTB*, f. 15b
Calers	*TB*, 20b, 15	*MTB*, f. 15b
Cambron	*TB*, 9b, 18	*MTB*, f. 15b
Candeil	*TB*, 20b, 16	*MTB*, f. 15b
Canonica	*TB*, 10b, 14	*MTB*, f. 15b
Capolago	*TB*, 21b, 20	*MTB*, f. 15b
Casamari	*TB*, 8b, 22	*MTB*, f. 16a
Casanova d'Abruzzo	*TB*, 19b, 22	*MTB*, f. 16a
Cashel	*TB*, 13b, 26	*MTB*, f. 16a
Cerreto	*TB*, 17b, 21	*MTB*, f. 16a
Chalade	*TB*, 12b, 1	*MTB*, f. 15b
Chaloché	*TB*, 10b, 17	*MTB*, f. 15b
Champagne	*TB*, 11b, 5	*MTB*, f. 15b
Charmoye	*TB*, 16b, 20	*MTB*, f. 16a
Charon	*TB*, 16b, 21	*MTB*, f. 16a
Châtelliers, Les	*TB*, 9b, 30	*MTB*, f. 16a

Châtillon	*TB*, 12b, 7	*MTB*, f. 16a
Chéhéry	*TB*, 12b, 6	*MTB*, f. 15b
Cheminon	*TB*, 12b, 4	*MTB*, f. 16a
Chérlieu	*TB*, 7b, 15	*MTB*, f. 15b
Chézery	*TB*, 12b, 12	*MTB*, f. 16a
Chiaravalle della Colomba	*TB*, 8b, 18	*MTB*, f. 16a
Chiaravalle di Milano	*TB*, 8b, 11	*MTB*, f. 16a
Clairmarais	*TB*, 8b, 24	*MTB*, f. 16a
Clairmont	*TB*, 9b, 24	*MTB*, f. 16a
Cleeve	*TB*, 16b, 12	*CB*, iii, 639
Coggeshall	*TB*, 11b, 1	*MTB*, f. 16b
Comber	*TB*, 19b, 13	*MTB*, f. 15b
Combermere	*TB*, 10b, 26	*MTB*, f. 16b
Conway	*TB*, 19b, 19	*MTB*, f. 14b
Corazzo	*TB*, 16b, 27	*MTB*, f. 16b
Corcomroe	*TB*, 11b, 10	*MTB*, f. 19b
Coupar Angus	*TB*, 16b, 3	*MTB*, f. 16b
Croxden	*TB*, 11b, 13	*MTB*, f. 22b
Culross	*TB*, 16b, 6	*MTB*, f. 21a
Cymmer	*TB*, 19b, 18	*MTB*, f. 15b
Deer	*TB*, 16b, 7	*MTB*, f. 16b
Disibodenberg	*TB*, 21b, 24	*MTB*, f. 19a
Doest, Ter	*TB*, 15b, 25	*MTB*, f. 15b
Dublin	*TB*, 11b, 21	*MTB*, f. 16b
Duinen, Ter	*TB*, 8b, 19	*MTB*, f. 16b
Dunbrody	*TB*, 11b, 23	*MTB*, f. 16b
Dundrennan	*TB*, 15b, 28	*MTB*, f. 16b
Eberbach	*TB*, 8b, 12	*MTB*, f. 16b
Écharlis, Les	*TB*, 12b, 11	*MTB*, f. 17a
Eldena	*TB*, 14b, 9	*MTB*, f. 17b
'Entela'	*TB*, 13b, 6	*MTB*, f. 17a
Ercsi		*MTB*, f. 25a
Espina, La	*TB*, 9b, 6	*MTB*, f. 21b
Esrom	*TB*, 9b, 23	*MTB*, f. 17a
Fermoy	*TB*, 11b, 9	*MTB*, f. 16a
Ferraria	*TB*, 16b, 26	*MTB*, f. 17a
Fiães	*TB*, 16b, 15	*MTB*, f. 17a
Fiastra	*TB*, 16b, 12	*MTB*, f. 16a
Foigny	*TB*, 7b, 11	*MTB*, f. 17b
Follina	*TB*, 14b, 13	*MTB*, f. 17a
Fontaine-Daniel	*TB*, 21b, 10	*MTB*, f. 17a
Fontaine-les-Blanches	*TB*, 10b, 25	*MTB*, f. 17a

Fontenay	*TB*, 7b, 10	*MTB*, f. 17a
Fontevivo	*TB*, 19b, 9	*MTB*, f. 17a
Fontfroide	*TB*, 20b, 14	*MTB*, f. 17a
Fontmorigny	*TB*, 9b, 19	*MTB*, f. 17a
Fossanova	*TB*, 16b, 22	*MTB*, f. 17a
Foucarmont	*TB*, 10b, 19	*MTB*, f. 17a
'Foulkeronde'	*TB*, 14b, 18	*MTB*, f. 17a
Fountains	*TB*, 8b, 5	*MTB*, f. 17a
Froidmont	*TB*, 12b, 22	*MTB*, f. 17a
Furness	*TB*, 10b, 18	*MTB*, f. 17a
Galeso	*TB*, 18b, 13	*MTB*, f. 17b
Gard, Le	*TB*, 12b, 26	*MTB*, f. 17b
Gerka	*TB*, 17b, 9	*MTB*, f. 18a
Glanawydan	*TB*, 19b, 4	*MTB*, f. 22a
Glenluce	*TB*, 16b, 11	*MTB*, f. 17b
Grâce-Dieu, La		
(Charente Maritime)	*TB*, 8b, 8	*MTB*, f. 17b
Graiguenamanagh	*TB*, 11b, 15	*MTB*, f. 21a
Grandpré	*TB*, 20b, 25	*MTB*, f. 17b
Grandselve	*TB*, 9b, 9	*MTB*, f. 17b
Grey Abbey	*TB*, 16b, 5	*MTB*, f. 18a
Gutnalia	*TB*, 13b, 20	*MTB*, f. 17b
Hautcrêt	*TB*, 8b, 30	*MTB*, f. 14a
Hautecombe	*TB*, 8b, 9	*MTB*, f. 14a
Haute-Fontaine	*TB*, 12b, 3	*MTB*, f. 14a
Hauterive	*TB*, 12b, 25	*MTB*, f. 14a
Heisterbach	*TB*, 16b, 17	*MTB*, f. 17b
Himmerod	*TB*, 8b, 6	*MTB*, f. 17b
Holmcultram	*TB*, 13b, 18	*MTB*, f. 17b
Holycross	*TB*, 18b, 30	*CB*, iii, 641
Hovedøy	*TB*, 17b, 15	*MTB*, f. 17b
Hulton	*TB*, 11b, 19	*MTB*, f. 23a
Igny	*TB*, 7b, 12	*MTB*, f. 23a
Ihlo	*TB*, 14b, 23	*MTB*, f. 20b
Inch	*TB*, 14b, 15	*MTB*, f. 23a
Inishlounaght	*TB*, 18b, 29	*MTB*, f. 22a
Isenhagen	*TB*, 15b, 12	*MTB*, f. 23a
Isle-Dieu	*TB*, 14b, 30	*MTB*, f. 17b
Jerpoint	*TB*, 19b, 6	*MTB*, f. 17b
Jervaulx	*TB*, 11b, 25	*MTB*, f. 18a
Junqueira	*TB*, 21b, 12	*MTB*, f. 18a
Kappel	*TB*, 18b, 5	*MTB*, f. 15b

Kilbeggan	*TB*, 18b, 27	*MTB*, f. 15a
Kilcooly	*TB*, 19b, 11	*MTB*, f. 14a
Killenny	*TB*, 19b, 28	*MTB*, f. 22b
Kinloss	*TB*, 16b, 2	*MTB*, f. 18a
Kirkstall	*TB*, 17b, 13	*MTB*, f. 18a
Kirkstead	*TB*, 17b, 7	*MTB*, f. 18a
Klaarkamp	*TB*, 10b, 3	*MTB*, f. 16a
Knardrup		*MTB*, f. 20a
Kołbacz	*TB*, 21b, 4	*MTB*, f. 16b
Lafões	*TB*, 10b, 10	*MTB*, f. 21a
Lannoy	*TB*, 11b, 6	*MTB*, f. 15a
Legno	*TB*, 16b, 28	*MTB*, f. 21b
Lieu-Dieu	*TB*, 11b, 11	*MTB*, f. 18a
Llantarnam	*TB*, 19b, 20	*CB*, iii, 640
Longpont	*TB*, 7b, 17	*MTB*, f. 18b
Longuay	*TB*, 8b, 17	*MTB*, f. 18b
Longvillers	*TB*, 10b, 27	*MTB*, f. 18b
Loos	*TB*, 9b, 21	*MTB*, f. 18a
Louth Park	*TB*, 17b, 8	*MTB*, f. 19b
Lyse	*TB*, 17b, 11	*MTB*, f. 18b
Maceira-Dão	*TB*, 20b, 10	*MTB*, f. 18b
Margam	*TB*, 9b, 14	*MTB*, f. 18b
Marienstatt	*TB*, 16b, 18	*MTB*, f. 18b
Marienwalde		*MTB*, f. 19a
Marmosoglio	*TB*, 16b, 25	*MTB*, f. 18b
Matina	*TB*, 14b, 3	*MTB*, f. 18b
Meaux	*TB*, 17b, 14	*MTB*, f. 19a
Medmenham	*TB*, 17b, 19	*MTB*, f. 18a
Meira	*TB*, 9b, 2	*MTB*, f. 19a
Mellifont	*TB*, 21b, 26	*MTB*, f. 18b
Melón	*TB*, 8b, 29	*MTB*, f. 19a
Melrose	*TB*, 15b, 26	*MTB*, f. 18b
Menterna		*MTB*, f. 20b
Midleton	*TB*, 19b, 2	*MTB*, f. 16b
Monasteranenagh	*TB*, 18b, 21	*MTB*, f. 18b
Monasterevin	*TB*, f. 19b, 7	*MTB*, f. 20a
Monfero	*TB*, 19b, 29	*MTB*, f. 19a
Montederramo	*TB*, 9b, 26	*MTB*, f. 19a
Mont-Ste-Marie	*TB*, 10b, 9	*MTB*, f. 19a
Moreruela	*TB*, 8b, 2	*MTB*, f. 19a
Mores	*TB*, 9b, 28	*MTB*, f. 19a
Mortemer	*TB*, 12b, 21	*MTB*, f. 19a

Moureilles	*TB*, 9b, 25	*MTB*, f. 19a
Moutier-en-Argonne	*TB*, 12b, 5	*MTB*, f. 19a
Neath	*TB*, 10b, 21	*MTB*, f. 19a
Newbattle	*TB*, 15b, 30	*MTB*, f. 19a
Newminster	*TB*, 17b, 6	*MTB*, f. 19a
Newry	*TB*, 18b, 24	*MTB*, f. 23a
Noara	*TB*, 18b, 11	*MTB*, f. 19a
Nogales	*TB*, 16b, 13	*MTB*, f. 19a
Noirlac	*TB*, 8b, 15	*MTB*, f. 16b
Nydala	*TB*, 9b, 4	*MTB*, f. 19a
Oliwa	*TB*, 21b, 9	*MTB*, f. 19b
Øm	*TB*, 13b, 24	*MTB*, f. 16a
Orval	*TB*, 12b, 2	*MTB*, f. 14b
Osera	*TB*, 8b, 28	*MTB*, f. 23a
Otterberg	*TB*, 17b, 28	*MTB*, f. 19b
Ourscamp	*TB*, 7b, 14	*MTB*, f. 23a
Oya	*TB*, 10b, 6	*MTB*, f. 19a
Palazzolo	*TB*, 14b, 11	*MTB*, f. 19b
Paris (St Bernard's)*	*TB*, 13b, 25	
Pásztó	*TB*, 15b, 23	*MTB*, f. 19b
Pérouse, La		*MTB*, f. 19b
Piedra	*TB*, 9b, 27	*MTB*, f. 19b
Pierres, Les	*TB*, 10b, 1	*MTB*, f. 19b
Pilis	*TB*, 15b, 22	*MTB*, f. 19b
Pipewell	*TB*, 17b, 18	*MTB*, f. 19b
Poblet	*TB*, 20b, 18	*MTB*, f. 19b
Ponza	*TB*, 14b, 12	*MTB*, f. 18a
Pornó	*TB*, 12b, 10	*MTB*, f. 19b
Pozega		*MTB*, f. 17b
Prée, La	*TB*, 9b, 10	*MTB*, f. 19b
Prières	*TB*, 17b, 5	*MTB*, f. 20a
Quarr	*TB*, 10b, 24	*MTB*, f. 16a
Quartazzola	*TB*, 18b, 3	*MTB*, f. 19b
Real, La	*TB*, 20b, 22	*MTB*, f. 18b
Reclus, Le	*TB*, 16b, 19	*MTB*, f. 20a
Reigny	*TB*, 7b, 13	*MTB*, f. 20a
Revesby	*TB*, 13b, 8	*MTB*, f. 20a
Rievaulx	*TB*, 8b, 1	*MTB*, f. 20a
Ripalta di Puglia	*TB*, 20b, 3	*MTB*, f. 20a
Robertsbridge	*TB*, 20b, 24	*MTB*, f. 19b
Roccadia	*TB*, 18b, 12	*MTB*, f. 20a
Roccamadore	*TB*, 18b, 17	*MTB*, f. 20a

Roche	*TB*, 17b, 16	*MTB*, f. 20a
Rufford	*TB*, 15b, 20	*MTB*, f. 20a
Rufiniani*	*TB*, 15b, 9	*MTB*, f. 20a
Ruhe	*TB*, 14b, 21	*MTB*, f. 20a
Rushen			*CB*, iii, 639
Säby	*TB*, 20b, 5	*MTB*, f. 20b
Saddell	*TB*, 15b, 6	*MTB*, f. 20b
Sagittario	*TB*, 18b, 9	*MTB*, f. 20a
S. Agostino de Montalto	*TB*, 19b, 25	*MTB*, f. 20b
St. André-de-Gouffern	*TB*, 10b, 20	*MTB*, f. 20b
S. Angelo in Frigido	*TB*, 15b, 8	*MTB*, f. 20b
St Angelus in Constantinople*	*TB*, 16b, 23	*MTB*, f. 20b
S. Bernardo in Vanencia[5]*		*MTB*, f. 20b
St Bernard-sur-l'Escaut	*TB*, 20b, 26	*MTB*, f. 18b
Santes Creus	*TB*, 14b, 24	*MTB*, f. 16b
S. Galgano	*TB*, 18b, 8	*MTB*, f. 21a
S. Gaudenzio	*TB*, 15b, 14	*MTB*, f. 20b
S. Giusto di Tuscania	*TB*, 18b, 6	*MTB*, f. 21a
Szent Gotthárd	*TB*, 12b, 8	*MTB*, f. 17b
S. Maria de Caritate	*TB*, 19b, 23	*MTB*, f. 21b
S. Maria de Gloria		*MTB*, f. 17b
S. Maria dell' Arco	*TB*, 17b, 1	*MTB*, f. 14b
S. Maria delle Paludi	*TB*, 10b, 11	*MTB*, f. 19b
S. Maria dell' Ospedale del Piave	*TB*, 17b, 26	*MTB*, f. 17b
S. Maria de Zagrabia	*TB*, 15b, 15	*MTB*, f. 18a
S. Maria Incoronata	*TB*, 16b, 29	*MTB*, f. 21a
S. Maria Maddalena alla Cava	*TB*, 17b, 24	*MTB*, f. 16a
S. Michele alla Verruca	*TB*, 21b, 17	*MTB*, f. 22b
S. Michele a Quarto	*TB*, 21b, 18	*MTB*, f. 20a
S. Pantaleone del Monte Faeta	*TB*, 18b, 19	*MTB*, f. 21a
S. Pastore e S. Matteo	*TB*, 14b, 14	*MTB*, f. 21a
S. Salvatore a Settimo	*TB*, 18b, 20	*MTB*, f. 21a
S. Spirito della Valle	*TB*, 16b, 30	*MTB*, f. 21a
S. Spirito di Palermo	*TB*, 18b, 10	*MTB*, f. 21a
S. Stefano del Bosco	*TB*, 16b, 24	*MTB*, f. 21a
S. Stefano del Corno	*TB*, 17b, 25	*MTB*, f. 16b
S. Trinità della Magione*	*TB*, 18b, 16	*MTB*, f. 21b

SS. Vito e Salvo	*TB*, 14b, 10	*MTB*, f. 21a	
Sala	*TB*, 14b, 4	*MTB*, f. 20b	
Salzedas	*TB*, 9b, 8	*MTB*, f. 20b	
Sambucina	*TB*, 18b, 7	*MTB*, f. 20a	
Sandoval	*TB*, 20b, 8	*MTB*, f. 20b	
Savigny	*TB*, 7b, 8	*MTB*, f. 21b	
Sawley	*TB*, 17b, 17	*MTB*, f. 20b	
Sawtry	*TB*, 16b, 8	*MTB*, f. 20b	
Schönau	*TB*, 14b, 8	*MTB*, f. 20b	
Seiça	*TB*, 20b, 11	*MTB*, f. 21b	
Sept-Fons	*TB*, 12b, 13	*MTB*, f. 21b	
Sibton	*TB*, 16b, 9	*MTB*, f. 21b	
Signy	*TB*, 12b, 15	*MTB*, f. 21b	
Sobrado	*TB*, 9b, 1	*MTB*, f. 21b	
Soleuvre	*TB*, 9b, 13	*MTB*, f. 22b	
Sorø	*TB*, 21b, 1	*MTB*, f. 21b	
Stanley	*TB*, 11b, 14	*MTB*, f. 22a	
Strata		*MTB*, f. 22a	
Strata Florida	*TB*, 19b, 15	*MTB*, f. 21b	
Strata Marcella	*TB*, 19b, 16		*CB*, iii, 640
Stratford Langthorn	*TB*, 10b, 28	*MTB*, f. 22a	
Sweetheart	*TB*, 15b, 16		*CB*, iii, 641
Swineshead		*MTB*, f. 21b	*CB*, iii, 639
Tamarães	*TB*, 20b, 12	*MTB*, f. 21a	
Tarouca	*TB*, 8b, 4	*MTB*, f. 21a	
Tautra	*TB*, 17b, 20	*MTB*, f. 22a	
Tilty	*TB*, 16b, 10		*CB*, iii, 639
Tironneau	*TB*, 11b, 12	*MTB*, f. 22a	
Toplica	*TB*, 10b, 12	*MTB*, f. 16b	
Torigny	*TB*, 11b, 16	*MTB*, f. 22a	
Tracton	*TB*, 19b, 17	*MTB*, f. 22a	
Trappe, La		*MTB*, f. 22a	
Tre Fontane	*TB*, 8b, 27	*MTB*, f. 20b	
Trois-Fontaines	*TB*, 7b, 9	*MTB*, f. 22a	
'Ulnesti'	*TB*, 14b, 6	*MTB*, f. 23a	
Valasse, Le	*TB*, 11b, 8	*MTB*, f. 23a	
Valbonne	*TB*, 20b, 19	*MTB*, f. 22b	
Valdedíos	*TB*, 19b, 10	*MTB*, f. 22a	
Valdeiglesias	*TB*, 20b, 7	*MTB*, f. 22b	
Valdieu	*TB*, 17b, 29	*MTB*, f. 22a	
Valence	*TB*, 10b, 13	*MTB*, f. 22a	
Valldigna		*MTB*, f. 22b	

Valle Crucis	*TB*, 13b, 30	*MTB*, f. 19a
Valparaiso	*TB*, 10b, 4	*MTB*, f. 22b
Valroy	*TB*, 12b, 16	*MTB*, f. 22b
Val-St-Lambert	*TB*, 12b, 18	*MTB*, f. 22b
Val Serena	*TB*, 21b, 7	*MTB*, f. 22b
Varnhem	*TB*, 20b, 4	*MTB*, f. 22b
Vaucelles	*TB*, 8b, 3	*MTB*, f. 22b
Vauclair	*TB*, 8b, 7	*MTB*, f. 22a
Vaudey	*TB*, 17b, 12	*MTB*, f. 22a
Vaux-de-Cernay	*TB*, 10b, 16	*MTB*, f. 22b
Vega, La	*TB*, 20b, 1	*MTB*, f. 23a
Vieuville	*TB*, 11b, 3	*MTB*, f. 22b
Villeneuve	*TB*, 17b, 4	*MTB*, f. 22b
Villers-en-Brabant	*TB*, 9b, 12	*MTB*, f. 22b
Vitskøl	*TB*, 14b, 22	*MTB*, f. 22b
Warden	*TB*, 15b, 27	*MTB*, f. 22a
Whalley	*TB*, 11b, 18	*MTB*, f. 22b
Whitland	*TB*, 8b, 26	*MTB*, f. 15a
Woburn	*TB*, 17b, 10	*MTB*, f. 23a
Zirc	*TB*, 10b, 5	

Generation of Morimond[6]

'Abbacia in Grecia'*	*TB*, 23b, 3	*MTB*, f. 23a
Abbey Dore	*TB*, 27b, 1	*MTB*, f. 25a
Acquafredda	*TB*, 13b, 27	*MTB*, f. 23b
Aiguebelle	*TB*, 22b, 13	*MTB*, f. 23b
Alcántara*	*TB*, 27b, 24	*MTB*, f. 23b
Aldersbach	*TB*, 25b, 4	*MTB*, f. 23a
Altenberg	*TB*, 22b, 9	*MTB*, f. 28a
Altzelle	*TB*, 24b, 11	*MTB*, f. 23b
Amelunxborn	*TB*, 24b, 6	*MTB*, f. 23b
Backenrode	*TB*, 28b, 17	*MTB*, f. 23b
Baix, La	*TB*, 26b, 27	*MTB*, f. 25a
Baumgarten	*TB*, 25b, 24	*MTB*, f. 24a
Baumgartenberg	*TB*, 13b, 7	*MTB*, f. 24a
Beaulieu (Cyprus)	*TB*, 23b, 12	*MTB*, f. 23b
Beaupré-en-Lorraine	*TB*, 22b, 11	*MTB*, f. 23b
Bellevaux	*TB*, 22b, 1	*MTB*, f. 23b
Belmont*	*TB*, 22b, 22	*MTB*, f. 23b
Bénissons-Dieu, La (Haute Garonne)	*TB*, 26b, 26	*MTB*, f. 23b

Berdoues	*TB*, 22b, 15	*MTB*, f. 23b
Bildhausen	*TB*, 25b, 6	*MTB*, f. 23b
Bithaine	*TB*, 22b, 6	*MTB*, f. 23b
'Bolhams'	*TB*, 27b, 10	*MTB*, f. 24a
	(also):	Accts., 5 entries
Bonaval	*TB*, 26b, 19	*MTB*, f. 24a
Bonnefont	*TB*, 22b, 16	*MTB*, f. 24a
Bors Monostor	*TB*, 14b, 29	*MTB*, f. 26a
Bouchet	*TB*, 26b, 5	*MTB*, f. 24a
Bouillas	*TB*, 13b, 15	*MTB*, f. 26b
Boulbonne	*TB*, 26b, 23	*MTB*, f. 24a
Bredelar	*TB*, 24b, 29	*MTB*, f. 24a
Bronnbach	*TB*, 23b, 21	*MTB*, f. 24a
Buch	*TB*, 24b, 16	*MTB*, f. 24a
Buków	*TB*, 27b, 14	*MTB*, f. 24a
Byszewo-Korónowo	*TB*, 28b, 25	*MTB*, f. 24a
Calatrava*	*TB*, 23b, 2	*MTB*, f. 24a
Casalvolone	*TB*, 25b, 23	*MTB*, f. 24b
Charité, La	*TB*, 23b, 14	*MTB*, f. 24a
Chorin	*TB*, 15b, 13	*MTB*, f. 24b
Clairefontaine	*TB*, 22b, 7	*MTB*, f. 24b
Clairlieu	*TB*, 25b, 11	*MTB*, f. 24b
Creste, La	*TB*, 22b, 2	*MTB*, f. 24b
Czikádor	*TB*, 25b, 15	*MTB*, f. 24b
Daphni[7]	*TB*, 23b, 16	*MTB*, f. 25b
Dargun	*TB*, 24b, 27	*MTB*, f. 24b
Doberan	*TB*, 24b, 26	*MTB*, f. 24b
Dobrilugk	*TB*, 24b, 20	*MTB*, f. 25a
Dünamünde	*TB*, 24b, 12	*MTB*, f. 26b
Eaunes	*TB*, 26b, 16	*MTB*, f. 23b
Ebrach	*TB*, 22b, 4	*MTB*, f. 25a
Écurey	*TB*, 24b, 3	*MTB*, f. 25a
Engleszell	*TB*, 28b, 16	*MTB*, f. 24b
Escale-Dieu, L'	*TB*, 22b, 14	*MTB*, f. 27b
Eusserthal	*TB*, 25b, 26	*MTB*, f. 28a
Falkenau	*TB*, 27b, 29	*MTB*, f. 28a
Feniers	*TB*, 23b, 31	*MTB*, f. 25a
Feuillants, Les	*TB*, 24b, 1	*MTB*, f. 25a
Fitero	*TB*, 13b, 16	*MTB*, f. 23a
Flaran	*TB*, 26b, 3	*MTB*, f. 25a
Franquevaux	*TB*, 22b, 18	*MTB*, f. 25a
Frienisberg	*TB*, 23b, 7	*MTB*, f. 23b

Fürstenfeld	TB, 27b, 5	MTB, f. 24a
Fürstenzell	TB, 27b, 8	MTB, f. 24a
Gemelnice	TB, 14b, 25	MTB, f. 25a
Georgenthal	TB, 22b, 17	MTB, f. 26a
Gimont	TB, 26b, 13	MTB, f. 25a
Gotteszell	TB, 27b, 7	MTB, f. 24b
Grâce-Dieu, La (Doubs)	TB, 23b, 27	MTB, f. 25a
Grünhain	TB, 28b, 21	MTB, f. 25a
Gumiel		MTB, f. 27a
Haina	TB, 25b, 21	MTB, f. 23a
Hardehausen	TB, 24b, 7	MTB, f. 25b
Haute-Seille	TB, 25b, 10	MTB, f. 23b
Heiligenkreuz	TB, 22b, 8	MTB, f. 27a
Heilsbronn	TB, 25b, 1	MTB, f. 25b
Henryków	TB, 24b, 14	MTB, f. 25b
Herrenalb	TB, 23b, 20	
Herrera	TB, 26b, 12	MTB, f. 25a
Hiddensee	TB, 29b, 11	MTB, f. 26a
Himmelpfort		MTB, f. 24b
Hradište	TB, 25b, 8	MTB, f. 25b
Hude	TB, 28b, 26	MTB, f. 26b
Huerta	TB, 26b, 14	MTB, f. 26b
Isle-en-Barrois	TB, 24b, 2	MTB, f. 25b
Jędrzejów	TB, 22b, 21	MTB, f. 23b
Kaisheim	TB, 23b, 18	MTB, f. 24b
Kamieniec		MTB, f. 20a
Kamp	TB, 22b, 3	MTB, f. 24a
Königsbrunn		MTB, f. 25a
Koprzywníca	TB, 28b, 1	MTB, f. 24b
Kostanjevica		MTB, f. 25b
Krzeszów		MTB, f. 25a
Ląd	TB, 25b, 20	MTB, f. 25b
Langheim	TB, 25b, 3	MTB, f. 25b
Lehnin	TB, 24b, 15	MTB, f. 26a
Leire	TB, 26b, 7	MTB, f. 27b
Lekno-Wągrowiec	TB, 29b, 1	MTB, f. 25b
Lieu-Croissant	TB, 23b, 17	MTB, f. 26a
Lilienfeld	TB, 25b, 17	MTB, f. 24a
Lockum	TB, 24b, 19	MTB, f. 26a
'Locus Anseris'	TB, 26b, 21	MTB, f. 26a
Lubiąź	TB, 24b, 10	MTB, f. 26a
Lucelle	TB, 23b, 5	MTB, f. 26a

Marienfeld	*TB*, 24b, 28	*MTB*, f. 24a
Marienthal	*TB*, 25b, 18	*MTB*, f. 28a
Matallana	*TB*, 26b, 10	*MTB*, f. 26a
Maulbronn	*TB*, 23b, 19	*MTB*, f. 26a
Michaelstein	*TB*, 24b, 8	*MTB*, f. 25b
Mogila	*TB*, 24b, 13	*MTB*, f. 24b
Monsalud de Córcoles	*TB*, 26b, 6	*MTB*, f. 26a
Monthéron	*TB*, 23b, 15	*MTB*, f. 27b
Morimondo Coronato	*TB*, 22b, 10	*MTB*, f. 26a
Nepomuk	*TB*, 25b, 2	*MTB*, f. 26b
Neuberg	*TB*, 29b, 10	*MTB*, f. 26a
Neubourg	*TB*, 23b, 6	*MTB*, f. 26a
Neu Dobrilugk	*TB*, 27b, 28	*MTB*, f. 26a
Neuenkamp	*TB*, 27b, 16	*MTB*, f. 26a
Neuzelle	*TB*, 29b, 8	*MTB*, f. 26a
Obra		*MTB*, f. 26b
Oliva, La	*TB*, 26b, 2	*MTB*, f. 26b
Osek	*TB*, 24b, 23	*MTB*, f. 26b
Ovila	*TB*, 26b, 30	*MTB*, f. 26b
Padis	*TB*, 28b, 18	*MTB*, f. 26b
Pairis	*TB*, 23b, 9	*MTB*, f. 26b
Palazuelos	*TB*, 26b, 20	*MTB*, f. 26b
Paradyż		*MTB*, f. 26b
Pelplin	*TB*, 27b, 12	*MTB*, f. 26a
Peyrignac	*TB*, 26b, 24	*MTB*, f. 26b
Pforta	*TB*, 28b, 23	*MTB*, f. 26b
Plasy	*TB*, 25b, 7	*MTB*, f. 26b
Pontifroid	*TB*, 29b, 12	*MTB*, f. 26b
Przemęt	*TB*, 28b, 19	*MTB*, f. 28a
Raitenhaslach	*TB*, 23b, 23	*MTB*, f. 27a
Reifenstein	*TB*, 24b, 18	*MTB*, f. 27a
Rein	*TB*, 24b, 30	*MTB*, f. 27a
Reinfeld	*TB*, 24b, 24	*MTB*, f. 27a
Riddagshausen	*TB*, 24b, 25	*MTB*, f. 27a
Rioseco	*TB*, 26b, 22	*MTB*, f. 27a
Rosières	*TB*, 23b, 13	*MTB*, f. 27a
Rudy	*TB*, 28b, 11	*MTB*, f. 27a
Rueda	*TB*, 26b, 17	*MTB*, f. 27a
Sacramenia	*TB*, 25b, 29	*MTB*, f. 27a
Salvatio	*TB*, 22b, 23	*MTB*, f. 27a
St Benoît-en-Woëvre	*TB*, 23b, 29	*MTB*, f. 27a
Santa Fe	*TB*, 15b, 18	*MTB*, f. 21a

Sanctus Johannes in Nemore*	*TB*, 27b, 20	*MTB*, f. 27b
S. Maria del Mirteto	*TB*, 23b, 28	*MTB*, f. 27a
Svaty Pole	*TB*, 27b, 9	*MTB*, f. 27a
S. Prudencio	*TB*, 26b, 8	*MTB*, f. 27b
St. Stephen in Constantinople*	*TB*, 23b, 26	*MTB*, f. 27b
S. Tommaso di Torcello	*TB*, 23b, 25	*MTB*, f. 27b
Sancta Trinitas de Refech*	*TB*, 27b, 21	*MTB*, f. 27b
Sankt Urban	*TB*, 23b, 11	*MTB*, f. 27b
Salem	*TB*, 23b, 8	*MTB*, f. 27a
Säusenstein	*TB*, 29b, 9	*MTB*, f. 28a
Sauvelade		*MTB*, f. 27b
Saya	*TB*, 26b, 11	*MTB*, f. 27a
Scharnebeck	*TB*, 26b, 9	*MTB*, f. 27b
Schlägl	*TB*, 14b, 7	*MTB*, f. 21b
Schöntal	*TB*, 23b, 22	*MTB*, f. 27b
Sedlec	*TB*, 24b, 21	*MTB*, f. 28b
Silvacane	*TB*, 22b, 20	*MTB*, f. 27b
Sittichenbach	*TB*, 24b, 9	*MTB*, f. 27b
Skalice	Accts., f. 20a, col. 2	
'So[m]pnova	*TB*, 29b, 3	*MTB*, f. 27b
	(also):	Accts., 3 entries
Stams	*TB*, 27b, 3	*MTB*, f. 27b
Stična	*TB*, 28b, 5	
Stolpe	*TB*, 27b, 13	*MTB*, f. 27b
Sulejów	*TB*, 22b, 24	*MTB*, f. 27b
Szczyrzycz	*TB*, 28b, 10	*MTB*, f. 24b
Szepes	*TB*, 28b, 13	*MTB*, f. 24b
Tennenbach	*TB*, 23b, 24	*MTB*, f. 24b
Theuley	*TB*, 22b, 5	*MTB*, f. 27b
Valbuena	*TB*, 22b, 19	*MTB*, f. 28a
Vale Royal		*CB*, iii, 641
Valsainte	*TB*, 27b, 19	*MTB*, f. 28a
Vaux-en-Ornois	*TB*, 23b, 30	*MTB*, f. 28a
Vaux-la-Douce	*TB*, 25b, 12	*MTB*, f. 25a
Velehrad	*TB*, 25b, 9	*MTB*, f. 28a
Veruela	*TB*, 25b, 30	*MTB*, f. 23b
Viktring	*TB*, 25b, 25	*MTB*, f. 28a
Villelongue	*TB*, 26b, 25	*MTB*, f. 28a
Villers-Bettnach	*TB*, 22b, 12	*MTB*, f. 28a

Vizovice		*MTB*, f. 27b
Volkerode	*TB*, 24b, 5	*MTB*, f. 28b
Vyšší Brod	*TB*, 28b, 8	*MTB*, f. 23b
Wąchok	*TB*, 23b, 1	*MTB*, f. 24a
'Walcesa'	*TB*, 28b, 29	*MTB*, f. 28a
Walderbach	*TB*, 24b, 21	*MTB*, f. 28a
Waldsassen	*TB*, 24b, 17	*MTB*, f. 28a
Walkenried	*TB*, 24b, 4	*MTB*, f. 28a
Werschweiler	*TB*, 25b, 27	*MTB*, f. 28a
Wettingen	*TB*, 27b, 26	*MTB*, f. 26a
Wilhering	*TB*, 25b, 5	*MTB*, f. 25b
Zbraslav	*TB*, 27b, 27	*MTB*, f. 23b
Žďár	*TB*, 27b, 4	*MTB*, f. 27b
Zinna	*TB*, 25b, 19	*MTB*, f. 24b
Zlatá Koruna	*TB*, 28b, 14	*MTB*, f. 24b
Zwettl	*TB*, 25b, 13	*MTB*, f. 28b

NOTES TO APPENDIX

1.   Incorporated into the Order in 1379, under the generation of Cîteaux, *MTB*, f. 12a.

2.   Vallemagne and Ulmet were united some time in the fourteenth century, *MTB*, f. 12b. See Franceschini, 'Un registro cisterciense della fine del sec. XIV', 125.

3.   'Barona destruca est', *MTB*, f. 12b.

4.   The community moved from Outremer to the neighbourhood of Genoa after the fall of Acre, *Orig.*, 217-18. Jubin occurs regularly in the Accounts of 1337-47.

5.   Founded 1381, *Orig.*, 273.

6.   See the list by Anselme Dimier, appended to H.P. Eydoux, 'L'Église abbatiale de Morimond', *Analecta Sacri Ordinis Cisterciensis*, 14 (1958) 112-16.

7.   Both references are to *Laurus,* which was most probably another name for Daphni. See J. Richard, ' "Laurum": une abbaye cistercienne fantôme', *Bulletin de l'École des Chartres*, 129 (1971) 409-10.

BIBLIOGRAPHIES

1. MANUSCRIPT SOURCES

Dijon, *Archives Départementales de la Côte d'Or.*
11 H 151-61; 163-6 (various rents).
11 H 1160 (Accounts of the Order for 1337-47; various Accounts of the bursar of Cîteaux).

Troyes, *Archives Départementales de l'Aube.*
3 H 148 (list of rents).
3 H 153 (Innocent VI and the Order; Audit of 1390).
3 H 154 (Innocent VI and the Order).
3 H 157 (Documents relating to rents).

Sens, *Bibliothèque municipale.*
MS 129 (the *dossier* of 1483-6).

Modena, *Biblioteca Estense.*
MS Latino 142 (The Modena Tax Book).

Copenhagen, The Royal Library.
MS Thott 138 (Tabula Cisterciensis).

2. PRINTED SOURCES

Baluz, E., *Vitae Paparum Avenionensium,* ed. G. Mollat, 4 vols. Paris, 1916-24.
Benedict XII, *Lettres closes et patentes intéressant les pays autre que la France,* eds. J.M. Vidal and G. Mollat (Bibliothèque des Écoles françaises d'Athènes et de Rome, 2 ter), 2 vols. Paris, 1935-50.
Benedict XII, *Lettres closes, patentes, et curiales se rapportant à la France,* ed. G. Daumet, (Bibliothèque des Écoles françaises d'Athènes et de Rome, 2), 3 vols. Paris, 1899-1920.
Benedict XII, *Lettres communes,* ed. J. Vidal, (Bibliothèque des Écoles

françaises d'Athènes et de Rome, 2 bis), 3 vols. Paris, 1902-11.

Calendar of Close Rolls preserved in the Public Record Office, 8 (1343-6). London, 1904.

Charters of the Abbey of Coupar Angus, ed. D.E. Easson, (Publications of the Scottish History Society, 40, 41), 2 vols. Edinburgh, 1947.

Chronica de Melsa, ed. E.A. Bond, (Rolls Series, 43), 3 vols. London, 1866-9.

Clement V, *Regestum,* eds. the monks of St. Benedict, 8 vols. Rome, 1885-8.

Clement VI, *Lettres closes, patentes, et curiales, intéressant les pays autre que la France,* ed. E. Deprez and G. Mollat, (Bibliothèque des Écoles françaises d'Athènes et de Rome), in progress. Paris, 1960-

Clement VI, *Lettres closes, patentes, et curiales se rapportant à la France,* eds. E. Deprez, J. Glenisson, and G. Mollat, (Bibliothèque des Écoles françaises d'Athènes et de Rome 3), 2 vols. Paris, 1901-61.

Codex Dunensis sive Diplomatum et Chartarum Medii Aevi amplissima Collectio, ed. J.M.B.C. Kervyn de Lettenhove, (Commission royale d'Histoire). Brussels, 1875.

Comptes du Trésor 1296, 1316, 1384, 1477, ed. M.R. Fawtier. Paris, 1930.

Die Ausgaben der apostolischen Kammer unter Benedikt XII, Klemens VI, und Innozenz VI, ed. K.H. Schäfer. Paderborn, 1914.

Die Einnahmen der apostolischen Kammer unter Innozenz VI, ed. H. Hoberg. Paderborn, 1955.

Griesser, P. Bruno, 'Statuten von Generalkapiteln ausserhalb Cîteaux– Wien 1393 und Heilsbronn 1398', *Cistercienser Chronik,* 62 (1955) 65-83.

Griesser, P. Bruno, 'Unbekannte Generalkapitelstatuten', *Cistercienser Chronik,* 64 (1957) 1-22, 41-60.

Innocent VI, *Lettres secrètes et curiales,* eds. P. Gasnault, M.H. Laurent, N. Gotteri, (Bibliothèque des Écoles françaises d'Athènes et de Rome, 4 bis) 4 vols. Paris, 1959-76.

Innocent VI, *Lettres closes, patentes, et curiales, se rapportant à la France,* ed. E. Deprez, (Bibliothèque des Écoles françaises d'Athènes et de Rome, 4). Paris, 1909.

Inventaire d'anciens comptes royaux dressé par Robert Mignon, ed. C.V. Langlois. Paris, 1899.

Johannis de Fordun Chronica Gentis Scotorum, ed. W.F. Skene, 2 vols. Edinburgh, 1871-2.

John XXII, *Lettres communes,* ed. G. Mollat (Bibliothèque des Écoles françaises d'Athènes et de Rome, 1 bis), 16 vols. Paris, 1904-47.

Krausen, E., 'Generalkapitel ausserhalb Cîteaux während des grossen

Schismas', *Cistercienser Chronik,* 63 (1956) 7-11.

La codification cistercienne de 1202, ed. B. Lucet, Rome, 1964.

Les codifications cisterciennes de 1237 et de 1257, ed. B. Lucet. Paris, 1977.

Les journaux du Trésor de Charles IV le Bel, ed. J. Viard. Paris, 1917.

Les journaux du Trésor de Philippe IV le Bel, ed. J. Viard. Paris, 1940.

Les journaux du Trésor de Philippe de Valois, ed. J. Viard. Paris, 1899.

Les plus anciens textes de Cîteaux, eds. J. Bouton and J. van Damme. Achel, 1974.

Manrique, A., *Cisterciensium seu verius Ecclesiasticorum annalium a condito Cistercio,* 4 vols. Lyon, 1642-59.

Monasticon Praemonstratense, ed. N. Backmund, 3 vols. Straubing, 1949-56.

Nomasticon Cisterciense seu antiquiores ordinis Cisterciensis constitutiones, (second edn.), ed. H. Séjalon. Solesmes, 1892.

Peregrinatio Hispanica, ed. M. Cocheril, 2 vols. Paris, 1970.

Rotuli Parliamentorum, ed. J. Strachey and others, 6 vols. London, 1767-77.

Statuta capitulorum generalium ordinis Cisterciensis 1116-1768, ed. J.M. Canivez, 8 vols. Louvain, 1933-41.

Taxae pro communibus servitiis, ed. H. Hoberg. Rome, 1949.

The Coucher Book of Furness Abbey, ed. J.C. Atkinson, (Chetham Society, 9, 11, 14, 74, 76, 78), 6 vols. Manchester, 1886-1919.

The Tax Book of the Cistercian Order, eds. A.O. Johnsen and H.P. King, (Det Norske Videnskaps-Akademi II, Hist.-Filos Klasse Avhandlinger Ny serie, No. 16). Oslo, 1979.

Valois, N., 'Un plaidoyer du xive siècle en faveur des cisterciens', *Bibliothèque de l'Ecole des Chartes,* 69 (1908) 353-368.

3.   MODERN WORKS

Anselme, le père, *Histoire Genéalogique et Chronologique de la Maison Royale de France etc.,* 9 vols. Paris, 1726-33.

Bedini, B.G., *Breve Prospetto delle Abbazie Cisterciensi d'Italia.* Rome, 1964.

Buczek, Daniel S., 'Medieval Taxation: the French Crown, the Papacy, and the Cistercian Order 1190-1320', *Analecta Cisterciensia,* 25 (1969) 42-106.

Buczek, Daniel S., ' "Pro defendendis Ordinis": The French Cistercians and Their Enemies', *Studies in Medieval Cistercian History presented to Jeremiah O' Sullivan,* 88-109 (see below).

Canivez, J.M., 'Cîteaux (Abbaye)', *Dictionnaire d'Histoire et de Géographie Ecclésiastiques,* 12 (1953) 852-874.

Canivez, J.M., 'Cîteaux (Ordre)', *Dictionnaire d'Histoire et de Géographie Ecclésiastiques,* 12 (1953) 874-997.

Canivez, J.M., 'Clairvaux', *Dictionnaire d'Histoire et de Géographie Ecclésiastiques,* 12 (1953) 1050-1061.

Cazelles, R., 'Quelques réflexions à propos des mutations de la monnaie roayle française', *Le Moyen Âge* 72 (1966) 83-105, 251-78.

Cowan, I.B., *The Parishes of Medieval Scotland* (Scottish Record Society, 93). Edinburgh, 1967.

Cowan, I.B. and Easson, D.E., *Medieval Religious Houses: Scotland.* London, 1976.

Dautrey, Phillippe, 'Croissance et Adaptation chez les Cisterciens au 13e siècle', *Analecta Cisterciensia,* 22 (1976) 122-215.

De Ganck, Roger, 'Les pouvoirs de l'Abbé de Cîteaux de la bulle "Parvus Fons" (1265) à la Révolution Française', *Analecta Cisterciensia,* 27 (1971) 4-63.

Denton, J.H., *Robert Winchelsey and the Crown 1294-1313.* Cambridge, 1980.

Desmond, L.A., 'The Statute of Carlisle and the Cistercians', *Studies in Medieval Cistercian History Presented to Jeremiah O'Sullivan,* 138-162 (see below).

Dictionnaire des Monastères Cisterciens, tome 1, par M. Cocheril; tome 2 (compléments) par E. Manning. Rochefort, 1976, 1979.

Elm, Kaspar, and others, eds., *Die Zisterzienser. Ordensleben zwischen Ideal und Wirklichkeit* (Schriften des Rheinischen Museumsamtes Nr. 10). Cologne, 1981.

Eubel, C., *Hierarchia Catholica Medii Aevi,* 1. Münster, 1913.

Eydoux, H.P., 'L'Église abbatiale de Morimond', *Analecta Sacri Ordinis Cisterciensis,* 14 (1958) 3-111. Annexe par A. Dimier, 112-16.

Favier, J., *Phillipe le Bel.* Paris, 1978.

Fournial, E., *Histoire Monétaire de l'Occident Médievale.* Paris, 1970.

Franceschini, A., 'Un Registro Cisterciense della Fine del sec. xiv', *Ravennatensia,* 9 (1981) 121-32.

Grieve, M., *A Modern Herbal.* London, 1931, reprinted 1980.

Guillemain, B., *La Cour Pontificale d'Avignon 1306-76.* Paris, 1966.

Gwynn, A. and Hadcock, R.N., *Medieval Religious Houses: Ireland.* London, 1970.

Hadcock, R.N. and Knowles, M.D., *Medieval Religious Houses: England and Wales.* London, 1971.

Harper-Bill, C., 'Cistercian visitation in the late Middle Ages: the case of Hailes Abbey', *Bulletin of the Institute of Historical Research,*

53 (1980) 103-114.

Henneman, J.B., *Royal Taxation in Fourteenth Century France, France, 1322-56*. Princeton, 1971.

Henneman, J.B., *Royal Taxation in Fourteenth Century France, 1356-76*. Philadelphia, 1976.

Hermans, V., 'Notes historiques sur le Procureur Géneral de l'Ordre de Cîteaux', *Analecta Cisterciensia*, 24 (1968) 143-52.

Janauschek, L., *Originum Cisterciensium tomus, 1*. Vienna, 1877.

King, A.A., *Cîteaux and Her Eldest Daughters*. London, 1954.

King, H.P., 'Cistercian Financial Organisation 1335-92', *Journal of Ecclesiastical History*, 24 (1973) 127-43.

King, H.P., 'Coupar Angus and Cîteaux', *Innes Review*, 27 (1976) 49-69.

King, H.P., 'Materials for a Financial History of the Cistercian Order to 1486', *Bulletin of the Institute of Historical Research*, 50 (1977) 20-9.

Kłoczowski, J., 'Les Cisterciens en Pologne du xiie au xiiie siècle', *Cîteaux*, 21 (1970) 111-34.

Krausen, E., Zakar, P., Vongrey, F., and Hervay, F., 'Kritische Bemerkungen zum "Atlas de l'Ordre Cistercien" von Frédéric van der Meer', *Analecta Sacri Ordinis Cisterciensis*, 22 (1966) 279-90; 23 (1967) 115-52.

Kuhn-Rehfus, M., 'Zisterzienserinnen in Deutschland', in: Elm, ed., *Die Zisterzienser*, 125-47 (see above).

Lecler, J., *Vienne* (Histoire des Conciles Oecuméniques, 8). Paris, 1964).

Lekai, Louis J., 'An Unknown French "Janauschek" of the Eighteenth Century', *Analecta Cisterciensia*, 33 (1977) 177-90.

Lekai, Louis J., *The Cistercians, Ideal and Reality*, Kent, Ohio, 1977.

Lucas, H.S., 'The great European Famine of 1315, 1316, and 1317', in: E.M. Carus-Wilson, ed., *Essays in Economic History*, 2:49-72. London, 1962.

Mahn, J.B., *Le Pape Benoît XII et les Cisterciens*. Paris, n.d.

Mahn, J.B., *L'Ordre Cistercien et son Gouvernement des Origines au Milieu du xiiie siècle*. Paris, 1941.

Marilier, J., 'Catalogue des Abbés de Cîteaux pour les 13e et 14e siècles', *Cistercienser Chronik*, 63 (1956) 1-6.

Meade, W.E., *The English Mediaeval Feast*. London, 1967.

Mollat, G., *The Popes at Avignon*, transl. from ninth edn. (1949). London, 1963.

Monasticon Belge, ed. Usmer Berlière and others. Maredsous, Liége, 1890- (in progress).

Müller, G., 'Der Fleischgenuss im Orden', *Cistercienser Chronik*, 18 (1906) *passim.*

Müller, G., 'Studien über das Generalkapitel', *Cistercienser Chronik*, 12-20 (1900-8) *passim.*

Nicholson, R., *Scotland—the Later Middle Ages.* Edinburgh, 1974.

Olsen, T.H., *Dacia og Rhodos.* Copenhagen, 1962.

Prestwich, M., 'Early fourteenth century exchange rates', *Economic History Review*, 32 (1979) 470-82.

Renouard, Y., 'La capacité du tonneau bordelais au moyen âge', *Annales du Midi*, 65 (1953) 395-403.

——, 'La consommation des grands vins de Bourgogne et du Bourbonnais à la cour pontificale d'Avignon', *Annales de Bourgogne*, 24 (1952) 221-44.

Renouard, Y., 'Le compagnie commerciali fiorentine del Trecento (dai documenti dell' Archivo Vaticano)', *Archivio Storico Italiano*, 96 (1938) 41-68, 163-79.

Renouard, Y., 'Le grand commerce des vins de Gascogne au moyen âge', *Revue Historique*, 221 (1959) 261-304.

Renouard, Y., *Les Relations des Papes d'Avignon et des Compagnies Commerciales et Bancaires de 1316 à 1378.* Paris, 1941.

Renouard, Y., 'Recherches complémentaires sur la capacité du tonneau bordelais au moyen âge', *Annales du Midi*, 68 (1956) 195-207.

Richard, J., *Répertoire Numérique des Archives Départementales antérieures à 1790*, Côte d'Or, Archives Ecclésiastiques, Série H— Clergé Régulier 11 H—Abbaye de Cîteaux, Dijon, 1950.

Riley-Smith, J., *The Knights of St. John in Jerusalem and Cyprus.* London, 1967.

Rouse, Richard H., 'Cistercian aids to study in the thirteenth century', *Studies in Medieval Cistercian History*, 2 (Cistercian Studies Series, 24). Kalamazoo, 1976, 123-34.

Saraman, C. and Mollat, G., *La Fiscalité Pontificale en France au xive siècle* (Bibliothèque des Écoles françaises d'Athènes et de Rome, 96). Paris, 1905.

Schneider, A., ed., *Die Cistercienser, Geschichte, Geist, Kunst.* Cologne, 1974.

Schrader, T., *Die Rechenbücher der Hamburgischen Gesandten in Avignon 1338-55.* Hamburg, 1907.

Spufford, P. and Wilkinson, W., *Interim Listing of the Exchange Rates of Western Europe* (typescript). Keele, 1977.

Stouff, L., *Ravitaillement et Alimentation en Provence aux xive et xve siècles.* Paris, 1970.

Strayer, J.R. and Taylor, C.H., *Studies in Early French Taxation.* Cambridge, Mass., 1939.

Strayer, J.R., *The Reign of Philip the Fair.* Princeton, 1980.

Studies in Mediaeval Cistercian History presented to Jeremiah F. O'Sullivan (Cistercian Studies Series, 13). Spencer, Mass., 1971.

Suhle, A., *Deutsche Münz- und Geldgeschichte von den Anfängen bis zum 15 Jahrhundert.* Munich, 1970.

Talbot, C.H., 'Cîteaux and Scarborough', *Studia Monastica,* 2 (1960) 95-158.

Telesca, W.J., 'Jean de Cirey and the question of an abbot-general in the Order of Cîteaux in the fifteenth century', *Studies in Mediaeval Cistercian History,* 2 (Cistercian Studies Series, 24): 186-207. Kalamazoo, 1976.

Van der Meer, F., *Atlas de l'Ordre Cistercien.* Paris–Brussels, 1965.

Watson, A.M., 'Back to gold—and silver', *Economic History Review,* 20 (1967) 1-34.

White, L., *Latin Monasticism in Norman Sicily,* Cambridge, Mass., 1938.

Wienand, V., 'Die Cistercienserinnen', in: Schneider, ed., *Die Cistercienser;* 341-62 (see above).

Willi, D., 'Die Cistercienser Päpste, Kardinäle, und Bischöffe', *Cistercienser Chronik,* 23-24 (1911-12) *passim.*

Winter, F., *Die Cistercienser des Nordöstlichen Deutschlands.* Gotha, 1868.

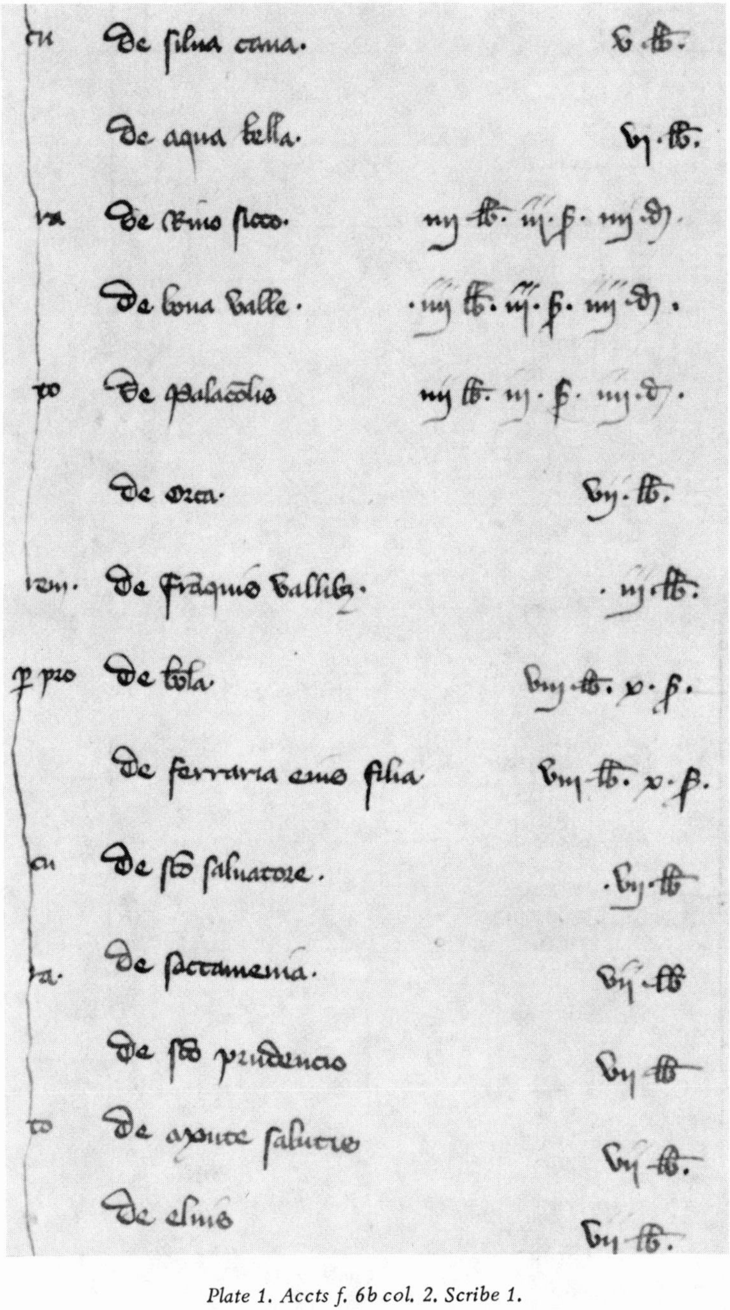

Plate 1. Accts f. 6b col. 2. Scribe 1.

De salem ——————————————— xxvi. lb.

De chaudiaf ——————————————— xxiij. lb.

De puns ——————————————— xxij. lb

De luzeli ——————————————— x. lb.

De stampis ——————————————— xxij. lb.

De cesura ——————————————— xxiij. lb.

De maustelli ——————————————— xxxij. lb.

De sancto Urbano ——————— viij. lb.

De nouo castro ——————— xij lb

De aurora ——————————— iij lb. x. s

De bello prato cutteri ——————— iiij lb.

De claro loco ——————————— ij. lb.

De cella principis ——————— iiij. lb.

De balsini ——————————— viij lb.

De eberiaco ——————————— viij lb.

De pomoniik. ——————————— xxiij. lb.

De lausti ——————————— xxij. lb.

De campo principis ——————— v. lb.

Plate 2. Accts f. 15a col. 1. Scribe 2.

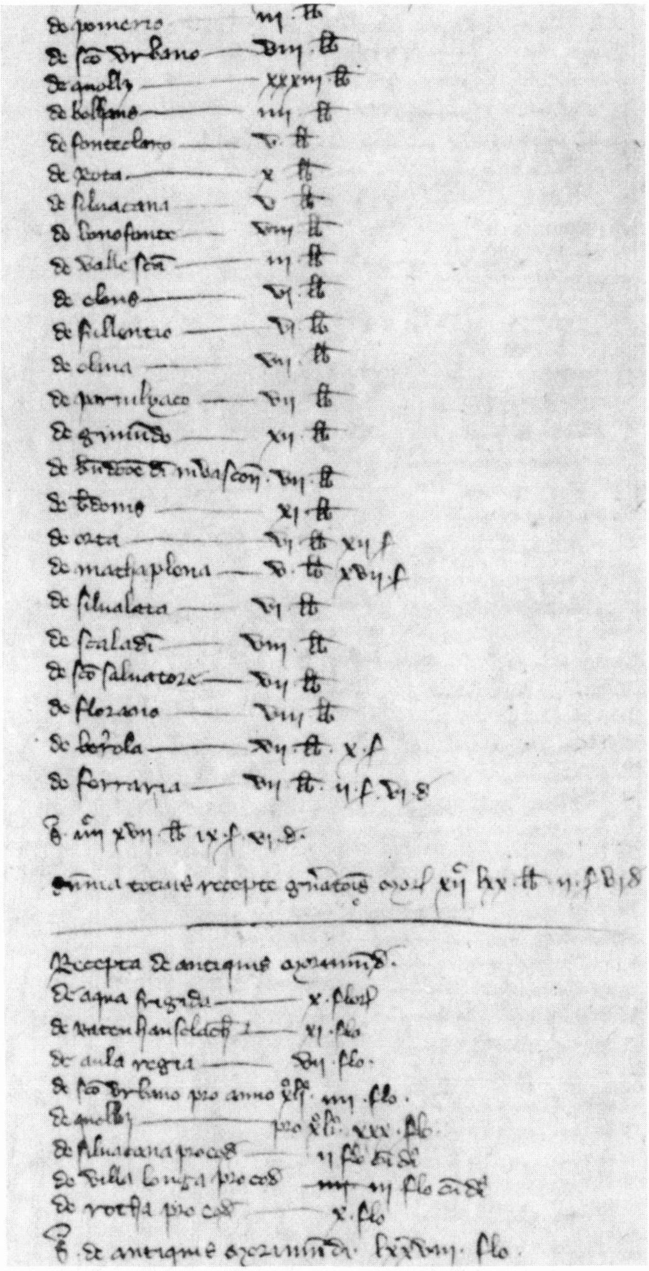

De pomerio — iij ℔
De sco Vrbano — viij ℔
De anollis — xxxiiij ℔
De bolseno — iiij ℔
De fontebono — v ℔
De rota — x ℔
De siluacana — v ℔
De bonofonte — viij ℔
De valle sca — iij ℔
De cluno — vj ℔
De sillencio — vj ℔
De olina — xiij ℔
De paruilpaco — vij ℔
De grimado — xij ℔
De [...] de ribascon — vij ℔
De bono — xj ℔
De orta — vij ℔ xij s
De machaplona — v ℔ xviij s
De siluatera — vj ℔
De scalast — viij ℔
De sco saluatore — vij ℔
De florario — vij ℔
De berola — xij ℔ x s
De ferraria — viij ℔ ij s vj d

Summa iiij xx vij ℔ ix s xj d

Summa totius recepte granatoru[m] ccc xij xx ℔ ij s vj d

──────────────

Recepta de antiquis expensis.
De aqua regia — x flor
De vatenhanselati [...] — xj flo
De aula regia — viij flo
De sco Vrbano pro anno [...] iij flo
De anollis — pro [...] xxx flo
De siluacana pro cast — ij flo [...]
De villa longa pro cast — iiij ij flo [...]
De rocha pro cast — x flo
Summa de antiquis expensis — lxxviij flo

Plate 3. Accts f. 22b col. 2, Scribe 3.

CISTERCIAN PUBLICATIONS INC.
Kalamazoo, Michigan

TITLES LISTING

THE CISTERCIAN FATHERS SERIES

THE WORKS OF BERNARD OF CLAIRVAUX

THE WORKS OF WILLIAM OF SAINT THIERRY

THE WORKS OF AELRED OF RIEVAULX

THE WORKS OF GILBERT OF HOYLAND

THE WORKS OF JOHN OF FORD

Texts and Studies in the Monastic Tradition

* Temporarily out of print   † Forthcoming

* *Temporarily out of print*   † *Forthcoming*